THE SPANISH CIVIL WAR

*This book is dedicated to
the men and women of the International Brigades
who fought and died
fighting fascism in Spain.*

THE SPANISH CIVIL WAR

1936-39

Paul Preston

Weidenfeld and Nicolson
London

Illustrations – sources

We are grateful to the following Archives and private collectors for their cooperation in the illustration of this book:

Agencia Efe, Madrid – Agencia Keystone-Nemes, Madrid – A. Centelles i Ossó, Barcelona – Family of D. Luis Quintanilla – Fundación Pablo Iglesias, Madrid – M. González García, Madrid – Partido Comunista de España, Madrid – R. Sanz Lobato, Madrid – *Historia 16*, Madrid

Picture Research and Captions by Sheelagh Ellwood.

ISBN 0 297 79805 7

Weidenfeld and Nicolson Ltd
91 Clapham High Street, London SW4 7TA

Printed by Butler & Tanner Ltd
Frome and London

Contents

Preface

There have been several thousand books on the Spanish Civil War and many of them are extremely long. The present volume aims to provide the new reader with a managcable guide to the labyrinth. It is interpretative rather than descriptive, although ample use has been made of quotation to give a flavour of the period. It is not a book which sets out to find a perfect balance between both sides. I lived for several years under Franco's dictatorship. It was impossible not to be aware of the repression of workers and students, the censorship and the prisons. As late as 1975 political prisoners were still being executed. Despite what Franco supporters claim, I do not believe that Spain derived any benefit from the military rising of 1936 and the Nationalist victory of 1939. Many years devoted to the study of Spain before and during the 1930s have convinced me that, while many mistakes were made, the Spanish Republic was an attempt to provide a better way of life for the humbler members of a repressive society. Accordingly, there is little sympathy here for the Spanish right, but I hope there is some understanding.

My early interest in Spain was stimulated by the postgraduate seminar run at the University of Reading by Hugh Thomas. I have learned an enormous amount during my friendship with Herbert Southworth, who has always been prodigal with his hospitality and his knowledge. I also derived a lot from conversations over many years with Norman Cooper, Denis Smyth, Angel Viñas, Julián Casanova, Manuel González García, Jerónimo Gonzalo and Martin Blinkhorn. My friends Paul Heywood and Sheelagh Ellwood gave me marvellous support. My warm thanks go to Juliet Gardiner of Weidenfeld & Nicolson who encouraged me to undertake this book and then saw it through the press with common sense and sparkling good humour. My wife Gabrielle was, as ever, my shrewdest critic. With such a team of friends to help, it seems astonishing that any book could still have shortcomings. Unfortunately, it does and they are mine.

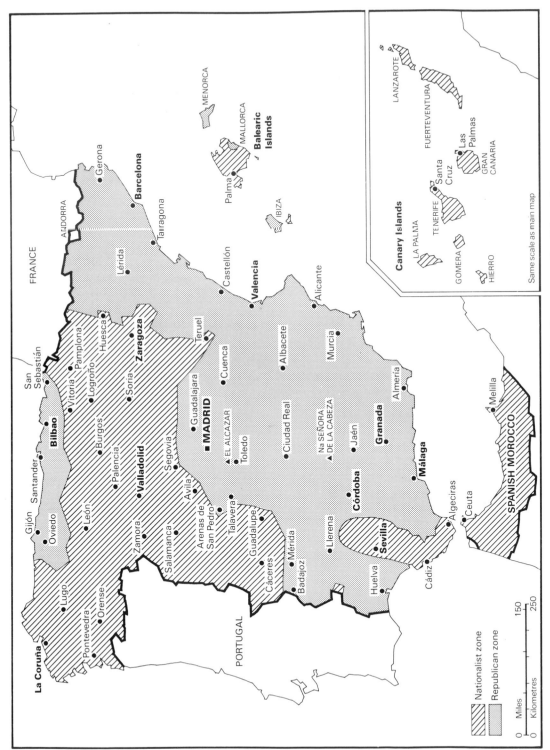

The division of Spain into Republican and Nationalist zones, as of 22 July 1936.

FRANCE

ANDORRA

San Sebastián

Bilbao

Gijón

Santander

Oviedo

Lugo

La Coruña

Pontevedra

Orense

León

Zamora

Salamanca

Vitoria

Pamplona

Logroño

Burgos

Palencia

Valladolid

Segovia

Ávila

Arenas de San Pedro

Soria

Huesca

Zaragoza

Lérida

Gerona

Barcelona

Tarragona

Castellón

Teruel

Cuenca

Guadalajara

MADRID

EL ALCÁZAR

Toledo

Talavera

Guadalupe

Cáceres

Mérida

Badajoz

Llerena

Ciudad Real

Na SEÑORA DE LA CABEZA

Albacete

Valencia

Alicante

Murcia

Almería

Jaén

Granada

Córdoba

Sevilla

Huelva

Cádiz

Algeciras

Ceuta

Málaga

Melilla

SPANISH MOROCCO

PORTUGAL

MENORCA

MALLORCA

Balearic Islands

Palma

IBIZA

Canary Islands

LANZAROTE

FUERTEVENTURA

LA PALMA

TENERIFE

Santa Cruz

Las Palmas

GRAN CANARIA

GOMERA

HIERRO

Same scale as main map

Nationalist zone

Republican zone

Miles

Kilometres

0   150

0   250

viii

Introduction

The Civil War Fifty Years On

In geographical and human scale, let alone in the scale of technological horrors, the Spanish Civil War has been dwarfed by later conflicts. Nonetheless, it has generated over fifteen thousand books, a literary epitaph which puts it on a par with the Second World War. In part, that reflects the extent to which, even after 1939, the war continued to be fought between Franco's victorious Nationalists and the defeated and exiled Republicans. Even more, and certainly as far as foreigners were concerned, the survival of interest in the Spanish tragedy was closely connected with the sheer longevity of its victor. General Franco's uninterrupted enjoyment of a dictatorial power seized with the aid of Hitler and Mussolini was an infuriating affront to opponents of fascism the world over. Moreover, the destruction of democracy in Spain was not allowed to become just another fading remnant of the humiliations of the period of appeasement. Far from trying to heal the wounds of civil strife, Franco worked harder than anyone to keep the war a live and burning issue both inside and outside Spain.

Reminders of Francoism's victory over international communism were frequently used to curry favour with the outside world. This was most dramatically the case immediately after the Second World War, when frantic efforts were made to dissociate Franco from his erstwhile Axis allies. This was done by stressing his enmity to communism and playing down his equally vehement opposition to liberal democracy and socialism. Throughout the Cold War, the irrefutable anti-communism of the Nationalist side in the Civil War was used to build a picture of Franco as the bulwark of the Western system, the 'Sentinel of the West' in the phrase coined by his propagandists. Within Spain itself, memories of the war and of the bloody repression which followed it were carefully nurtured in order to maintain what has been called 'the pact of blood'. The dictator was supported by an uneasy coalition of the highly privileged, landowners, industrialists and bankers; of what might be called the 'service classes' of Francoism, that is, those members of the middle and working classes who, for whatever reasons – opportunism, conviction or wartime geographical loyalty – threw in their lot with the regime; and finally of those ordinary Spanish Catholics who supported the Nationalists as the defenders of religion and law and order. Reminders of the war were useful to rally the wavering loyalty of any or all of these groups.

The most privileged usually remained aloof from the dictatorship and disdainful of its propaganda. However, those who were implicated in the regime's networks of corruption and repression, the beneficiaries of the killings and the pillage, were especially susceptible to hints that only Franco stood between them and the revenge of their victims. In any case, for many who worked for the dictator, as policemen or Civil Guards, as humble *serenos* (night-watchmen) or *porteros* (doormen), in the giant bureaucracy of Franco's single party, the *Movimiento*, in its trade union organization, or in its huge press network, the Civil War was a crucial part of their *curriculum vitae* and of their value system. They were to make up what in the 1970s came to be known as the *bunker*, the die-hard Francoists who were prepared to fight for the values of the Civil War from the rubble of the Chancellery. A similar, and more dangerous, commitment came from the praetorian defenders of the legacy of what Spanish rightists refer to broadly as *el 18 de julio* (from the date of the military rising of 1936). Army officers had been educated since 1939 in academies where they were taught that the military existed to defend Spain from communism, anarchism, socialism, parliamentary democracy and regionalists who wanted to destroy Spain's unity. Accordingly, after Franco's death the *bunker* and its military supporters were to attempt once more to destroy democracy in Spain in the name of the Nationalist victory in the Civil War.

For these ultra-rightists, Nationalist propaganda efforts to maintain the hatreds of the Civil War were perhaps gratuitous. However, the regime clearly thought them essential for the less partisan Spaniards who rendered Franco a passive support ranging from the grudging to the enthusiastic. The Catholics and members of the middle classes who had been appalled by the view of Republican disorder and anti-clericalism generated by the rightist press were induced to turn a blind eye to the more distasteful aspects of a bloody dictatorship by constant and exaggerated reminders of the war. Within months of the end of hostilities, a massive 'History of the Crusade' was being published in weekly parts, glorifying the heroism of the victors and portraying the vanquished as the dupes of Moscow, as either squalidly self-interested or the blood-crazed perpetrators of sadistic atrocities. Until well into the 1960s a stream of publications, many aimed at children, presented the war as a religious crusade against communist barbarism.

Beyond the hermetically sealed frontiers of Franco's Spain, the defeated Republicans and their foreign sympathizers rejected the Francoist interpretation that the Civil War had been a battle of the forces of order and true religion against a Jewish-Bolshevik-Masonic conspiracy. Instead, they maintained consistently that the war was the struggle of an oppressed people seeking a decent way of life against the opposition of Spain's backward landed and industrial oligarchies and their Nazi and Fascist allies. Unfortunately, bitterly divided over the reasons for their defeat, they could not present as monolithically coherent a view of the war as did their Francoist opponents. In a way that weakened their collective voice, but immeasurably enriched the literature of the Spanish Civil War, they were side-tracked into vociferous debate about whether they might have beaten the Nationalists if only they had unleashed the popular revolutionary war advocated by anarchists and Trotskyists, as opposed to mounting the conventional war effort imposed by the all-powerful Communists of the PCE (Partido Comunista de España). Ever since, their debate has engaged Republican sympathizers unable to come to terms with the leftist defeat; and it has raged anew, scoured for parallels, in the light of the national liberation struggles in Vietnam, Cuba, Chile and Nicaragua.

Death and destruction were the inevitable companions of military conquest, but not even those who, in 1936, had conspired against the Republic had envisaged a conflict so long, so devastating and so bloody. Above, corpses in the streets of Barcelona on 19 July 1936; below, the remains of a house in the village of Durango, on the Vizcaya front.

The relevance of the Civil War to Franco's supporters and to left-wingers throughout the world does not fully explain the much wider fascination which the Spanish conflict still exercises today. In the aftermath of the Second World War, Korea and Vietnam, it can only seem like small beer. As Raymond Carr, the doyen of British Hispanists, has pointed out, compared to Hiroshima or Dresden the bombing of Guernica seems 'a minor act of vandalism'. Yet it has provoked more savage polemic than virtually any incident in the Second World War. That is not, as some would have, because of the power of Picasso's painting but because Guernica was the *first* total destruction of an undefended civilian target by aerial bombardment. Accordingly, the Spanish Civil War is burned into the European consciousness not simply as a rehearsal for the bigger world war to come, but because it presaged the opening of the floodgates to a new and horrific form of modern warfare that was universally dreaded.

It was because they shared the collective fear of what defeat for the Spanish Republic might mean that men and women, workers and intellectuals, went to join the International Brigades. The left saw clearly in 1936 what for another three years even the democratic right chose to ignore: that Spain was the last bulwark against the horrors of Hitlerism. In a Europe still unaware of the crimes of Stalin, the Communist-organized brigades seemed to be fighting for much that was worth saving in terms of democratic rights and trade union freedoms. The volunteers believed that by fighting fascism in Spain they were also fighting it in their own countries. Hindsight about the sordid power struggles in the Republican zone between the Communists on the one hand and the Socialists, the anarchists and the quasi-Trotskyist Partido Obrero de Unificación Marxista (POUM) on the other cannot diminish the idealism of the individuals concerned. There remains something intensely tragic about Italian and German refugees from Mussolini and Hitler finally being able to take up arms against their persecutors, only to be defeated again.

To dwell on the impact of the horrors of the Spanish war and on the importance of the defence against fascism is to miss one of the most positive factors of the Republican experience: the attempt to drag Spain into the twentieth century. In the drab Europe of the depression years, what was happening in Republican Spain seemed an exciting experiment. Orwell's celebrated comment acknowledged this: 'I recognized it immediately as a state of affairs worth fighting for.' The cultural and educational achievements of the Spanish Republic were only the best-known aspects of a social revolution which had an impact on the contemporary world such as Cuba and Chile never quite attained in the 1960s. Spain was not only nearby, but its social experiments were taking place in a context of widespread disillusion with the failures of capitalism. By 1945, the fight against the Axis had become linked with the preservation of the old world. During the Spanish Civil War, however, the struggle against fascism was still seen as merely the first step to building a new egalitarian world out of the depression. In the event, the exigencies of the war effort and internecine conflict stood in the way of the full flowering of the industrial and agrarian collectives of the Republican zone. Nevertheless, there was, and is, something inspiring about the way in which the Spanish working class faced the dual tasks of war against the old order and of construction of the new. The anarchist leader, Buenaventura Durruti, best expressed this spirit when he told a reporter, 'We are not afraid of ruins, we are going to inherit the earth. The bourgeoisie may blast and ruin their world before they leave the stage of history. But we carry a new world in our hearts.'

All of this is perhaps to suggest that interest in the Spanish Civil War is made up of

The Spanish Civil War gave rise to a surge of cultural creativity
of which Picasso's *Guernica* is probably the most famous
manifestation. Many artists and writers may have felt, like the
Peruvian writer César Vallejo, that 'the shifts of politics had never
depended on what the intellectuals said or did'. Yet, at the same
time, they also felt, as he did, a deep moral, political and
aesthetic compulsion to express their sense of involvement, both
in their work and in their active support of one or the other of
the ideological positions in conflict.

Nationalist propaganda poster which linked the defence of traditional values (bottom) to the more contemporary fascist ambitions of Franco's allies (top).

nostalgia on the part of contemporaries of right and left and political romanticism on the part of the young. After all, there is a strong case to be made for presenting the Spanish Civil War as the 'the last great cause'. It was not for nothing that the Civil War inspired the greatest writers of its day in a manner not repeated in any subsequent war. However, nostalgia and romanticism aside, it is impossible to exaggerate the sheer historical importance of the Spanish war. Beyond its climactic impact on Spain itself, the war was very much the nodal point of the 1930s. Baldwin and Blum, Hitler and Mussolini, Stalin and Trotsky all had substantial parts in the Spanish drama. The Rome-Berlin Axis was clinched in Spain at the same time as the inadequacies of appeasement were ruthlessly exposed. It was above all a Spanish war, or rather a series of Spanish wars; yet it was also the great international battleground of fascism and communism. And while Colonel von Richthofen practised in the Basque Country the *Blitzkrieg* techniques he was later to perfect in Poland, agents of the Soviet NKVD (People's Commissariat for Internal Affairs) re-enacted the Moscow trials on the 'Trotskyists' of the POUM.

Nor is the Spanish conflict without its contemporary relevance. The war arose out of the violent opposition of the privileged and their foreign allies to the reformist attempts of liberal Republican-Socialist governments to ameliorate the daily living conditions of the most wretched members of society. The parallels with Chile in the 1970s or Nicaragua today hardly need emphasizing. Equally, the ease with which the Spanish Republic was destabilized by skilfully provoked disorder is not without sombre echoes in Italy, or even Spain, in the 1980s. Fortunately, Spanish democracy survived in 1981 the attempts to overthrow it, made by military men nostalgic for a Francoist Spain of victors and vanquished. In the same year that marks the fiftieth anniversary of the Spanish Civil War, a war which would see Spain suffer nearly forty years of international ostracism, the country has been formally admitted into the European Community. There is perhaps no better time to remember a violent and bloody Spain which has perhaps gone for ever.

'Franco has all the qualities the good soldier must have: courage, intelligence, military spirit, enthusiasm, dedication to work, the spirit of sacrifice and a virtuous life', wrote Millán Astray in 1922 of Franco's exploits in Morocco. The qualities he had shown in the colonial wars ensured that, by 1936, he was viewed by the middle classes as the saviour of Spain from revolution.

1

A Divided Society: Spain before 1930

The origins of the Spanish Civil War lie far back in the country's history. The notion that political problems could be solved more naturally by violence than by debate was firmly entrenched in a country in which for a thousand years civil war has been, if not exactly the norm, then certainly no rarity. The war of 1936-9 was the fourth such conflict since the 1830s. The religious 'crusade' propaganda of the Nationalists joyfully linked it with the Christian *Reconquista* of Spain from the Moors. On both sides, heroism and nobility vied with primitive cruelty and brutality in a way that would not have been out of place in a medieval epic. Yet, in the last resort, the Spanish Civil War is a war firmly rooted in the modern period. Leaving aside the dimension given to the war by the interference of Hitler, Mussolini and Stalin, the myriad Spanish conflicts which erupted in 1936 – regionalists against centralists, anti-clericals against Catholics, landless labourers against *latifundistas*, workers against industrialists – have in common the struggles of a society in the throes of modernization.

To understand Spain's progress to the bloodshed of 1936 it is necessary to make a fundamental distinction between the long-term structural origins and the immediate political causes. In the hundred years before 1930 it was possible to discern the gradual and immensely complex division of the country into two broadly antagonistic social blocks. However, when the Second Republic was established on 14 April 1931 amid scenes of popular rejoicing, few Spaniards outside of the lunatic fringes of the extreme left and right, the conspiratorial monarchists and the anarchists, believed that the country's problems could only be solved by resort to violence. Five years and three months later, large sections of the population believed that war was inevitable. Moreover, a substantial proportion of them felt that war would be a good thing. Accordingly, it is necessary to establish exactly what happened between 14 April 1931 and 18 July 1936 to bring about that change. Nevertheless, the political hatreds which polarized the Second Republic in those five and a quarter years were a reflection of the deep-rooted conflicts of Spanish society.

It is a central theme of this book that the Civil War was the culmination of a series of uneven struggles between the forces of reform and reaction which had dominated Spanish history since 1808. There is a curious pattern in Spain's modern history, arising from a frequent *desfase*, or lack of synchronization, between the social reality and the political power structure ruling over it. Periods in which reactionary elements have attempted to use political and military power to hold back social progress have inevitably been followed by outbursts of revolutionary fervour. In the 1850s, the 1870s, between 1917 and 1923, and above all during the Second Republic, efforts have been made to bring Spanish politics into line with the country's social reality. This has inevitably involved attempts to introduce fundamental reform, especially on the land, and to redistribute wealth. Such moves have in turn provoked reactionary efforts to stop the clock and reimpose the traditional balance of social and economic power. Thus were progressive movements crushed by General O'Donnell in 1856, by General Pavía in 1874 and by General Primo de Rivera in 1923.

Accordingly, the Civil War of 1936-9 represented the ultimate expression of the attempts by reactionary elements in Spanish politics to crush any reform that might threaten their privileged position. The recurring dominance of reactionary elements was a consequence of the continued power of the old landed oligarchy and the parallel weakness of the progressive bourgeoisie. A concomitant of the tortuously slow and uneven development of industrial capitalism in Spain was the existence of a numerically small and politically insignificant commercial and manufacturing class. Spain did not experience a classic bourgeois revolution in which the structures of the *ancien régime* were broken. The power of the monarchy, the landed nobility and the Church remained more or less intact well into the twentieth century. Unlike Britain and France, nineteenth-century Spain did not see the establishment of a democratic polity with the flexibility to absorb new forces and to adjust to major social change. That is not to say that Spain remained a feudal society, but rather that the legal basis for capitalism was established without there being a political revolution. Accordingly, with the obvious difference that her industrial capitalism was extremely feeble, Spain followed the pattern established by Prussia.

Indeed, even until the 1950s, capitalism in Spain was predominantly agrarian. Spanish agriculture is immensely diverse in terms of climate, crops and land-holding systems. There have long existed areas of commercially successful small and medium farming operations, especially in the lush, wet hills and valleys of those northern regions which also experienced industrialization, Asturias, Catalonia and the Basque Country. However, throughout the nineteenth century and for the first half of the twentieth, the dominant sectors in terms of political influence were, broadly speaking, the large landowners. In the main the *latifundia*, the great estates, are concentrated in the arid central and southern regions of New Castile, Extremadura and Andalusia, although there are also substantial *latifundios* to be found scattered in Old Castile and particularly in Salamanca. The political monopoly of the landed oligarchy was periodically challenged by the emasculated industrial and mercantile classes with virtually no success. Until well after the civil war, the urban *haute bourgeoisie* was obliged to play the role of junior partner in a working coalition with the great *latifundistas*. Despite sporadic industrialization and a steady growth in the national importance of the political representatives of the northern industrialists, power remained squarely in the hands of the landowners.

There was never any strong possibility in Spain that industrialization and political modernization would coincide. In the first half of the nineteenth century the progressive impulses, both political and economic, of the Spanish bourgeoisie were irrevocably diverted. The removal of feudal restrictions on land transactions combined with royal financial problems in the 1830s and the 1850s to liberate huge tracts of aristocratic, ecclesiastical and common lands. This not only diminished any impetus towards industrialization but, by helping to expand the great estates, also created intense social hatreds in the south. The newly released land was bought up by the more efficient among existing landlords and by members of the commercial and mercantile bourgeoisie attracted by its cheapness and social prestige. The latifundia system was consolidated and the new landlords were keen for a return on their investment. Unwilling to engage in expensive projects of irrigation, they preferred instead to build their profits on the exploitation of the great armies of landless day-labourers, the *braceros* and *jornaleros*. The departure of the more easy-going clerics and nobles of an earlier age, together with the enclosure of common lands, removed most of the social palliatives which had hitherto kept the poverty-stricken south from upheaval. Paternalism was replaced by repression when the Civil Guard was created as a rural armed police with the principal function of guarding the big estates from the labourers who worked on them. Thus, the strengthening of the landed oligarchy exacerbated an explosive social situation which could only foster the reactionary tendencies of the owners. At the same time, the syphoning into the land of the capital of the merchants of the great seaports, and of the Madrid bankers, correspondingly weakened their interest in modernization.

Continued investment in land and widespread intermarriage between the urban bourgeoisie and the landed oligarchy debilitated those forces committed to reform. The feebleness of the Spanish bourgeoisie as a potentially revolutionary class was underlined in the period from 1868 to 1874, which culminated in the chaos of the First Republic. With population growth in the middle of the century increasing pressure on the land, unskilled labourers had flocked to the towns and swelled the mob of unemployed, who were highly sensitive to increases in bread prices. Hardly less wretched was the position of the urban lower middle class of teachers, officials and shopkeepers. Conditions were perhaps worst in the Catalan textile industry, which produced all the horrors of nascent capitalism: long hours, child labour, overcrowding and low wages. When the American Civil War cut off supplies of cotton in the 1860s, the consequent rise in unemployment combined with a depression in railway construction to drive the urban working class to desperation. In 1868 this popular discontent combined with a movement of middle-class and military resentment of the clerical and ultra-conservative leanings of the monarchy. A number of *pronunciamientos* by liberal army officers, together with urban riots, led to its overthrow. The two movements were ultimately contradictory. The liberals were terrified to find that their constitutionalist rebellion had awakened a revolutionary movement of the masses. To make matters worse, a rebellion began in Spain's richest surviving colony, Cuba. The chosen replacement monarch, Amadeo of Savoy, abdicated in despair in 1873. In the ensuing vacuum, the First Republic was established after a number of working-class risings, an intolerable threat to the established order which was crushed by the army in December 1874.

In many respects, 1873–74 was to Spain what 1848–49 had been elsewhere in Europe. Having plucked up the courage to challenge the old order, the bourgeoisie was frightened out of its reforming ambitions by the spectre of proletarian disorder. When the army restored the monarchy in the person of Alfonso XII, reform was abandoned in return for social peace. The subsequent balance of forces between the landed oligarchy, the urban bourgeoisie and the remainder of the population was perfectly represented by the political system of the 1876 monarchical restoration. Two political parties, the Conservative and the Liberal, represented the interests of two sections of the landed oligarchy, respectively the wine and olive growers of the south and the wheat growers of the centre. The differences between them were slight. They were both monarchist and were divided not on social issues but over free trade and, to a much lesser extent, over religion. The northern industrial bourgeoisie was barely represented within the system but was, for the moment, content to devote its activities to economic expansion in an atmosphere of stability.

It was virtually impossible for any political aspirations to find legal expression outside these two great oligarchical parties. Liberal and Conservative governments followed one another with soporific regularity. When results were not faked in the Ministry of the Interior, they were fixed at the local level. The system of electoral falsification rested on the social power of local town bosses or *caciques* (a South American Indian word meaning 'chief'). In the northern smallholding areas, the *cacique* was usually a moneylender, one of the bigger landlords, a lawyer or even a priest, who held mortgages on the small farms. In the latifundia areas, New Castile, Extremadura or Andalusia, the *cacique* was the landowner or his agent, the man who decided who worked and therefore did not starve. *Caciquismo* ensured that the narrow interests represented by the system were never seriously threatened.

On occasion, over-zealous local officials would produce majorities adding up to more than 100 per cent of the electorate. It was not unknown for results to be published before the elections took place. As the century wore on, casual falsification became somewhat more difficult and, if the requisite number of peasant votes could not be mustered, the *caciques* were said sometimes to register the dead in the local cemetery. In consequence, politics became an exclusive minuet danced out by a small privileged minority. The nature of politics in the period of *caciquismo* is illustrated by the celebrated story of the *cacique* of Motril in the province of Granada. When the coach with the election results arrived from the provincial capital, they were brought to him in the local *casino* (club). Leafing through them, he pronounced to the expectant hangers-on the following words: 'We the Liberals were convinced that we would win these elections. However, the will of God has decreed otherwise.' A lengthy pause. 'It appears that we the Conservatives have won the elections.' Excluded from organized politics, the hungry masses could choose only between apathy and violence. The inevitable outbreaks of protest by the unrepresented majority were dealt with by the forces of order – the Civil Guard and, at moments of greater tension, the army.

Challenges to the system did arise, however, and they were linked to the painfully slow but inexorable progress of industrialization and to the brutal social injustices intrinsic to the latifundia economy. The 1890s were a period of economic depression which exacerbated the grievances of the lower classes, especially in the countryside. Land hunger was creating an increasingly desperate desire for change, the more so as the southern labourers came under the influence of anarchism. The arrival of anarchism in the 1860s had given a sense of hope and purpose to hitherto sporadic rural uprisings. Its message of justice and equality found eager converts among the starving day-labourers or *braceros*. They took part in outbreaks of sporadic violence, crop burnings and strikes. In January 1892 an army of *braceros*, armed only with scythes and sticks but driven by hunger, seized the town of Jerez. Anarchism also took root in the small workshops of the highly fragmented Catalan textile industry.

The system was rocked in 1898 by defeat at the hands of the USA and the loss of the remnants of empire, including Cuba. This was to have a catastrophic effect on the Spanish economy, especially in Catalonia for whose products Cuba had been a protected market. Barcelona was the scene of sporadic strikes and acts of terrorism by both anarchists and government *agents provocateurs*. Moreover, by the turn of the century, the growth of coal, steel and textile industries in the north saw the emergence of a militant industrial proletariat. In the two decades before the First World War, the working-class aristocracy of printers and craftsmen from the building and metal trades in Madrid, the steel and shipyard workers in Bilbao, and the coalminers of Asturias began to swell the ranks of the Partido Socialista Obrero Español, (PSOE), the Socialist Party founded in 1879, and its trade union organization, the Unión General de Trabajadores (UGT). Surprisingly, however, when the inevitable explosion came it was precipitated not by the rural anarchists or the urban working class but by the industrial bourgeoisie. Nevertheless, once the crisis started, proletarian ambitions came into play in such a way as to ensure that the basic polarization of Spanish political life became starker than ever.

The geometric symmetry of the Restoration system, with political power concentrated in the hands of those who also enjoyed the monopoly of economic power, was shattered by the coming of the First World War. Not only were political passions aroused by a bitter debate about whether Spain should intervene and on which side, accentuating growing divisions within the Liberal and Conservative parties, but massive social upheaval came in the wake of the war. The fact that Spain was a non-belligerent put her in the economically privileged position of being able to supply both the Entente and the Central Powers with agricultural and industrial products. Coalmine owners from Asturias, Basque steel barons and shipbuilders, Catalan textile magnates, all experienced a wild boom which constituted the first dramatic take-off for Spanish industry. The balance of power within the economic élite shifted somewhat. Agrarian interests remained pre-eminent but industrialists were no longer prepared to tolerate their subordinate political position. Their dissatisfaction came to a head in June 1916 when the Liberal Minister of Finance, Santiago Alba, attempted to impose a tax on the notorious war profits of northern industry without a corresponding measure to deal with those made by the agrarians. Although the move was blocked, it so underlined the arrogance of the landed élite that it precipitated a bid by the industrial bourgeoisie to carry through political modernization.

The discontent of the Basque and Catalan industrialists had already led them to mount challenges to the Spanish establishment by sponsoring regionalist movements. Now the reforming zeal of industrialists enriched by the war coincided with a desperate need for change from a proletariat impoverished by it. Boom industries attracted rural labour to towns where the worst conditions of early capitalism prevailed. This was especially true of Asturias and the Basque Country. At the same time, massive exports created shortages, rocketing inflation and plummeting living standards. The Socialist UGT and the anarcho-syndicalist Confederación Nacional del Trabajo (CNT) were drawn together in the hope that a joint general strike might bring about free elections and then reform. While industrialists and workers pushed for change, middle-rank army officers were protesting at low wages, antiquated promotion structures and political corruption. A bizarre and short-lived alliance was forged in part because of a misunderstanding about the political stance of the army.

Military complaints were couched in the language of reform which had become fashionable after Spain's loss of empire in 1898. Known as 'Regenerationism', it associated the defeat of 1898 with political corruption. Ultimately, 'Regenerationism' was open to exploitation by either the right or the left since among its advocates there were those who sought to sweep away the degenerate *caciquista* system by democratic reform and those who planned simply to crush it by the authoritarian solution of 'an iron surgeon'. However, in 1917 the officers who mouthed 'Regenerationist' clichés were acclaimed as the figureheads of a great national reform movement. For a brief moment workers, capitalists and the military were united in the name of cleansing Spanish politics of the corruption of *caciquismo*. Had the movement been successful in establishing a political system capable of permitting social adjustment, the Civil War would not have been necessary. As things turned out, the great crisis of 1917 merely consolidated the power of the entrenched landed oligarchy.

Despite a rhetorical coincidence of their calls for reform, the ultimate interests of workers, industrialists and officers were contradictory and the system survived by skilfully exploiting these differences. The Prime Minister, the Conservative Eduardo Dato, conceded the officers' economic demands. He then provoked a strike of Socialist railway workers, forcing the UGT to act before the CNT was ready. Now at peace with the system, the army was happy to defend it in August 1917 by crushing the striking Socialists with considerable bloodshed. Alarmed by the prospect of militant workers in the streets, the industrialists dropped their own demands for political reform and, lured by promises of economic modernization, joined in a national coalition government in 1918 with both Liberals and Conservatives. Yet again the industrial bourgeoisie had abandoned its political aspirations and allied with the landed oligarchy out of a fear of the lower classes. Short-lived though it was to be, the coalition symbolized the slightly improved position of industrialists in a reactionary alliance still dominated by the landed interest.

By 1917, Spain was divided more starkly even than before into two mutually hostile social groups, with landowners and industrialists on one side and workers and landless labourers on the other. Only one numerous social group was not definitively aligned within this broad cleavage: the smallholding peasantry. Significantly, in the years before and during the first World War, efforts were being made to mobilize Catholic farmers in defence of big landholding interests. With anarchism and Socialism making headway among the urban workers, the more far-sighted landowners were anxious to stop the spread of the poison to the countryside. Counter-revolutionary syndicates were financed by landlords from 1906, but the process was systematized after 1912 by a group of dynamic Catholics led by Angel Herrera, the *éminence grise* of political Catholicism in Spain before 1936. Through his organization of determined social Christian activists, the Asociación Católica Nacional de Propagandistas (ACNP), Herrera helped set up a series of provincial Catholic Agrarian Federations which tried to prevent impoverished farmers from turning to the left by offering them credit facilities, agronomic expertise, warehousing and machinery in return for their adoption of virulent anti-socialism. Many of those recruited were to play an important role when the landed oligarchy was forced to seek more modern forms of defence in the 1930s, first by voting for the legalist parties of the right during the Second Republic and later by fighting for Franco.

General Miguel Primo de Rivera y Orbaneja.

H.R.H. Alfonso de Borbón, seen here posing for an official portrait, ascended the Spanish throne as Alfonso XIII on 17 May 1902, at the age of sixteen. His romantic, personalist and militarist concept of the monarchy proved to be totally inappropriate to the social, political and economic upheavals of early twentieth century Spain.

In the aftermath of the crisis of 1917, however, the existing order survived, in part because of the organizational naïvety of the left but more because of its own ready recourse to armed repression. The defeat of the urban Socialists in 1917 did not mark the end of the assault on the system. From 1918 to 1921, in the so-called *trienio bolchevique*, the anarchist day-labourers of the south took part in a series of risings. Eventually put down by a combination of the Civil Guard and the army, the strikes and land seizures of these years intensified the social resentments of the rural south. At the same time urban anarchists were also coming into conflict with the system. Northern industrialists, having failed to invest their war profits in modern plant and rationalization, were badly hit by the postwar resurgence of foreign competition. The Catalans in particular tried to ride the recession with wage cuts and lay-offs. They countered the consequent strikes with lock-outs and hired gunmen. The anarchists retaliated in kind and, from 1919 to 1921, the streets of Barcelona witnessed a terrorist spiral of provocations and reprisals. It was obvious that Restoration politics were no longer an adequate mechanism for defending the economic interests of the ruling classes.

On 23 September 1923, a *coup d'état* was carried out by General Miguel Primo de Rivera. Ostensibly, Primo came to power to put an end to disorder and to prevent an embarrassing report by a parliamentary commission from causing discomfort to the King. However, as Captain-General of Barcelona and intimate of the Catalan textile barons, Primo was fully aware of the anarchist threat to them. Moreover, coming from a large landowning family in the south, he had also experienced the peasant risings of 1918-21. He was thus the ideal praetorian defender of the coalition of industrialists and landowners which had been consolidated during the great crisis of 1917. Initially, his dictatorship had two great advantages: a general revulsion against the chaos of the previous six years, and an upturn in the European economy. He outlawed the anarchist movement and made a deal with the UGT whereby it was given a monopoly of trade union affairs. A massive public works programme, which involved a significant modernizing of Spanish capitalism and the building of a road and rail infrastructure that would be fully exploited only thirty years later, gave the impression that liberty was being traded in for prosperity.

The Primo de Rivera dictatorship was to be regarded in later years as a golden age by the Spanish middle classes, and became a central myth of the reactionary right. Paradoxically, however, its short-term effect was to discredit the very idea of authoritarianism in Spain. This fleeting phenomenon was born partly of Primo's failure to use the economic breathing space to construct a lasting political replacement for the decrepit constitutional monarchy, but more immediately it sprang from his alienation of the powerful interests which had originally supported him. A genial eccentric with a Falstaffian approach to political life, he governed by a form of personal improvisation which ensured that he bore the blame for his regime's failures. Although by 1930 there was hardly a section of Spanish society that he had not offended, his most crucial errors led to the estrangement of industrialists, landowners and the army. Attempts to standardize the army's promotion system outraged the officer corps. The Catalan bourgeoisie was antagonized by an offensive against regionalist aspirations. Northern industrialists were even more enraged by the collapse of the peseta in 1928, which they attributed to his inflationary public spending. Perhaps most importantly, the support of Primo's fellow landowners was lost when efforts were made to introduce into rural areas arbitration committees for wages and working conditions. At the end of January 1930 Primo resigned.

There was no question of a return to the pre-1923 political system. Apart from the fact that it had fallen into disrepute by the time Primo seized power, significant changes had taken place in the attitudes of its personnel. Among the senior politicians death, old age and, above all, resentment of the King's cavalier abandonment of the constitution had taken their toll. Of the younger men, some had opted for the republican movement, partly out of pique, partly out of a conviction that the political future lay in that direction. Others, especially those Conservatives who had followed the authoritarian implications of 'Regenerationism' to the logical extreme, had thrown themselves wholeheartedly into the service of the dictator. For them, there could be no going back. Their experiences under Primo had left them entrenched in the view that the only feasible solution to the problems faced by the right was a military monarchy. They would form the general staff of the extreme right in the Second Republic and were to provide much of the ideological content of the Franco regime.

In desperation, therefore, Alfonso XIII turned to another general, Dámaso Berenguer. His mild dictatorship floundered in search of a formula for a return to constitutional monarchy but was undermined by republican plots, working-class agitation and military sedition. When he held municipal elections on 12 April 1931, Socialists and liberal middle-class republicans swept the board in the main towns while monarchists won only in the rural areas where the social domination of the *caciques* remained intact. Faced by the questionable loyalty of both army and Civil Guard, the King took the advice of his counsellors to depart gracefully before he was thrown out by force. The attitude of the military reflected the hope of a significant section of the upper classes that by sacrificing the King it would be possible to contain the desires for change of both the progressive bourgeoisie and the left. That was to be an impossible ambition without some concessions in the area of land reform.

The conflicts of the *trienio bolchevique* had been silenced by repression from 1919 to 1920 and by the Primo de Rivera dictatorship, but they continued to smoulder. The violence of those years had ended the uneasy *modus vivendi* of the agrarian south. The repression had intensified the hatred of the *braceros* for the big landowners and their estate managers. By the same token, the landlords were outraged by insubordinate behaviour of the day-labourers, whom they considered to be almost subhuman. Accordingly, the elements of paternalism which had previously mitigated the daily brutality of the *braceros'* lives came to an abrupt end. The gathering of windfall crops, the watering of beasts, even the collection of firewood were deemed to be 'collective kleptomania' and were prevented by the vigilance of armed guards. In consequence, the new Republic was to inherit a situation of sporadic social war in the south which was dramatically to diminish its possibilities of establishing a regime of co-existence. Nevertheless, with goodwill on both sides, everything, even peace, was possible in 1931. Within weeks of the Republic being established, however, it was clear that among the erstwhile supporters of Alfonso XIII and within the anarchist movement there was anything but goodwill towards Spain's new democracy.

Above: All over Spain, thousands of people came onto the streets to celebrate the declaration of the Second Republic on 14 April 1931. The photograph shows the huge crowd which gathered in the Plaza de Cibeles, in the centre of Madrid.

Left: The candidacy of D. Niceto Alcalá Zamora for President of the new Republic was approved by 362 of the total of 446 parliamentary representatives. In the photograph, Alcalá Zamora (seated, centre) converses with the Papal *nuncio* Monsgr. Tedeschini while, to the right, Cardinal Vidal i Barraquer talks with Manuel Portela Valladares, former Development Minister during the reign of Alfonso XIII.

2

The Leftist Challenge: 1931-33

The coming of the Second Republic signified a threat to the most privileged members of society and raised inordinate hopes among the most humble. Ultimately, the new regime was to fail because it neither carried through its threatened reforms nor fulfilled the utopian expectations of its most fervent supporters. The success of the right in blocking change would so exasperate the rural and urban working classes as to undermine their faith in parliamentary democracy. Once that happened, and once the left had turned to revolutionary solutions, the rightist determination to destabilize the Republic would be enormously facilitated. Yet, given the failures of both the monarchy and the Dictatorship, the majority of Spaniards had been prepared in 1931 to give the Republic a chance. However, behind the superficial goodwill, there was potentially savage conflict over the scale of the social and economic reform it should pursue or, to use the jargon of the day, over what the 'content' of the Republic should be. In this sense, the seeds of war were buried near the surface of a Republic which was the source of hope to the left and of fear to the right.

Before 1931, social, economic and political power in Spain had all been in the hands of the same groups, the components of the reactionary coalition of landowners, industrialists and bankers. The challenge to that monopoly mounted by the disunited forces of the left between 1917 and 1923 had exposed the deficiencies of the Restoration monarchy. The defence of establishment interests was then entrusted to the military dictatorship of General Primo de Rivera. Because of its failure, the idea of an authoritarian solution to the problems facing the beleagured oligarchy was briefly discredited. Moreover, the coming of the Republic found the right temporarily bereft of political organization. Accordingly, the upper classes and large sectors of the middle classes acquiesced in the departure of Alfonso XIII because they had little alternative. They did so in the hope that, by sacrificing a King and tolerating a President, they might protect themselves from greater unpleasantness in the way of social and economic reform.

However, the establishment of the Republic meant that for the first time political power had passed from the oligarchy to the moderate left. This consisted of representatives of the most reformist section of the organized working class, the Socialists and a mixed bag of petty-bourgeois Republicans, some of whom were idealists and many of whom were cynics. Together, they hoped, despite considerable disagreement over the finer details, to use state power to create a new Spain by destroying the reactionary influence of the Church and the army, by sweeping away the structure of the latifundia estates and by meeting the autonomy demands of Basque and Catalan regionalists. However, social and economic power, ownership of the land and control over those who worked it, of the banks and industry remained unchanged. Those who held that power were united with the Church and the army in being determined to prevent any attacks on property, religion or national unity. They were quick to find a variety of ways in which to defend their interests. Ultimately the Spanish Civil War was to grow out of the efforts of the progressive leaders of the Republic to carry out reform against the wishes of the most powerful sections of society.

When the King fled power was assumed by the Provisional Government, whose composition had been agreed in August 1930 when Republican and Socialist opponents of the King had met and forged the Pact of San Sebastian. The Prime Minister was Niceto Alcalá Zamora, a landowner from Cordoba and an ex-minister of the King. The Minister of the Interior was Miguel Maura, the son of the celebrated Conservative politician Antonio Maura. Both Alcalá Zamora and Maura were Catholic conservatives and served as a guarantee to the upper classes that the Republic would remain within the bounds of reason. The remainder of the cabinet was made up of centre and left Republicans and reformist Socialists, unanimous in their desire to build a Republic for all Spaniards. Inevitably, therefore, the coming of the parliamentary regime constituted far less of a change than was either hoped for by the rejoicing crowds in the streets or feared by the upper classes.

Socialist ambitions were restrained. The PSOE leadership hoped that the political power that had fallen into their hands would permit the improvement of the living conditions of the southern *braceros*, the Asturian miners and other sections of the working class. They realized that the overthrow of capitalism was a distant dream. What the most progressive members of the new Republican-Socialist coalition failed to perceive at first was the stark truth that the great *latifundistas* and the mineowners would regard any attempt at reform as an aggressive challenge to the existing balance of social and economic power. However, in the days before they realized that they were trapped between the impatient mass demand for significant reform and the dogged hostility to change of the rich, the Socialists approached the Republic in a spirit of self-sacrifice and optimism. In Madrid on 14 April members of the Socialist Youth Movement prevented assaults on buildings associated with the right, especially the royal palace. The Socialist ministers acquiesced in Maura's refusal to abolish the Civil Guard – a hated symbol of authority to workers and peasants. Also, in a gesture to the wealthy classes, the Socialist Minister of Finance, Indalecio Prieto, announced that he would meet all the financial obligations of the Dictatorship.

However, the potential state of war between the proponents of reform and the defenders of the existing order was not to be ignored. Rightist hostility to the Republic was quickly revealed. Prieto announced at the first meeting of ministers that the financial position of the regime was being endangered by a large-scale withdrawal of wealth from the country. Even before the Republic had been established, followers of General Primo de Rivera had been trying to build barricades against liberalism and republicanism. They started to collect money from aristocrats, landowners, bankers and industrialists to publicize authoritarian ideas, to finance conspiratorial activities and to buy arms. They realized that the Republic's commitment to improving the living conditions of the poorest members of society inevitably threatened them with a major redistribution of wealth. At a time of world depression, wage increases and the cost of better working conditions could not simply be absorbed by higher profits.

From the end of April to the beginning of July the Socialist Ministers of Labour, Francisco Largo Caballero, and of Justice, Fernando de los Ríos, issued a series of decrees which aimed to deal with the appalling situation in rural Spain, shattered by a drought during the 1930-31 season and thronged by returning emigrants. De los Ríos rectified the imbalance in rural leases which favoured the landlords. Eviction was made almost impossible and rent rises blocked while prices were falling. Largo Caballero's measures were much more dramatic. The so-called 'decree of municipal boundaries' prevented the hiring of outside labour while local workers in a given municipality remained unemployed. It struck at the landowners' most potent weapon, the power to break strikes and keep down wages by the import of cheap blackleg labour. In early May, Largo Caballero did something that Primo de Rivera had not been able to do: he introduced arbitration committees for rural wages and working conditions, which had previously been subject only to the whim of the owners. One of the rights now to be protected was the newly introduced eight-hour day. Given that, previously, the *braceros* had been expected to work from sunup to sundown, this meant that owners would either have to pay overtime or else employ more men to do the same work. Finally, in order to prevent the owners sabotaging these measures by lock-outs, a decree of obligatory cultivation prevented them taking their land out of operation. Preparations were also set in train for a sweeping law of agrarian reform.

The response of the right was complex. In general, its powerful press networks began to present the Republic as responsible for all the centuries-old problems of the Spanish economy and as the fount of mob violence. At a local level, landlords simply ignored the new legislation, letting loose their armed retainers on the trade union officials who complained. More specifically, there were two broad responses, known at the time as 'accidentalist' and 'catastrophist'. The 'accidentalists' took the view that forms of government, republican or monarchical, were 'accidental' as opposed to fundamental. What really mattered was the social content of a regime. Thus, inspired by Angel Herrera, the leader of the Asociación Católica Nacional de Propagandistas, the 'accidentalists' adopted a legalist tactic. Under a dynamic leader, the ACNP stalwart, José María Gil Robles, the old Catholic Agrarian Federations were forged into an organization called Acción Popular. Its few elected deputies used every possible device to block reform in the parliament or Cortes. Massive and extraordinarily skilful efforts of propaganda were made to persuade the smallholding farmers of northern and central Spain that the agrarian reforms of the Republic damaged their interests every bit as much as those of the big landowners. The Republic was presented to the conservative Catholic smallholders as a Godless, rabble-rousing instrument of Soviet Communism poised to steal their lands and dragoon their wives and daughters into an orgy of obligatory free love. With their votes thereby assured, by 1933 the legalist right was to wrest political power back from the left.

At the same time, the various 'catastrophist' groups were fundamentally opposed to the Republic and believed that it should be overthrown by some great catastrophic explosion or uprising. It was their view which was to prevail in 1936, although it should not be

Above: Smoke pours from the windows of the convent church of the Trinitarian nuns in Madrid, one of several church buildings set on fire in May 1931 as a gesture of anti-clericalism.

Left: Shortly after the proclamation of the Republic, on 1 May 1931, the head of the Catholic Church in Spain, Cardinal Pedro Segura y Saez, published a pastoral letter in which he openly condemned the new régime and urged all Catholics not to be passive bystanders to the advance of 'the enemies of Jesus Christ'. As a result, he was expelled from Spain on 13 June 1931. He is seen here being escorted to the car which waits to take him to exile.

forgotten that the contribution of the 'accidentalists' in stirring up anti-Republican masses was crucial for Franco's war effort. There were three principal 'catastrophist' organizations. The oldest was the Traditionalist Communion of the Carlists, anti-modern advocates of a theocracy to be ruled on earth by warrior priests. Antiquated though its ideas were, it was well supplied with supporters among the farmers of Navarre and had a fanatical militia called the *Requeté* which was to receive training in Mussolini's Italy. The best financed and ultimately the most influential of the 'catastrophists' were the one-time supporters of Alfonso XIII and General Primo de Rivera. These Alfonsine monarchists, with their journal *Acción Española* and their political party Renovación Española, were the general staff and the paymasters of the extreme right. Both the rising of 1936 and the structure and ideology of the Francoist state owed an enormous amount to the Alfonsines. Finally, there were a number of unashamed fascist groups, which finally coalesced between 1933 and 1934 under the leadership of the Dictator's son, José Antonio Primo de Rivera, as Falange Española. Also subsidized by Mussolini, the rank-and-file Falangists supplied the cannon-fodder of the 'catastrophist' option, attacking the left and provoking the street fights which permitted other groups to denounce the 'disorder' of the Republic.

Among the Republic's enemies two of the most powerful were the Church and the army. Both were to be easily drawn into the anti-Republican right, in part because of errors made by the Republic's politicians. On 7 May the Archbishop of Toledo, Cardinal Segura, declared war on the Republic in a pastoral letter calling on Catholics to take up arms against the destroyers of religion. This did nothing to soften the Republican view that the Church was the bulwark of black reaction. Thus, on 11 May, when a rash of church burning spread through Madrid, Malaga, Seville, Cadiz and Alicante, the cabinet refused to call out the Civil Guard. Manuel Azaña, the immensely talented left Republican Minister of War, proclaimed that 'all the convents in Madrid are not worth the life of one Republican', a phrase which was so built on by the rightist press as to persuade its middle-class readership that Azaña somehow approved of the actual burnings. On 22 May full religious liberty was declared. The monarchist daily *ABC* and the Catholic *El Debate* howled abuse and were briefly closed down by the government.

Several issues were to cause friction between the Republic and the armed forces, but none more than the new regime's readiness to concede regional autonomy. On 14 April Colonel Macià, the leader of the Catalan Esquerra Republicana de Catalunya (Republican Left of Catalonia), declared an independent Catalan republic. A deputation from Madrid persuaded him to await government action by promising a rapid statute of autonomy. Inevitably, this aroused the suspicions of the army, which had shed so much blood in the fight against Catalan separatism. To make matters worse the Minister of War, Azaña, began in May to prepare reforms to cut down the inflated officer corps and to make the army more efficient. It was thereby hoped to reduce the political ambitions of the armed forces. It was a necessary reform and, in fact, a generous one, since the 8,000 surplus officers were retired on full pay. However, since the reform involved the abolition of the army's jurisdiction over civilians thought to have insulted it, many officers regarded it as a savage attack. Those that were retired, having refused to take the oath of loyalty to the Republic, were left with the leisure to plot against the regime.

Azaña was misquoted to the effect that he planned to pulverize (*triturar*) the army. The rightist press made much of this and thereby confirmed military hostility. In fact, far from depriving the army of funds and equipment, Azaña, who had made a lifetime study of civil-military relations, merely ensured that the military budget would be used more efficaciously. If anything, Azaña tended to be punctilious in his treatment of a chaotic and inefficient force which compared poorly with the armies of countries like Portugal or Romania. Ironically, the military readiness of the Spanish Army in 1936 owed as much to the efforts of Azaña as to those of his successor, the rightist José María Gil Robles. Azaña was converted by the right's propaganda machine into the bogey of the military because he wanted to provide Spain with a non-political army. For the right, the army existed above all to defend their social and economic interests. Azaña therefore was presented as a corrupt monster, determined to destroy the army, as he was allegedly determined to destroy the Church, because it was part of the Jewish-Bolshevik-Masonic conspiracy to do so. Curiously, he had a much higher regard for military procedures than his predecessor General Primo de Rivera. A general who presumed to 'interpret the widespread feeling of the nation' to Azaña was told forthrightly, 'Your job is merely to interpret regulations.' That was not how Spanish generals expected to be treated by civilians.

The first major political contest of the Republic had taken place before the right was properly organized. The June 1931 elections were won by the Socialists in coalition with the left Republicans. Republicanism tended to be a movement of intellectuals and the petty bourgeoisie, more an amorphous improvised grouping than a united left-wing force. The only centre grouping, the Radicals, had on the other hand started out as a genuine mass movement in Barcelona in the early years of the century. Led by the fiery orator and corrupt machine politician Alejandro Lerroux, the Radicals were to become progressively more conservative and anti-Socialist as the Republic developed. They did immense damage to the Republic by their readiness to opt for the winning side at any given time. The polarization brought about by the pendulum effect of a big left-wing victory in the 1931 elections followed by an equally dramatic rightist triumph in 1933 was greatly intensified by the fact that the Radicals had changed sides.

The centrifugal dynamic of Republican politics was in itself the inadvertent consequence of a set of electoral regulations which were drawn up in such a way as to avoid the political fragmentation of the Weimar Republic. To ensure strong government majorities, in any given province 80 per cent of the seats were given to the party or list with most votes over 40 per cent of those cast. The other 20 per cent block of seats went to the list that was second past the post. Accordingly, small fluctuations in the number of votes cast could lead to massive swings in the number of parliamentary seats actually won. The pressure to form coalitions was obvious. The 1931 elections therefore registered a heavy victory for the united Socialists, the left Republicans and the Radicals. The former gained 250 seats, Alejandro Lerroux's Radicals 90, and the somewhat heterogeneous right 80. By 1933, however, the success of rightist tactics in blocking reform and the consequent disappointment of the left-wing rank and file had provoked a significant realignment of forces. By then the anarchists who had voted for the leftist parties in 1931 were committed to abstention. The Socialists had so lost faith in the possibilities of bourgeois democracy that they refused to make a coalition with the left Republicans. The apparatus of the state was thus allowed to slip out of the grasp of the left in the November 1933 elections.

That change was a reflection of the enormity of the task that had faced the 1931 parliament, known as the Constituent Cortes because its primary task was to give Spain a new constitution. For the Republic to survive, it had to increase wages and cut unemployment. Unfortunately, the regime was born at the height of the world depression. With agricultural prices falling, landowners had let land fall out of cultivation. The landless labourers, who lived near starvation at the best of times, were thus in a state of revolutionary tension. Industrial and building workers were similarly hit. To make matters worse, the wealthy classes were hoarding or exporting their capital. This posed a terrible dilemma for the Republican government. If the demands of the lower classes for expropriation of the great estates and take-overs of the factories were met, the army would probably rise to destroy the Republic. If revolutionary disturbances were put down in order to appease the upper classes, the government would find the working class arrayed against it. In trying to tread the middle course, the Republican-Socialist coalition ended up enraging both sides.

This was demonstrated within a week of the Cortes' first session. A general strike called by the anarchists led to thousands of CNT telephone workers leaving work. The strike achieved its most notable successes in Seville and Barcelona, and was an intense embarrassment to the government which was anxious to prove its ability to maintain order. The Ministry of Labour declared the strike illegal, and the Civil Guard was called in. In Seville, the CNT attempted to convert the strike into an insurrection. Miguel Maura, Minister of the Interior, decided on drastic action: martial law was declared and the army sent in to crush the strike. The revolutionary nature of the strike frightened the upper classes, while the violence with which it was put down - 30 killed and 200 wounded - confirmed the anarchists in their hostility to the Republic. The CNT was increasingly falling under the domination of the Federación Anarquista Ibérica (FAI), the secret organization founded in 1927 to maintain the ideological purity of the movement. In the summer of 1931, there was a split between the orthodox unionists of the CNT and FAI members who advocated continuous revolutionary violence. The FAI won the internal struggle and the more reformist elements of the CNT were effectively expelled. The bulk of the anarcho-syndicalist movement was left in the hands of those who felt that the Republic was no better than either the monarchy or the dictatorship of Primo de Rivera. Thereafter, and until the CNT was uneasily reunited in 1936, the anarchists embarked on a policy of 'revolutionary gymnastics', anti-Republican insurrectionary strikes which invariably failed because of lack of co-ordination and fierce repression, but enabled the rightist press to identify the Republic with violence and upheaval.

In the autumn of 1931, however, before the waves of anarchist agitation were fully under way, the Cortes was occupied with the elaboration of the new constitution. After an earlier draft by the conservative politician Angel Ossorio y Gallardo had been rejected, a new constitutional committee, under the Socialist law professor, Luis Jiménez de Asua, met on 28 July. It had barely three weeks to draw up its draft. In consequence, some of its unsubtle wording was to give rise to three months of acrimonious debate. Presenting the project on 27 August, Jiménez de Asua described it as a democratic, liberal document with great social content. An important Socialist victory was chalked up by Luis Araquistain, later to be one of Largo Caballero's radical advisers, when he prevailed on the chamber to accept article 1, which read 'Spain is a republic of workers of all classes.' Article 44 stated that all the wealth of the country must be subordinate to the economic interests of the nation and that all property could be expropriated, with compensation, for reasons of social utility. Indeed, the constitution, finally approved on 9 December 1931, was as democratic, laic, reforming and liberal on matters of regional autonomy as

Above: The leader of the right wing Confederation of Autonomous Rightist Parties (CEDA), José María Gil Robles, addresses a meeting of his followers during the election campaign of November 1933. The ladies who accompany him on the platform were to be able to vote for the first time that year.

Left: Among the competitors for right-wing votes in 1933 was José Antonio Primo de Rivera, portrayed here in the uniform of the national chief of the fascist party he founded on 29 October 1933, *Falange Española.*

the Republicans and Socialists could have wished. It appalled the most powerful interests in Spain, landowners, industrialists, churchmen and army officers.

The opposition of the conservative classes to the constitution crystallized around articles 44 and 26. The latter concerned the cutting off of state financial support for the clergy and religious orders; the dissolution of orders, such as the Jesuits, that swore foreign oaths of allegiance; and the limitation of the Church's right to wealth. The Republican-Socialist coalition's attitude to the Church was based on the belief that, if a new Spain was to be built, the stranglehold of the Church on many aspects of society must be broken. That was a reasonable perception, but it failed to take into account the sensibilities of Spain's millions of Catholics. Religion was not attacked as such, but the Constitution was to put an end to the government's endorsement of the Church's privileged position. To the right, the religious settlement of the constitution was a vicious onslaught on traditional values. The debate on article 26, the crucial religious clause, provoked the first major conflict of the Republic and began the polarization which was to end in civil war. At a meeting in Ledesma (Salamanca), José María Gil Robles, leader of Acción Popular, declared, 'While anarchic forces, gun in hand, spread panic in government circles, the government tramples on defenceless beings like poor nuns.'

Indeed, the passing of the constitution marked a major change in the nature of the Republic. By identifying the Republic with the Jacobinism of the Cortes majority, the ruling coalition alienated many members of the Catholic middle classes. The right's view of the constitution as fiercely anti-clerical provoked it into organizing its forces at the same time as the union that had been made at San Sebastian in 1930 began to break up. Alcalá Zamora and Miguel Maura resigned in October 1931 and Azaña, who had risen to prominence during the debate, became Prime Minister. This upset Lerroux, who had been grooming himself for the job, and was excluded because of widespread fear in political circles that he would be unable to keep his hands out of the till. He went into opposition with his Radicals. Thus Azaña was forced to rely more heavily upon the Socialists. This in turn made it more difficult for him to avoid provoking the enmity of the right.

In fact, Azaña was caught between two fires: that of the left which wanted reform, and that of the right which rejected it. This was made apparent when he came to deal with the agrarian problem. Agrarian violence was a constant feature of the Republic. Based on the crippling poverty of rural labourers, it was kept at boiling point by the CNT. The anarchists, together with the Socialist Landworkers' Federation (FNTT: Federación Nacional de Trabajadores de la Tierra, founded in April 1930), were calling for expropriation of estates and the creation of collectives. The Republicans, as middle-class intellectuals, respected property and were not prepared to do this. Largo Caballero, as Minister of Labour since April 1931, had improved the situation somewhat. However, the limits of such piecemeal reform were starkly exposed in December 1931 when the Badajoz section of the FNTT called a general strike. It was in the main a peaceful strike, in accordance with the instructions of its organizers. In an isolated village called Castilblanco, however, there was bloodshed. When the strike was called the FNTT members in Castilblanco has already spent the winter without work. On 31 December, while they were holding a peaceful and disciplined demonstration, the Civil Guard started to break up the crowd. After a scuffle, a Civil Guard opened fire, killing one man and wounding two others. The hungry villagers, in a frenzy of fear, anger and panic, fell upon the four guards and killed them with stones and knives.

Almost before the cabinet had had time to come to terms with Castilblanco, there occurred an equally disturbing tragedy, this time in the north. At Arnedo, in Logroño, several workers were sacked from the local shoe factory at the end of 1931 for belonging to the UGT. At a public protest the Civil Guard opened fire, killing four women, a child, and a worker, besides wounding at least thirty more. The incident had all the appearance of an act of revenge for Castilblanco. Then in early 1932 an anarchist strike was put down with considerable severity, especially in Bajo Llobregat in Catalonia. There were arrests and deportations. Anarchist and Socialist workers were simply being exasperated at the same time as the right was confirmed in its belief that the Republic meant only chaos and violence. Nevertheless, the need for reform was self-evident, particularly in the rural south. There, despite promises of agrarian reform, conditions remained brutal. All over the south, many owners had declared war on the Republican-Socialist coalition by refusing to plant crops.

The response of the big landowners to reform measures had been rapid, both nationally and locally. Their press networks spouted prophecies of the doom that would ensue from government reforms while in reality they themselves simply went on as if the decrees had never been passed. What the vituperative outbursts of the landowners' organizations failed to stress was the extent to which Socialist measures remained little more than hopes on paper. There was virtually no machinery with which to enforce the new decrees in the isolated villages of the south. The social power consequent on being the exclusive providers of work, remained with the owners. The Civil Guard was skilfully cultivated by, and remained loyal to, the rural upper classes. Socialist deputies from the south regularly complained in the Cortes about the inability of the provincial civil governors to apply government legislation and to oblige the Civil Guard to side with the *braceros* rather than with landowners.

Throughout 1932, the FNTT worked hard to contain the growing desperation of its southern rank and file. With agrarian reform imminent, the landowners did not feel disposed to invest in their land. The law of obligatory cultivation was effectively ignored and labour was not hired to do the tasks essential for the spring planting. *Braceros* were refused work because they belonged to the landworkers' union. Nonetheless, the FNTT continued to adhere to a moderate line, and appealed to grassroots militants to refrain from extremism and not to expect too much from the forthcoming agrarian reform. Unfortunately, the statute drawn up by Marcelino Domingo, the new Minister of Agriculture, did little. After a painfully slow progress through the Cortes between July and September, it provided for the setting up of an Institute of Agrarian Reform to supervise the break-up of estates over 22.5 hectares. Therefore it did nothing for the smallholders of the north, and moreover, since it was extremely legalistic and riddled with loopholes and exceptions, it did little for the labourers of the south either. Largo described it as 'an aspirin to cure an appendicitis'. Moreover, if it did nothing to abate the revolutionary fervour of the countryside, it did even less to allay the hostility of right-wing landowners towards the Republic.

Another source of fierce opposition to the Republic was the statute of Catalan autonomy. Providing for a Catalan regional government, the *Generalitat*, the statute was regarded by the army and the conservative classes as an attack on national unity. In the Cortes, a determined Azaña battled it out with right-wing deputies. In fact, the statute of Catalan autonomy, drawn up by a coalition headed by Francesc Macià, the intransigent

Left: The monarchist General Sanjurjo (centre) with a group of officers in the Captaincy General of Sevilla where, in August 1932, he attempted a rising against the Republic.

Below: In December 1934, a number of prominent right-wing politicians formed an anti-Republican alliance, the National Bloc. Its leaders are seen here at a banquet.

Catalan nationalist, was far from the maximalism that had been expected by the Madrid politicians. Nevertheless, they were loath to allow the *Generalitat*, and particularly Macià, any real autonomy. They regarded his party, the Esquerra, as a short-lived and opportunistic coalition, dependent for its viability on the votes of the CNT rank and file. This did not prevent the right presenting Azaña's cabinet as hell-bent on destroying centuries of Spanish unity.

Away from the constitutional debates in the Cortes, the right demonstrated that it would not scruple to use violence to change the course of the Republic. Army officers enraged by the military reforms and autonomy statute were joined by monarchist plotters in persuading General José Sanjurjo that the country was on the verge of anarchy and ready to rise at his bidding. General Sanjurjo's attempted coup took place on 10 August 1932. Badly planned, it was easily defeated both in Seville, by a general strike of CNT. UGT and Communist workers, and in Madrid where the government, warned in advance, easily rounded up the conspirators. In a sense, this attack on the Republic by one of the heroes of the old regime, a monarchist general, benefited the government by generating a wave of pro-Republic fervour. The ease with which the *Sanjurjada*, as the fiasco was known, was snuffed out enabled the government to generate enough parliamentary enthusiasm to pass the agrarian reform bill and the Catalan statute of autonomy in September.

The government's prestige was at its height, yet the situation was much less favourable than it appeared. The *Sanjurjada* showed the hostility with which the army and the extreme right regarded the Republic. Moreover, while the government coalition was crumbling, the right was organizing its forces. This process was aided by the insurrectionism of the CNT. The rightist press did not make subtle distinctions between the CNT, the UGT and the FNTT. Although the CNT regarded the Republic as being 'as repugnant as the monarchy', its strikes and uprisings were blamed on the Republican-Socialist coalition which was working hard to control them. However, while the extreme right in the *pueblos* (villages) was content to engage in blanket condemnation of disorder, the more far-sighted members of the rural bourgeoisie, who had found a home in the Radical Party, were able to use the CNT's hostility towards the Socialists in order to drive wedges between the different working-class organizations. The most dramatic example of this process took place as a result of a nationwide revolutionary strike called by the CNT for 8 January 1933 and of its bloody repercussions in the village of Casas Viejas in the province of Cadiz. In the lock-out conditions of 1932, four out of five of all workers in Casas Viejas were unemployed for most of the year, dependent on charity, occasional roadmending and scouring the countryside for wild asparagus and rabbits. Their desperation, inflamed by an increase in bread prices, ensured a ready response on 11 January to the earlier CNT call for revolution. Their hesitant declaration of libertarian communism led to a savage repression in which twenty-four people died.

The rightist press was delighted. The subsequent smear campaign, in which the right-wing papers howled that the Republic was as barbaric, unjust and corrupt as all the previous regimes, ate into the morale of the Republican-Socialist coalition. The work of the government was virtually paralysed. Although the Socialists stood loyally by Azaña, who bore the brunt of rightist abuse for Casas Viejas, the incident heralded the death of the coalition, symbolizing as it did the government's failure to resolve the agrarian problem. Henceforth, at a local level the FNTT was to become more belligerent and its attitude filtered through into the Socialist Party in the form of a rejection of collaboration with the Republicans. The anarchists, meanwhile, stepped up the tempo of their revolutionary activities. The Radicals under Lerroux, ever anxious for power, drew increasingly to the right and began a policy of obstruction in the Cortes.

The latent violence at local level was transmitted to national politics, where increasing hostility developed between the PSOE and the newly created rightist group, the Confederación Española de Derechas Autónomas (CEDA). The new party, which had grown out of Acción Popular and at least forty other rightist groups, was the creation of José María Gil Robles. In his closing speech at the founding congress in Madrid, in February 1933, he told his audience:

> when the social order is threatened, Catholics should unite to defend it and safeguard the principles of Christian civilization.... We will go united into the struggle, no matter what it costs.... We are faced with a social revolution. In the political panorama of Europe I can see only the formation of Marxist and anti-Marxist groups. This is what is happening in Germany and in Spain also. This is the great battle which we must fight this year.

Later on the same day, at another meeting in Madrid, he said that he could not see anything wrong with thinking of fascism as a cure for the evils of Spain. The Socialists were convinced that the CEDA was likely to fulfil a fascist role in Spain, a charge only casually denied by the Catholic party, if at all. A majority in the PSOE led by Largo Caballero came to feel that if bourgeois democracy was incapable of preventing the rise of fascism, it was up to the working class to seek different political forms with which to defend itself.

In the meantime, throughout 1933, the CEDA spread discontent with the Republic in agrarian circles. Gil Robles specialized in double-edged pronouncements, and fuelled the Socialists' sensitivity to the danger of fascism. Weimar was persistently cited as an example by the right and as a warning by the left. Parallels between the German and Spanish Republics were not difficult to find. The Catholic press applauded the Nazi destruction of the German socialist and communist movements. Nazism was much admired on the Spanish right because of its emphasis on authority, the fatherland and hierarchy – all three central preoccupations of CEDA propaganda. More worrying still was that, in justification of the legalistic tactic in Spain, *El Debate* pointed out that Hitler had attained power legally. The paper frequently commented on Spain's need for an organization like those which had destroyed the left in Germany and Italy, and hinted that Acción Popular/CEDA could fulfil that role.

It was in such an atmosphere that elections were called for November. In contrast to 1931, this time the left went to the polls in disarray. The right, on the other hand, was able to mount a united and generally bellicose campaign. Gil Robles had just returned from the Nuremberg rally and appeared to be strongly influenced by what he had seen. Indeed, the CEDA election campaign showed that Gil Robles had learned his lessons well. Determined on victory at any price, the CEDA election committee decided for a single anti-Marxist counter-revolutionary front. Thus the CEDA had no qualms about going into the elections in coalition with 'catastrophist' groups such as Renovación Española and the Carlists or, in other areas, with the cynical and corrupt Radicals.

A vast amount of money was spent on the Right's election campaign. The CEDA's election fund was enormous, based on generous donations from the well-to-do like Juan March, the millionaire enemy of the Republic. The climax of the CEDA's campaign came in a speech given in Madrid by Gil Robles. His tone would only make the left wonder what a CEDA victory might mean for them:

> We must reconquer Spain.... We must give Spain a true unity, a new spirit, a totalitarian polity.... It is necessary now to defeat socialism inexorably. We must found a new state, purge the fatherland of judaizing Freemasons.... We must proceed to a new state and this imposes duties and sacrifices. What does it matter if we have to shed blood! ... We need full power and that is what we demand.... To realize this ideal we are not going to waste time with archaic forms. Democracy is not an end but a means to the conquest of the new state. When the time comes, either parliament submits or we will eliminate it.

The Socialists, who had decided to contest the elections on their own, could not match the massive propaganda campaign mounted by the right. Gil Robles dominated the campaign of the rightist coalition, as Largo Caballero did that of the Socialists, mirroring the radical extremism of his opponent. Declaring that only the dictatorship of the proletariat could carry out the necessary economic disarmament of the bourgeoisie, he delighted his supporters, but antagonized the right and helped justify its already aggressive stance. The PSOE also suffered from the post-Casas Viejas hostility of the anarchists, who abstained. Given the existing electoral law, the Socialists' tactical error of failing to ally with the left Republicans, together with the CEDA's readiness to make alliances, meant that it took twice as many Socialist votes to elect a deputy as rightist ones. The election results brought bitter disappointment to the Socialists, who won only fifty-eight seats. After local deals between the CEDA and the Radicals designed to take advantage of the electoral law, the two parties finished with 115 and 104 deputies respectively. The right had regained control of the apparatus of the state. It was determined to use it to dismantle the reforms of the previous two years. However, expectations had been raised during that time which could only ensure burning popular fury when the right put back the clock to before 1931.

3

Confrontation and Conspiracy: 1934-36

In the following two years, which came to be known as the *bienio negro*, Spanish politics were to be bitterly polarized. The November 1933 elections had given power to a right wing determined to avenge the injuries and indignities which it felt it had suffered during the period of the Constituent Cortes. This made conflict inevitable, since if the workers and peasants had been driven to desperation by the inadequacy of the reforms of 1931-2, then a government set on destroying these reforms could only force them into violence. At the end of 1933, 12 per cent of Spain's workforce was unemployed and in the south the figures were nearer 20 per cent. Employers and landowners celebrated the victory by cutting wages, sacking workers, evicting tenants and raising rents. Even before a new government had taken office, labour legislation was being blatantly ignored.

The outrage of the Socialists knew no bounds. Their own tactical error in not allying with the Republicans had made a crucial contribution to their electoral defeat. However, the PSOE was convinced that the elections had been fraudulent. In the south, they had good reason to believe that they had been swindled out of seats by the power of the *caciques* over the starving *braceros*. In Spain as a whole, the PSOE's one and a half million votes had won it fifty-eight seats in the Cortes, while the Radicals' eight hundred thousand votes had been rewarded with 104 seats. According to calculations made by the PSOE, the united parties of the right had together got 3,345,504 votes and 212 seats, while the disunited left had received 3,375,432 votes and only ninety-nine seats. Rank-and-file bitterness at unfairly losing the elections and outrage at the untrammelled offensive of the employers were all the greater because of the restraint and self-sacrifice that had characterized Socialist policy between 1931 and 1933. In response to the consequent wave of militancy, the Socialist leadership began to adopt a tactic of revolutionary rhetoric. Their vain hope was that they could both scare the right into limiting its belligerancy and persuade the President of the Republic, Niceto Alcalá Zamora, to call new elections.

Although he was not prepared to go that far, Alcalá Zamora did not invite Gil Robles to form a government despite the fact that the CEDA was the biggest party in the Cortes, albeit without an overall majority. The President suspected the Catholic leader of nurturing more or less fascist ambitions to establish an authoritarian, corporative state. Thus Alejandro Lerroux, as leader of the second largest party, became Prime Minister. Dependent on CEDA votes, the Radicals were to be the CEDA's puppets. In return for harsh social policies in the interests of the CEDA's wealthy backers, the Radicals were to be allowed to enjoy the spoils of office. The Socialists were appalled. Largo Caballero was convinced that in the Radical Party, there were those who 'if they have not been in jail, deserve to have been'. Once in government, they set up an office to organize the sale of state favours, monopolies, government procurement orders, licences and so on. The PSOE view was that the Radicals were hardly the appropriate defenders of the basic principles of the Republic against rightist assaults.

The first violent working-class protest, however, came from the anarchists. With irresponsible naïvety they called for an uprising on 8 December 1933. However, the government had been forewarned of the anarcho-syndicalists' plans, and it quickly declared a state of emergency. Leaders of the CNT and the FAI were arrested, press censorship was imposed, and syndicates were closed down. In traditionally anarchist areas, Aragon, the Rioja, Catalonia, the Levante, parts of Andalusia and Galicia, there were sporadic strikes, some trains were derailed and Civil Guard posts were assaulted. The movement was quickly over in Barcelona, Madrid and Valencia. In the Aragonese capital, Zaragoza, however, the rising did get off the ground. Workers raised barricades, attacked public buildings, and engaged in street fighting. The response of the government was to send in the Army, which took four days with the aid of tanks to crush the insurrection.

With a pliant Radical government in power, the success of Acción Popular's 'accidentalist' tactics could hardly have been more apparent. 'Catastrophism' was for the moment eclipsed. Nevertheless, the extreme right remained unconvinced by Gil Robles' democratic tactic and so continued to prepare for violence. Carlists were collecting arms and drilling in the north and the spring of 1934 saw Fal Conde, the movement's secretary, recruiting volunteers in Andalusia. In March, Carlist representatives went to see Mussolini who promised money and arms for a rising. The Alfonsine monarchists of Renovación Española were every bit as convinced that even a strong rightist government subject to the whims of the electorate in a democratic regime did not constitute an adequate long-term guarantee for their interests. The Alfonsine leader, Antonio Goicoechea, had accompanied the Carlists to Rome. In May 1934 the monarchists' most dynamic and charismatic leader, José Calvo Sotelo, returned after three years' exile. Henceforth the monarchist press, in addition to abusing Gil Robles' weakness, began increasingly to talk of the conquest of the state as the only certain road to the creation of a new authoritarian, corporative regime.

Even Gil Robles was having trouble controlling his forces. His youth movement, the Juventud de Acción Popular (JAP), was seduced by the German and Italian examples. Enormous fascist-style rallies were held at which Gil Robles was hailed with the cry '¡Jefe! ¡Jefe! ¡Jefe!' (the Spanish equivalent of *Duce*) in the hope that he might start a 'March on Madrid' to seize power. Monarchist hopes, however, centred increasingly on the openly fascist group of José Antonio Primo de Rivera, the Falange, as a potential source of shock troops against the left. As a landowner, an aristocrat and well-known socialite, José Antonio Primo de Rivera served as a guarantee to the upper classes that Spanish fascism would not get out of their control in the way of its German and Italian equivalents. The Falange, which merged in 1934 with the pro-Nazi Juntas de Ofensiva Nacional-Sindicalista of Ramiro Ledesma Ramos, remained during the Republican period essentially a small student group preaching a utopian form of violent nationalist revolution. Its importance lay in the role played by its political vandalism in working up the tension which would eventually erupt into the Civil War.

The Left was very aware of such developments and was determined to avoid the fate of the German and Austrian left. As 1934 progressed there were growing numbers of street battles between left and right. Events in the orthodox political arena did little to cool tempers. Lerroux resigned in April after Alcalá Zamora had hesitated to sign an amnesty bill which reinstated the officers involved in the Sanjurjo rising of 1932. Socialists and Republicans alike felt that the government was signalling to the Army that it could rise whenever it disliked the political situation. The left was already suspicious of the government's reliance on CEDA votes, since Gil Robles continued to refuse to swear his loyalty to the Republic. Moreover, since he made it quite clear that when he gained power he would change the constitution, the Left was coming to believe that strong action was necessary to prevent him doing so. In fact, even if Gil Robles was not quite as extreme as the left believed him to be, he managed to convey the impression that the Radical government, backed with CEDA votes, was intent on dismantling the Republic as it had been created in 1931.

In this context, it was difficult for the Socialist leadership to hold back its followers. Largo Caballero tended to give way to the revolutionary impatience of the masses, although his rhetoric, which they cheered to the echo, was unspecific and consisted largely of Marxist platitudes. No concrete relation to the contemporary political scene was ever made in Largo's speeches of early 1934 and no timetable for the future revolution was ever given. However, rank-and-file pressure for the radicalization of the Socialist movement, particularly from its youth movement, the Federación de Juventudes Socialistas (FJS), developed throughout 1934. This led to important divisions within the PSOE. The right wing of the party, led by the law professor Julián Besteiro, tried several tactics to slow down the process of bolshevization which was taking place within the party. This merely earned Besteiro the vehement hostility of the radical youth. The centre, led by Indalecio Prieto, reluctantly went along with the revolutionary tactic out of party loyalty. The young followers of Largo Caballero came to dominate the party and the UGT, with the organizations of the Socialist movement falling into their hands in quick succession.

Thus political tension grew throughout 1934. In March the anarchists held a four-week strike in Zaragoza to protest against the maltreatment of prisoners taken after the December rising. Then the CEDA made a sinister gesture in the form of a large rally of its youth movement, the JAP. The choice of Philip II's monastery of El Escorial as venue was an unmistakably anti-republican gesture. In driving sleet, a crowd of 20,000 gathered in a close replica of the Nazi rallies. They swore loyalty to Gil Robles, 'our supreme chief', and chanted '¡Jefe! ¡Jefe! ¡Jefe!' The JAP's nineteen-point programme was recited, with emphasis on point 2, 'our leaders never make mistakes', a direct borrowing from the Italian Fascists. One CEDA deputy declared that 'Spain has to be defended against Jews, heretics, Freemasons, liberals and Marxists.' Another, the deputy for Zaragoza, Ramón Serrano Suñer, brother-in-law of General Franco and later architect of the post-Civil War National-Syndicalist state, denounced 'degenerate democracy'. The high point of the rally was a speech by Gil Robles. His aggressive harangue was greeted by delirious applause and prolonged chanting of '¡Jefe!' 'We are an army of citizens ready to give our lives for God and for Spain', he cried. 'Power will soon be ours.... No one can stop us imposing our ideas on the government of Spain.'

The young revolutionaries of the FJS were convinced that Gil Robles was aiming to take over the government in order to bring the Republic to an end. Various Radical ministries were incapable of allaying the suspicion that they were merely Gil Robles' Trojan Horse. By repeatedly threatening to withdraw his support, Gil Robles provoked a series of cabinet crises as a result of which the Radical government was taking on an ever more conservative veneer. On each occasion, the more liberal elements of Lerroux's party would be impelled to quit the party, leaving the rump even more dependent on CEDA whims. The Radical minister who enjoyed Gil Robles' unalloyed trust was Rafael Salazar Alonso, the Minister of the Interior. He provoked a number of strikes throughout the spring and summer of 1934 which enabled him to pick off the most powerful unions one by one. The Radical-CEDA determination to undermine the Republic's most loyal support became clear when the government clashed successively with the Catalans and the Basques. The sympathy shown by the Constituent Cortes to autonomist aspirations was now dropped in favour of right-wing centralist bias. This was particularly the case with regard to Catalonia. Unlike the rest of Spain, Catalonia was governed by a truly Republican party, the Esquerra, now under Lluis Companys. In April, Companys passed an agrarian reform, the *Ley de Cultivos*, to protect tenants from eviction by landowners taking advantage of the central government's neglect of earlier agrarian legislation. The landlords appealed to Madrid and the reform was declared unconstitutional. Nevertheless, Companys went ahead and ratified it. Meanwhile, the government began to infringe the Basques' tax privileges and, in an attempt to silence protest, forbade their municipal elections. Such high-handed centralism could only confirm the left's fears of the Republic's rapid drift to the right.

Trouble increased during the summer. Rural labourers were suffering immense hardship through increased aggression from employers, and after much debate the FNTT called for a series of strikes, to be carried through in strict accordance with the law. While the strike action could hardly be considered revolutionary, Salazar Alonso was not prepared to lose this chance to strike a blow at the largest section of the UGT. His measures were swift and ruthless. Liberal and left-wing individuals in the country districts were arrested wholesale, including four Socialist deputies. This was a flagrant violation of articles 55 and 56 of the constitution. Several thousand peasants were loaded at gunpoint on to lorries and deported hundreds of miles from their homes and then left without food or money to make their own way back. Workers' centres were closed down and many town councils were removed, to be replaced by government nominees. Although most of the labourers arrested were soon released, emergency courts sentenced prominent workers' leaders to four or more years of imprisonment. The workers' societies in each village, the *Casas del Pueblo*, were closed and the FNTT was effectively crippled until 1936. In an uneven battle, the FNTT had suffered a terrible defeat. Salazar Alonso had effectively put the clock back to the 1920s in the Spanish countryside.

The politics of reprisal were beginning to generate an atmosphere, if not of imminent civil war, certainly of great belligerance. The left saw fascism in every action of the right; the right smelt revolution in every left-wing move. In the streets there were shots exchanged between Socialist and Falangist youths. Violent speeches were made in the Cortes and, at one point, guns were brandished. Government attacks on autonomy and the increasingly threatening attitude of the CEDA were driving the Socialists to play with the idea of a revolutionary rising to forestall the destruction of the Republic. The

The inhuman social and economic conditions suffered by Spain's rural working classes, particularly in the southern provinces of Andalucía, were at the root of the frequent violent clashes between peasants and Civil Guards. The figure of the Civil Guard, with his characteristic black leather cap (*tricornio*), was regarded by the rural populace as the agent of injustice and repression.

Catalan independence was declared in Barcelona during the revolutionary movement of October 1934. It was short-lived however, and order was quickly restored by governmental police and armed forces. Hundreds of people were arrested.

Popular Front poster produced for the electoral campaign of February 1936.

The official portrait of D. Manuel Azaña Díaz, architect of the Popular Front.

JAP held another rally in September, this time at Covadonga in Asturias, the starting point for the reconquest of Spain from the Moors. This was clearly a symbol of warlike aggression which foreshadowed the Francoist use of *Reconquista* imagery after 1936. Gil Robles spoke in violent terms of the need to crush the 'separatist rebellion' of the Catalans and the Basque Nationalists. The supreme '*Jefe*' of the JAP worked himself up to a frenzy of patriotic rhetoric and demanded that nationalist sentiment be exalted 'with esctasy, with paroxysms, with anything; I prefer a nation of lunatics to a nation of wretches'. There was more than a little provocation of the left in what was happening. Gil Robles was aware that the left considered him a fascist. He was also aware that it intended to prevent the CEDA coming to power, although he was confident that the left was not in a position to succeed in a revolutionary attempt. Constant police activity had revealed the most desultory preparations for a rising. Arms purchases by the left had been few and the authorities seem to have been well informed of them.

On 26 September the CEDA opened the crisis by announcing that it could no longer support a minority government. Lerroux's new cabinet included three CEDA ministers. The reaction of the Republican forces was abrupt: even the conservative Miguel Maura broke off relations with the President. The UGT called a general strike. In most parts of Spain, however, it was a failure largely because of the prompt action of the government in declaring martial law and arresting the hesitant Socialist leaders. In Barcelona events were more dramatic. Pushed by extreme Catalan nationalists, and alarmed by developments in Madrid, Companys proclaimed an independent state of Catalonia 'within the Federal Republic of Spain'. It was a protest against the fascist betrayal of the Republic. The CNT stood aside since it regarded the Esquerra as a purely bourgeois affair. In fact, the rebellion of the *Generalitat* was doomed when Companys refused requests to arm the workers. The only place where the Left's protest was not easily brushed aside was in Asturias. There, spontaneous rank-and-file militancy impelled the local PSOE leaders to go along with a revolutionary movement organized jointly by the UGT, the CNT and, belatedly, the Communists, united in the Alianza Obrera (Workers' Alliance). Its repression was entrusted to General Franco and the miners were reduced to submission by both heavy artillery attacks and bombing raids.

The Asturian rising marked the end for the Republic. To the Bloomsbury Group writer Gerald Brenan, who was living in self-imposed exile in Spain, it was 'the first battle of the Civil War'. The conflict did not end with the defeat of the miners. As their leader, Belarmino Tomás, put it, 'Our surrender today is simply a halt on the road, where we make good our mistakes, preparing for the next battle.' There could be no going back. The October revolution had terrified the middle and upper classes; and in their terror they took a revenge which determined the left that next time there must be no half measures. The Socialist movement was, in fact, badly scarred by the events of October. The repression unleashed in the aftermath of the October rising was truly brutal. Virtually the entire UGT executive was in jail. The Socialist press was silenced.

Nothing was done in the next fifteen months to reconcile the enmities aroused by the revolution and its repression. Despite the CEDA's much-vaunted aim of beating the revolution by a programme of social reform, proposals for moderate land reform and for tax reforms were defeated by right-wing intransigence. Indeed, Manuel Giménez Fernández, the CEDA Minister of Agriculture, encountered embittered opposition within his own party to his mildly reformist plans. He was denounced as 'the white Bolshevik'.

There was room only for the punishment of the October rebels. Gil Robles demanded the 'inflexible application of the law'. Companys was sentenced to thirty years' imprisonment. The thousands of political prisoners remained in jail. A vicious campaign was waged against Azaña in an unsuccessful attempt to prove him guilty of preparing the Catalan revolution. The Catalan autonomy statute was suspended.

Then, when the CEDA failed to secure the death penalty for two Asturian Socialist leaders, its three ministers resigned. Gil Robles resumed his tactic of provoking cabinet crises in order to weaken the Radicals, hoping to move crab-like towards the government. He was rewarded in early May when Lerroux's new government included five *Cedistas*, including Gil Robles himself as Minister of War. It was a period of open reaction. Landlords halved wages and order was forcibly restored in the countryside. Gil Robles purged the army of loyal Republican officers and appointed known opponents of the regime to high positions: Francisco Franco became Chief of the General Staff, Manuel Goded Inspector General, and Joaquín Fanjul Under-Secretary of War. In a number of ways – regimental reorganization, mechanization, equipment procurement – Gil Robles continued the reforms of Azaña and effectively prepared the army for its role in the Civil War.

In response to rightist intransigence the left was also growing in strength, unity and belligerence. In jail, political prisoners were soaking up revolutionary literature. Outside, the economic misery of large numbers of peasants and workers, the savage persecution of the October rebels and the attacks on Manuel Azaña combined to produce an atmosphere of solidarity among all sections of the left. Azaña and Indalecio Prieto began a campaign to ensure that the disunity behind the 1933 electoral defeat would not be repeated. Azaña worked hard to reunite the various tiny Republican parties, while Prieto concentrated on countering the revolutionary extremism of the Socialist left under Largo Caballero. A series of gigantic mass meetings was addressed by Azaña in the second half of 1935. The enthusiasm for left-wing unity shown by the hundreds of thousands who attended helped convince Largo Caballero to abandon his opposition to what eventually became the Popular Front. At the same time, the Communists, prompted by Moscow's desire for alliance with the democracies and frightened of being excluded, also used their influence with Largo in favour of the Popular Front. They knew that, in order to give it the more proletarian flavour that he wanted, Largo Caballero would insist on their presence. In this way, the Communists found a place in an electoral front which, contrary to rightist propaganda, was not, in Spain, a Comintern creation but the revival of the 1931 Republican-Socialist coalition. The left and centre left closed ranks on the basis of a programme of amnesty for prisoners, basic social and educational reform and trade union freedom.

When a combination of Gil Robles' tactic of erosion of successive cabinets and the revelation of two massive scandals involving followers of Lerroux led to the collapse of the Radicals, the CEDA leader assumed that he would be asked to form a government. Alcalá Zamora, however, had no faith in the CEDA leader's democratic convictions. After all, only some weeks previously, Gil Robles' youthful followers of the JAP had starkly revealed the aims of the legalist tactic in terms which called to mind the attitude of Goebbels to the 1933 elections in Germany: 'With the weapons of suffrage and democracy, Spain must prepare itself to bury once and for all the rotting corpse of liberalism. The JAP does not believe in parliamentarism, nor in democracy.' It is indicative of Alcalá

Zamora's suspicion of Gil Robles that throughout the subsequent political crisis he had the Ministry of War surrounded by Civil Guards and the principal garrisons and airports placed under special vigilance. Gil Robles was outraged, and in desperation he investigated the possibilities of staging a *coup d'état*. The generals that he approached, Fanjul, Goded, Varela and Franco, felt that, in the light of the strength of working-class resistance during the Asturian events, the Army was not yet ready for a coup.

Elections were announced for February 1936. Unsurprisingly, the election campaign was fought in a frenetic atmosphere. Already, at the end of the previous October, Gil Robles had requested a complete range of Nazi anti-Marxist propaganda pamphlets and posters, to be used as a model for CEDA publicity material. In practical terms, the right enjoyed an enormous advantage over the left. Rightist electoral finance dramatically exceeded the exiguous funds of the left. Ten thousand posters and 50 million leaflets were printed for the CEDA. They presented the elections in terms of a life-or-death struggle between good and evil, survival and destruction. The Popular Front based its campaign on the threat of fascism, the dangers facing the Republic and the need for an amnesty for the prisoners of October. The elections held on 16 February resulted in a narrow victory for the Popular Front in terms of votes, but a massive triumph in terms of power in the Cortes.

The left had won despite the expenditure of vast sums of money and the use of all the traditional devices of electoral chicanery on behalf of the right. Because the election results represented an unequivocal statement of the popular will, they were taken by many on the right as proving the futility of legalism and 'accidentalism'. The savagery of rightist behaviour during the *bienio negro* ensured that the left's tactical error of 1933 was unlikely to be repeated. The hour of the 'catastrophists' had struck. The CEDA's youth sections and many of the movement's wealthy backers were immediately convinced of the necessity of securing by violence what was unobtainable by persuasion. The elections marked the culmination of the CEDA attempt to use democracy against itself. This means that henceforth the right would be more concerned with destroying the Republic than with taking it over. Military plotting began in earnest.

Helpless in the midst of the conflict stood the government, weak and paralysed. Only Republicans sat in the Cabinet, because Largo Caballero was convinced that they would quickly exhaust their possibilities for reform and then there would have to be an exclusively Socialist cabinet. Accordingly, he used his immense influence to prevent the participation in the government of the more realistic Prieto. As long as Azaña was prime minister, authority could be maintained. Unfortunately, in May there was to occur a series of events which gave credence to the view that the most malignant of fates presided over Spain's destiny. In order to put together an even stronger team, Azaña and Prieto plotted to remove the more conservative Alcalá Zamora from the presidency. Azaña would be elevated to the presidency and Prieto take over as Prime Minister. The first part of the plan worked but not the second. Largo Caballero refused to support a government headed by Prieto. The consequences could not have been worse. A shrewd and strong Prime Minister, Azaña, was lost and, to make matters worse, on assuming the presidency, he increasingly withdrew from everyday politics. The new Prime Minister, Santiago Casares Quiroga, suffering from tuberculosis, was hardly the man to provide the determined leadership necessary in the circumstances.

Immediately the election results were known, exuberant workers had set about reaping revenge for the starvation and wage cuts of the *bienio negro* and for the brutal repression which had followed the Asturian rising. In any case, natural disaster intensified the social misery of the south. After drought in 1935, 1936 began with heavy rainstorms which slashed olive, wheat and barley production. Unemployment was rocketing and the election results had raised the hopes of the *braceros* to fever pitch. Throughout March, the Socialist landworkers' union, the FNTT, encouraged its members to take at its word the new government's proclaimed commitment to rapid reform. In Salamanca and Toledo, there were small-scale invasions of estates; in Cordoba and Jaen, peasants stole olives or cut down trees. The most substantial land seizures took place in Badajoz. In Yeste in the province of Albacete, seventeen peasants were killed by the Civil Guard when they attempted to cut wood on land that had once belonged to the village and had been taken from it by legal subterfuge in the nineteenth century. In general, what most alarmed the landlords was the assertiveness of labourers whom they expected to be servile but now found to be determined not to be cheated out of reform as they had between 1931 and 1933. Many landowners withdrew to Seville or Madrid, or even to Biarritz or Paris, where they enthusiastically joined, financed or merely awaited news of ultra-rightist plots against the Republic.

It was not only in rural areas that the middle and upper classes feared that a rising tide of 'red' violence was about to inundate society. The CEDA's failure to secure electoral success meant the end of moderation. The right turned from Gil Robles to the more belligerent José Calvo Sotelo, the monarchist leader. The '*Jefe*' of the CEDA, however, convinced that the legal road to corporativism was blocked, did everything possible to help those who were committed to violence. As he later boasted, he had already made an incalculable contribution to the creation of mass right-wing militancy. His efforts to block, and later to dismantle, reform had done much to undermine Socialist faith in the possibilities of bourgeois democracy. Now he handed over the CEDA's electoral funds to the head of the military conspiracy, General Emilio Mola. Gil Robles' day had passed, and nothing more starkly demonstrated the change in atmosphere than the startling rise of the Falange. Cashing in on middle-class disillusionment with the CEDA's legalism, it now expanded rapidly. Moreover, attracted by its code of violence, the bulk of the JAP went over *en masse*.

Falangist terror squads, trained in street fighting and assassination attempts, worked hard to create an atmosphere of disorder which would justify the imposition of an authoritarian regime. This helped to ensure the escalation of a spiral of mindless violence which rendered rational discussion impossible. At no time during the Second Republic was there a greater need for strong and decisive government. The young activists of right and left were clashing on the streets. Military plotters were working to overthrow the regime. Prieto realized, as did few others, that attempts at revolutionary social change would only enrage the middle classes and drive them to fascism and armed counter-revolution. Instead, he was convinced that the answer was to restore order and accelerate reform. He had plans to remove unreliable military commanders, reduce the power of the Civil Guard and disarm the fascist terror squads. He also was anxious to promote massive public works, irrigation and housing schemes and speed up agrarian reform. It was a project which, pursued with energy and will, might have prevented civil war. Largo Caballero, however, ensured that Prieto's vision would not be realized.

Indeed, while Prieto counselled caution, Largo Caballero did exactly the reverse.

Intoxicated by Communist flattery – *Pravda* had called him 'the Spanish Lenin' – he toured Spain, prophesying the inevitable triumph of the coming revolution to crowds of cheering workers. In March 1936 his grip on the PSOE had been considerably strengthened. His supporters gained control of the Agrupación Socialista Madrileña, the strongest section in the party. Then, on 16 March, he was elected president of the PSOE parliamentary minority. His grip on the party appeared unshakeable. Largo, however, then made a naïve error. Always obsessed with uniting the working class under PSOE hegemony, he acquiesced in the fusion of the Socialist and Communist movements. It meant the loss of 40,000 young Socialists of the FJS to the PCE. Santiago Carrillo, the FJS leader, had already drawn close to Moscow and started attending meetings of the Central Committee of the Communist Party.

In fact, though, it is debatable whether Largo Caballero was ever genuine in his revolutionary pronouncements. Always a pragmatist concerned to further the interests of his UGT members, Largo tended to 'lead from behind', going along with the rank and file less out of conviction than from a determination not to be out of step. For all the rhetoric, the only real weapon at the left's disposal in early 1936, the revolutionary general strike, was never used. Indeed, when serious proposals for revolution were made in April by Joaquín Maurín, one of the leaders of the quasi-Trotskyist POUM, he was scorned as a dangerous utopian by Largo Caballero's supporters. The divisions between Largo and Prieto ultimately weakened the Republic. The left wing of the party made regular statements about the death agony of capitalism and the inevitable triumph of socialism which Prieto, with some cause, regarded as insanely provocative. In fact, party discipline was maintained in such a way as to contribute to the stability of the Republican government. However, the May Day marches, the clenched-fist salutes, the revolutionary rhetoric and violent attacks on Prieto frightened elements of the middle classes into taking action to avoid their doom.

In fact, the Socialists were caught in a genuine dilemma. Prieto believed that strong reforming government was the only answer to the right's threats to the Republic. However, there was nothing about right-wing attitudes at the time to suggest that military conspiracy would have been voluntarily abandoned for anything less than social policies like those pursued under the Radical-CEDA coalition of 1934-5. Largo Caballero was convinced, after the experience of the Constituent Cortes, that a Republican-Socialist coalition such as Prieto advocated would be incapable of carrying out adequate measures. This division of opinion, exacerbated by personal animosity between Largo and Prieto, effectively paralysed the political initiative of the Socialist movement. That the strongest party of the Popular Front was not therefore able to participate actively in using the apparatus of the state to defend the Republic was all the more tragic in the light of the inefficacy of Casares Quiroga. The new Prime Minister was no match for the problems he was called upon to solve. Under constant attack in the Cortes from an angry right wing, harassed by the destruction of public order by the Falange and the anarchists, and undermined by the lack of Socialist support, Casares nonetheless seemed to have little appreciation of the gravity of the situation. He shrugged off Prieto's warnings about military plotters with the offensive comment, 'I will not tolerate your menopausic outbursts.'

The government could not therefore prevent politics degenerating into open conflict. While bombs were being planted and public officials murdered, there could be no

Above left: By mid-May 1936, General Emilio Mola Vidal had become the 'Director' of the military conspiracy, controlling the recruitment of participants, planning the execution of the proposed rising and sending secret instructions to the numerous officers involved in the plot throughout Spain.

Above right: On 14 July 1936, crowds of right-wingers gave the fascist salute at the funeral of Calvo Sotelo in Madrid.

Right: Francisco Franco Bahamonde's military character had been formed in the Foreign Legion during Spain's wars with Morocco. In the photograph, taken in 1921, Franco (then with the rank of Major) gives orders to his Captains before an attack on Ras-Medua, near the Spanish enclave of Melilla.

compromise. In the Cortes, the violence of speeches by José Calvo Sotelo or by the fiery Communist Dolores Ibárruri underlined the impossibility of any accord. In the street, the Falange was breaking up CEDA meetings, the Socialist Youth attacking the followers of Prieto. While Largo Caballero made empty prophecies of revolution, Calvo Sotelo talked in chillingly convincing terms of violent counter-revolution. The purpose of his speeches was to prevent any possible reconciliation between moderates on either side. Since parliamentary debates received full, uncensored press coverage, he dwelled on disorder – often generated by Falangists subsidized by his party – in order to persuade the middle classes of the need for military insurrection. Throughout the spring of 1936, Calvo Sotelo provided the army with a theory of political action and instilled in the right-wing masses an urgent sense of the need to confront the twin threats of 'communism' and 'separatism', both of which were presented as consubstantial with the Republic. His speeches provoked scuffles in the Cortes. On one occasion, a Socialist deputy offered to fight him in the street and called him a 'pimp'. On another, after declaring himself a fascist, he made an unmistakable overture to the army when he said that, 'The soldier who, faced with his destiny, is not prepared to rise for Spain and against anarchy is out of his mind.'

In fact, several generals had already decided that power should be taken away from a government which was both helpless to stop what they saw as the break-up of Spain at the hands of regional separatists, and responsible for policies that were undermining the structure of society. In consequence, they concluded that the time had come for a Primo de Rivera-style 'iron surgeon'. The high command, faced in 1936 by the chaos of the Popular Front, a chaos orchestrated by their rightist allies, felt no qualms about intervening in politics. The senior generals who could remember the Cuban disaster – men of Primo de Rivera's generation such as Sanjurjo and Queipo de Llano – had long since developed a haughty contempt for what they saw as the ineptitude of the professional politicians. The younger generals had little sense of loyalty to a regime which they believed to be impermanent. At all levels, there was a belief that the army had the right to intervene in politics to defend both the social order and the territorial integrity of Spain.

The conspiracy which broke out on 17–18 July 1936 was more carefully planned than any previous coup. The lesson of the *Sanjurjada* of 10 August 1932 had been well learned. It was that casual *pronunciamientos* would no longer work against a proletariat ready to use the weapon of the general strike. General Emilio Mola, the 'Director' of the plot, realized that there would have to be a co-ordinated seizure of power in the garrisons of all of Spain's fifty provinces and a swift subjugation of the organized working class. The preparation of the rising (*alzamiento*) was made more difficult by the efforts of the Republican government to neutralize suspect generals. Franco had been sacked as Chief of Staff and sent to the Canary Islands; Goded was transferred to the Balearic Islands; Mola, in command of the Army in Africa, was posted to the Navarrese capital, Pamplona. This last transfer was short-sighted, to say the least. Pamplona was the centre of Carlist monarchism, and of its militia force, the *Requeté*. Consequently, Mola found himself in an excellent place in which to organize plans for the mainland insurrection, although his relations with the Carlists were not without friction. The obvious figurehead was the veteran of African wars and earlier coups, General José Sanjurjo. Indeed, Sanjurjo played an important role in cementing the agreement between Mola and the Carlist leader, Manuel Fal Conde. José Antonio Primo de Rivera, imprisoned by the government in an attempt to control the *Falange*, was more cautious, but agreed lest his movement be left behind. However, the crucial impetus for the conspiracy came from junior officers sympathetic to authoritarian ideas.

Certain factors made the conspirators' task much easier than it might otherwise have been. The government continued to ignore the repeated warnings it received of the plot. The Director General of Security pointed the finger at Mola but no serious action was taken. One curious warning came from the pen of General Franco. On 23 June 1936 he wrote to Casares Quiroga a letter of labyrinthine ambiguity, both suggesting that the army would be loyal if treated properly and insinuating that it was hostile to the Republic. The clear implication was that, if only Casares would put Franco in charge, the plots could be dismantled. At that stage, Franco was some way back in the seniority stakes from some of the principal conspirators. In later years, his apologists were to spend many gallons of ink trying to explain away this letter, presenting it as either a skilful effort to put Casares off the scent or a last magnanimous peace-making gesture. It hardly mattered, since Casares took no more notice of Franco than he had of Prieto.

General Franco's letter was a typical example of his *retranca*, the hesitant peasant cunning associated with the natives of Galicia. His determination to be on the winning side without taking any substantial risks hardly set him aside as a likely charismatic leader. None the less, for several reasons, Mola and the other conspirators were loath to proceed without him. He had enormous influence in the officer corps, having been for a time Director of the Military Academy in Zaragoza as well as Chief of the General Staff under Gil Robles. In particular, he was greatly respected in the Spanish Moroccan Army, the country's toughest military force. The *Africanista* officers respected him for his icy ruthlessness; the Moorish troops because his numerous escapes from death convinced them that he possessed the mystical power of *baraka*, invulnerability. The coup could not possibly have a chance of succeeding without the Moroccan Army, and Franco was the obvious man to lead it. Moreover, his part in suppressing the working-class rebellions in Asturias in 1917 and 1934 had made him something of a hero among the more hysterical sections of the middle and upper classes. Yet, as the letter to Casares Quiroga indicated, in the early summer of 1936 Francisco Franco was a less determined plotter than might have been expected. He preferred to wait in the wings. His coy hesitations led his exasperated comrades to bestow upon him the ironic nickname of 'Miss Canary Islands 1936'. Sanjurjo was heard to say that the rising would go ahead 'with or without Franquito'.

When he finally decided to join in, Franco was given an important but second-rank role. The future Head of State after the coup triumphed was to be Sanjurjo. As technical mastermind of the plot, Mola was then expected to have a decisive role in the politics of the victorious regime. Then came a number of generals each of whom was assigned a region, among them Franco with Morocco. Several of them were of equal prominence to Franco, especially Joaquín Fanjul who was in charge of the rising in Madrid and Manuel Goded who was given Barcelona. Moreover, even if Franco had been *primus inter pares*, even if Sanjurjo and Mola had not outranked him in the conspiratorial hierarchy, his future in the post-coup polity could only lie in the shadow of the two charismatic politicians of the extreme right, José Calvo Sotelo and José Antonio Primo de Rivera. That situation was to change with astonishing rapidity and, in the eyes of some observers, with sinister symmetry.

Above: On 19 July 1936, the Dragon Rapide hired by Luis Bolín in England transported General Franco from the Canary Isles to Tetuán in Spanish Morocco. The photograph shows Franco and a group of other insurgent soldiers on his arrival in Africa.

Below: Franco stands by the plane which landed him in Seville on 6 August 1936. On his left, General Orgaz Yoldi.

Wherever the July 1936 rising was successful, Martial Law was declared and the red, gold and purple flag of the Republic was replaced with the red and gold flag of the Spanish monarchy. Here, the rebel standard is hoisted in Ceuta, while the flag of the legally constituted State lies over the balustrade.

A column of Carlist volunteers (*Requetés*), with their drummer and an army officer at the head, on their way to the battlefront. They believed they would be in Madrid within a week.

The rebel General Gonzalo Queipo de Llano was renowned for his nightly radio 'chats', broadcast over the regional network centred in Seville. In truth, his talks were inflammatory diatribes in which he terrified the populace loyal to the Republic with gory accounts of the Nationalist advance in Andalucía.

The white-bearded General Miguel Cabanellas Ferrer initiated the rising in Zaragoza. As the most senior General in the rebel zone, he was appointed head of the National Defence Committee created by the insurgents on 24 July 1936, although some of his colleagues (including Franco) were extremely wary of Cabanellas' Republican sympathies.

The arrangements for Franco's part in the coup were made as soon as his participation was finally confirmed. On 5 July the Marqués de Luca de Tena, owner of the monarchist daily *ABC*, instructed his London correspondent, the unpleasant Luis Bolín, to charter an aircraft to take Franco from the Canaries to Morocco where he was to take command of the Army of Africa. Bolín hired a De Havilland Dragon Rapide in Croydon and arranged for a set of apparently holidaying passengers to mask the aeroplane's real purpose. Douglas Jerrold, an English right-wing Catholic, was involved in the arrangements. In his autobiography, Jerrold wrote of his role in helping 'to save a nation's soul':

> We lunched at Simpson's and de la Cierva completed the party.
> 'I want a man and three platinum blondes to fly to Africa tomorrow.'
> 'Must there really be *three*?' I asked, and at that Bolín turned triumphantly to de la Cierva.
> 'I told you he would manage it.'
> I rang Hugh Pollard. 'Can you fly to Africa tomorrow with two girls?' I asked, and heard the expected reply.
> 'Depends upon the girls.'

Leaving Croydon on 11 July, the plane flew via Bordeaux and arrived in Casablanca on the following day. Three days later it arrived at the airport of Gando near Las Palmas on the island of Gran Canaria.

In the meantime, however, dramatic events had been taking place on the Spanish mainland. On the afternoon of 12 July Falangist gunmen had shot and killed a leftist officer of the Republican Assault Guards, Lieutenant José del Castillo. Castillo was number two on a blacklist of pro-Republican officers allegedly drawn up by the ultra-rightist Unión Militar Española, an association of conspiratorial officers linked to Renovación Española. The first man on the blacklist, Captain Carlos Faraudo, had already been murdered. Enraged comrades of Castillo responded with a dramatic and irresponsible reprisal. In the early hours of the following day, they set out to avenge his death by murdering a prominent right-wing politician. Failing to find Gil Robles, who was holidaying in Biarritz, they kidnapped and shot Calvo Sotelo. On the evening of the 13th, Indalecio Prieto led a delegation of Socialists and Communists to demand that Casares distribute arms to the workers before the military rose. The Prime Minister refused, but he could hardly ignore the fact that there was now virtually open war.

The political scandal that followed the discovery of Calvo Sotelo's body was enormous and played neatly into the hands of the military plotters. The murder provided graphic justification for their contention that Spain needed military intervention to save her from anarchy. It clinched the commitment of many ditherers and obscured the extent to which the coup of 17-18 July had been long in the making. It also deprived the conspirators of an important leader. As a powerful figure and a cosmopolitan rightist of wide experience, Calvo Sotelo would have been the senior civilian leader after the coup. Unlike the various ciphers that were to be used by Franco, he would have imposed his personality on the post-war state. However, now he was dead, and, even if no one could have judged it in such terms at the time, his death removed an important political rival to Franco.

In the short term, Calvo Sotelo's assassination gave a new urgency to plans for the uprising. Franco had acute immediate problems which took precedence over any long-term ambitions. As military commander of the Canary Islands, his headquarters were in Santa Cruz de Tenerife. The Dragon Rapide from Croydon had landed on Gran Canaria perhaps because it was nearer to mainland Africa, perhaps because of the low cloud which afflicts Tenerife, or perhaps because it was feared that Franco was being watched. In order to travel from Santa Cruz to Gran Canaria, Franco needed the authorization of the Ministry of War. Apparently his request for an inspection tour of Gran Canaria was turned down. The rising was scheduled to start on 17 July, so Franco would have to leave for Morocco on that day at the latest. In the event he did so, yet none of his biographers seem to regard it as odd that the Dragon Rapide should have been directed to Gran Canaria with confidence in Franco's ability to get there too. That he got there at all was the result of either an amazing coincidence or foul play.

On the morning of 16 July General Amado Balmes, military commander in Gran Canaria, and an excellent marksman, was shot in the stomach while trying out various pistols in a shooting range. Francoist historiography has played down the incident as a tragic, but fortunately timed, accident. To counter suggestions that Balmes was removed by members of the military conspiracy, Franco's official biographer claimed that Balmes was himself an important figure in the plot. Strangely, however, Balmes never figured in the subsequent pantheon of heroes of the 'Crusade'. Other sources suggest that Balmes was a loyal officer who had withstood intense pressure to join the rising. If that was true, he had, like many other Republican officers, put his life in mortal danger. It is virtually impossible now to say if his death was accidental, suicide or murder. What is certain is that he died at the exact moment urgently needed by Franco. The need to preside over the funeral gave Franco the perfect excuse to travel to Las Palmas on 17 July. Co-ordinated risings were planned to take place all over Spain on the following morning. However, indications that the conspirators in Morocco were about to be arrested led to the action being brought forward there to the early evening of 17 July. The garrisons rose in Melilla, Tetuan and Ceuta in Morocco. In the early morning of 18 July Franco and General Luis Orgaz took over Las Palmas. The Spanish Civil War had begun.

The suppression of General Fanjul's rebellion in Madrid left the Montaña barracks littered with corpses. Some were of rebel soldiers who had committed suicide. Others, such as those photographed here in the inner courtyard, were those of the victims of popular anger.

4

'The Map of Spain Bleeds': From Coup d'État to Civil War

The plotters had not foreseen that their rising would turn into a long civil war. Their plans had been for a rapid *alzamiento* to be followed by a military directory like that established in 1923, and they had not counted on the strength of working-class resistance. It was only in certain areas, however, that there was certainty of success. In Pamplona the Carlist population turned the coup into a popular festival, thronging the streets and shouting *¡Viva Cristo Rey!* (Long live Christ the King). The conservative ecclesiastical towns of Leon and Old Castile – Burgos, Salamanca, Zamora, Segovia and Avila – fell almost without struggle, although it took Generals Saliquet and Ponte nearly twenty-four hours to crush the Socialist railway workers of Valladolid. According to the *Diario de Burgos* of 20 July, 'The Assault and Civil Guards joined in the Movement from the first moment.' In the Canary Islands, the local press displayed a misplaced optimism typical of the Nationalist zone in the early days of the war. It was announced in the *Gaceta de Tenerife* on 21 July that José Antonio Primo de Rivera (actually in a Republican jail in Alicante) was marching on Madrid with a column of Falangists, that Azaña had been arrested in Santander and that Mola had seized the Ministry of the Interior in Madrid.

In the Catholic heartlands where the risings had enjoyed instant success, blood soon started to flow with the blanket repression of Republicans of all kinds. It was not just the region's relatively few anarchists, Communists and Trotskyists who were rounded up and shot, but also moderate Socialists and centre-left Republicans. General Mola had foreseen that terror behind the lines would play a crucial role when he issued the following announcement to his fellow conspirators: 'It will be borne in mind that our action will have to be very violent, in order to crush a strong and well-organized enemy as soon as possible. Hence, all leaders of political parties, societies, or unions not pledged to the Movement will be imprisoned: such people will be administered exemplary punishment so that movements of rebellion or strikes will be strangled.' Those who claimed to be rising in defence of law and order and of eternal Catholic values inaugurated a savage purge of leftists and Freemasons which was to leave a smouldering legacy of hatred in the area for over forty years.

Outside the areas which in a sense had been secured for the right twenty years previously by the success of the Catholic Agrarian Federations and during the Republic

51

A major of the Civil Guard is arrested by Republican militiamen in Guadalajara. Here, as in Madrid, the Civil Guard did not support the rising.

by the propaganda efforts of Acción Popular, there were Nationalist victories gained against hostile populations by various combinations of surprise, trickery and the swift crushing of working-class resistance. Thus, in Oviedo, Colonel Antonio Aranda, pretending to be loyal to the Republic, convinced local miners' leaders that they could safely despatch their men to help relieve Madrid. Once their trains had left, Aranda declared for the rebellion. Determined officers in Galicia took Vigo and La Coruña after heavy fighting with the unarmed population. Remarkable successes were achieved in Andalusia, but the way that they were won suggested that a long and bloody struggle was ahead. Of all the various conflicts which had contributed to the outbreak of the Spanish Civil War, none had been fiercer than the agrarian war in the south. In consequence, once the outbreak of hostilities removed all restraints, latent social hatreds ensured that in the villages and towns of Andalusia and Extremadura horrific cruelties would be unleashed.

In the rural districts, the local *braceros*, fervent supporters of the Republic, were usually able to overpower small Civil Guard garrisons. Cruel reprisals were then often taken, both against the landowners not rich enough to have removed themselves to the safety of Seville or the south of France, and against the priests who had legitimized the tyranny of the *caciques* and *latifundistas*. Then, within days of the *alzamiento*, the local branches of the Socialist FNTT and of the CNT went about collectivizing the big estates. The stores of the great *cacique* families were broken open and their flour, hams and olive oil distributed by the revolutionary committees. The special pastures given over to the breeding of fighting bulls, a caprice of the owners which had contributed to local misery, were ploughed over. In the months before new crops would be available, plans were made by the local revolutionary committees to slaughter the bulls for food. Strictly rationed, it was hoped that they would keep everyone fed until the harvest. For most of them, used to a meagre diet of bread and *gazpacho* (a soup made of onions, peppers and garlic) augmented by the occasional rabbit, it was the first time they had ever tasted beef. However, retribution in the villages would not be long behind once the major Andalusian cities had fallen to the rebels.

A general strike in Cadiz seemed to have won the town for the workers, but after a fierce encounter the rebel garrison gained control. Cordoba, Huelva, Seville and Granada all fell after savage elimination of working-class opposition. Seville, the Andalusian capital and the most revolutionary southern city, fell to the eccentric General Gonzalo Queipo de Llano in remarkable fashion. Queipo de Llano was related by marriage to Alcalá Zamora and had been a fervent supporter of the Republic in 1931. Having been involved in the abortive military rising of December 1930 with which Republicans, Socialists and left-wing army officers had hoped to overthrow Alfonso XIII, he was not entirely trusted by the rebels. However, posing initially as a loyalist, he browbeat the local garrison into joining the rising by suddenly announcing, gun in hand, 'I have come to tell you that the time has come to decide whether you support your comrades in arms or the government that is leading Spain to ruin.' He then surrounded the civil governor's office with artillery and destroyed working-class resistance by swift motorized machine-gun raids into the slums of the Triana district. Moorish mercenaries, the *Regulares*, were given a free hand to loot and to butcher men, women and children. On 25 July Queipo signed a declaration that all the leaders of any labour union on strike would 'immediately be shot' as well as 'an equal number of carefully chosen rank-and-file members'.

Events in Granada were equally bloody and typical of the Nationalist determination to

54

win by the application of terror. The working-class district of the Albaicín was shelled and bombed. When control of the city centre was assured, the military authorities allowed the Falangist 'Black Squad' to sow panic among the population by taking leftists from their homes at night and shooting them in the cemetery. In the course of the war about 5,000 civilians were shot in Granada. The caretaker of the cemetery went mad and was committed to an asylum. One of the most celebrated victims of rightist terror, not just in Granada but in all of Spain, was the poet Federico García Lorca. Years later, the Francoists were to claim that Lorca had died because of an apolitical private feud related to his homosexuality. In fact, Lorca was anything but apolitical. In ultra-reactionary Granada, his sexuality had given him a sense of apartness which had grown into a sympathy for those on the margins of respectable society. In 1934 he had declared, 'I will always be on the side of those who have nothing.' His itinerant theatre *La Barraca* was inspired by a sense of social missionary zeal. Lorca regularly signed anti-fascist manifestos and was connected with organizations such as International Red Aid.

In Granada itself, he was closely connected with the moderate left. His views were well known and it would not have escaped the notice of the town's oligarchs that he considered the Catholic conquest of Moorish Granada in 1492 to have been a disaster. Flouting a central tenet of Spanish right-wing thinking, Lorca believed that the conquest had destroyed a unique civilization and created 'a wasteland populated by the worst bourgeoisie in Spain today'. When rightists hunting for 'reds' began to look for him, he took refuge in the home of his friend, the Falangist poet Luis Rosales. It was there that he was arrested by the sinister Ramón Ruiz Alonso, a prominent member of the local CEDA who had hitched his cart to the Falange. Having been denounced as a Russian spy by Ruiz Alonso, Federico García Lorca was shot at dawn on 19 August 1936. The cowardly murder of a great poet was, however, merely a drop in an ocean of political slaughter.

Even those areas which had been won by the rebels had produced sufficient popular hostility to suggest that a major war of conquest was called for if the rebels were to gain control of all of Spain. Nonetheless, General Mola declared optimistically in Burgos,

> The government which was the wretched bastard of liberal and Socialist concubinage is dead, killed by our valiant army. Spain, the true Spain, has laid the dragon low, and now it lies writhing on its belly and biting the dust. I am now going to take up my position at the head of the troops and it will not be long before two banners – the sacred emblem of the Cross and our own glorious flag – are waving together in Madrid.

Nevertheless, the scale of working-class resistance suggested that if the government had taken the decisive action of issuing guns to the workers the rising might have been crushed at birth. Understandably, however, the moderate liberal cabinet of Santiago Casares Quiroga had refused to do so. In part this was because the Prime Minister seemed not to believe that the situation was serious. It also derived from a reluctance to hand over power to working-class organizations which would be unlikely to hand it back once the military rising had been crushed. Then valuable time was lost in a search for a compromise solution. Left-wing demonstrations calling for arms were ignored, guaranteeing the success of the rising in many places.

Casares Quiroga resigned on 18 July, and President Azaña called on the moderate centre Republican Diego Martínez Barrio to form a government to negotiate with the rebels. This enraged the left, which regarded him as a conservative. Martínez Barrio telephoned

D. Diego Martínez Barrio, who, for a few hours on 19 July 1936, occupied the position of Republican Prime Minister.

In their suppression of the rising in Barcelona, the members of the Presidential Guard (*Mozos de Escuadra*) were assisted by a number of civilians, although the Chief of Police refused to make a general distribution of arms. The two citizens accompanying a *Mozo* in this photograph had probably volunteered with their own firearms.

Mola twice in Pamplona, assuring him that his government would pursue a more right-wing policy and reimpose law and order. Mola refused the new Prime Minister's offers of the post of Minister of War in his government. On the following day, Martínez Barrio was replaced by José Giral, a left Republican follower of Azaña. After his Minister of War, General José Miaja, also tried unsuccessfully to negotiate Mola's surrender, Giral quickly grasped the nature of the situation and took the crucial step of authorizing the arming of the workers. Yet in many places an equally decisive role was played by the forces of order, the Assault Guards and the Civil Guards. Where they remained loyal, and they usually did so in cities of substantial proletarian strength, the rebels were usually defeated.

On the same afternoon, General Joaquín Fanjul, aided by some Falangists, tried to start the rising in Madrid from the Montaña barracks. His troops were immediately surrounded by a vast crowd of workers reinforced by loyal Assault Guards. After white flags were flown, the Madrileños advanced on the barracks to accept its surrender, only to be fired on. Infuriated, they murdered several of the officers when the barracks was captured at noon on 20 July. In the euphoria of the moment, it was seen as the equivalent of the storming of the Bastille during the French Revolution. Among the crowd was Valentín Gonzalez, a road mender from Extremadura, who was shortly to acquire fame as 'El Campesino', the peasant soldier. The left-wing parties of Madrid then formed militias and columns set off to repel General Mola's troops at the Somosierra pass north of the capital. In the fierce fighting there 'El Campesino' emerged as a potential military leader. Other spontaneous left-wing militiamen from the capital headed south to reverse the success of the rising in Toledo. With loyal regular troops they captured the town, but the rebels under Colonel José Moscardó retreated into the Alcázar, the impregnable fortress which dominates both Toledo and the river Tagus which curls around it.

In Barcelona, Companys refused to issue arms but depots were seized by the CNT. In the early hours of 19 July rebel troops began to march on the city centre. They were met by anarchists and the local Civil Guard which, decisively, had stayed loyal. The CNT stormed the Atarazanas barracks, where the rebels had set up headquarters. When General Goded arrived by seaplane from the Balearic Islands to join them, the situation was already lost. Captured, he was forced to broadcast an appeal to his followers to lay down their arms. This was a vital victory for the government, for it ensured that all of Catalonia would remain loyal.

The losses of Fanjul in Madrid and Goded in Barcelona were not entirely unforeseeable blows for the Nationalists. Both generals had realized that they faced immensely difficult tasks. However, as Mola and other successful conspirators awaited the arrival of General Sanjurjo from his Portuguese exile to lead a triumphal march on Madrid, they received some entirely unexpected bad news. Sanjurjo had been killed in bizarre circumstances. On 19 July Juan Antonio Ansaldo, a famous air ace and monarchist playboy who had once organized Falangist terror squads, had arrived in Estoril at the summer house where General Sanjurjo was staying. Ansaldo claimed later to have been sent by Mola to collect Sanjurjo but there is no corroborating evidence for this. His tiny Puss Moth biplane seemed an odd choice for the mission. Moreover, the far more suitable Dragon Rapide used by Franco had arrived in Lisbon at the same time almost certainly with a view to picking up Sanjurjo. When Ansaldo arrived, he announced dramatically to an enthusiastic group of Sanjurjo's hangers-on that he was placing himself at the orders of the Spanish

Above: During August and September 1936, a total of 14,000 Legionnaires and Moroccan troops were transported across the Straits of Gibraltar. The top photograph shows the quayside at Ceuta, where the S.S. *Alicante*, loaded with troops, is about to depart for the Spanish mainland.

Below: In Madrid, as in Barcelona, the loyalty to the Republic of the Civil Guard was crucial to the failure of the rising. A group of militiamen and Civil Guards are seen here during the first days of the war in Madrid.

Chief of State. Overcome with emotion at this theatrical display of public respect, Sanjurjo agreed to travel with him.

To add to the problems posed by the minuscule scale of Ansaldo's aeroplane, the Portuguese authorities now intervened. Although Sanjurjo was legally in the country as a tourist, the Portuguese government did not want trouble with Madrid. Accordingly, Ansaldo was obliged to clear customs and depart alone from the airport of Santa Cruz. He was then to return towards Estoril and collect Sanjurjo at a disused racetrack called La Marinha at Boca do Inferno (the mouth of hell) near Cascaes. In addition to his own rather portly self, Sanjurjo had, according to Ansaldo, a large suitcase containing uniforms and medals for his ceremonial entry into Madrid. The wind forced Ansaldo to take off recklessly in the direction of some trees. The overweight aircraft had insufficient lift to prevent the propellor clipping the tree tops. It crashed and burst into flames. Sanjurjo died although his pilot escaped virtually unhurt. Contrary to Ansaldo's version, it has recently been claimed in Portugal that the crash was the result of an anarchist bomb. Whatever the cause, it was to have a profound impact on the course of the war and on the career of General Franco. It was later asserted that Sanjurjo would have pushed for an early negotiated settlement before the battle fronts hardened, although this seems unlikely given Mola's rejection of Martínez Barrio's peace overtures, and it was not something that would have found a sympathetic response among the revolutionary masses of the Republican zone. More concretely, however, with Fanjul and Goded eliminated, the demise of Sanjurjo left only General Mola in a position of authority over Franco. Mola's position as 'Director' of the rising was in any case matched by Franco's control of the Moroccan Army which was increasingly emerging as the cornerstone of Nationalist success. Apart from Mola the only other challenger to Franco's growing pre-eminence was the Falangist leader, José Antonio Primo de Rivera, but he was in a Republican prison in Alicante.

In these early days of the war, it is unlikely that even the quietly ambitious Franco would have been thinking of anything but winning the war. The death of Sanjurjo merely served as a reminder that the *alzamiento* was far from the instant success that the conspirators had hoped for. The rebels controlled about a third of Spain in a huge block including Galicia, Leon, Old Castile, Aragon and part of Extremadura, together with isolated enclaves like Oviedo, Seville and Cordoba. They had the great wheat-growing areas, but the main centres of both heavy and light industry in Spain remained in Republican hands. The revolt had collapsed in Madrid, Barcelona, Valencia, Malaga and Bilbao. The insurgents therefore had quickly to evolve a plan of attack to conquer the rest of Spain. Since Madrid was seen as the hub of Republican resistance, their strategy was to take the form of drives on the Spanish capital by Mola's northern army and Franco's African forces. The rebels, however, confronted unexpected problems. The columns sent by Mola had not anticipated being halted at the Sierra north of Madrid by the untrained workers' militias from the capital. The northern army was also impeded by lack of arms and ammunition. Franco's army was paralysed by the problem of transport across the Straits of Gibraltar. Sea passage was impossible, since the Straits were controlled by Republican warships whose crews had mutinied against their rebel officers. In the face of these difficulties, the rebels turned to fellow rightists abroad for help.

On 19 July, Luis Bolín had set off for Rome to ask Mussolini for transport planes. While Bolín was still travelling, Franco managed to prevail upon the Italian Consul in

Tangiers to send a telegram to Rome with a request for twelve bombers or civilian transport aircraft. Mussolini simply scribbled at the bottom of the telegram 'NO'. On a second desperate telegram from Franco, the *Duce* wrote only 'FILE'. Bolín arrived in Rome on 21 July. Despite initial sympathy from the new Italian foreign minister, Count Galeazzo Ciano, he did not receive the assistance that he had hoped for. However, at that point Mussolini received a plea for aid from the exiled Spanish King, Alfonso XIII. The *Duce* told him that he 'would not permit the establishment of a Soviet regime in Spain'. While he was still in a bellicose mood, he received on 24 July a more prestigious delegation sent by General Mola. It consisted of prominent monarchists including Antonio Goicoechea, the head of Renovación Española who had visited Rome in March 1934, and the intellectual Pedro Sáinz Rodríguez. Mussolini was already on the warpath at the news that the French were about to aid the Republic. Accordingly, Ciano was able to respond positively and promised twelve Savoia-81 bombers. He insisted, however, that they be paid for in cash before their delivery. The necessary sum, over £1,000,000, was provided within a matter of days by the millionaire smuggler Juan March. The bombers were despatched on 29 July, although three of the twelve crashed before arrival.

On 22 July a further request for aid had been sent to Hitler through two Nazi businessmen resident in Spanish Morocco, Adolf Langenheim and Johannes Bernhardt. When they arrived in Germany Hitler was staying at Villa Wahnfried, the Wagner residence, while attending the annual Wagnerian festival in Bayreuth. He received Franco's emissaries on his return from a performance of *Die Walküre*. They brought a terse letter from General Franco requesting rifles, fighter planes and anti-aircraft guns. Hitler's initial reaction to the letter was to note the lack of any mention of transport planes, and to comment, 'That's no way to start a war.' However, after an interminable harangue about the Bolshevik threat he decided, against the advice of Goering, to launch what he called *Unternehmen Feuerzauber* (Operation Magic Fire), apparently still under the influence of the closing pages of the opera he had just attended. There was no continuity between Hitler's spontaneous decision and the long-standing contacts there had been between the Nazi *Ausland-Organization* (Foreign Affairs Organization) and Spanish rightists. These contacts were exposed when the Barcelona offices of the *Ausland-Organization* were ransacked by anarchists. The documents seized were published in 1937 as *The Nazi Conspiracy in Spain*. However, Operation Magic Fire was the real start of German intervention in the Spanish conflict. Hitler thereby turned a *coup d'état* that was going wrong into a bloody and prolonged civil war. With thirty Junkers JU-52 transport aircraft to join the Italian bombers, there was soon an air ferry of troops from Morocco to Seville and within ten days 15,000 troops were transported across. By 6 August, there were troopships crossing the Straits under Italian air cover. The Germans also sent some Heinkel fighters and volunteer pilots from the Luftwaffe. Within a week the rebels were receiving regular supplies of ammunition and armaments from both Hitler and Mussolini.

The arrival of foreign aid now enabled the Nationalist rebels to undertake two campaigns which considerably improved their situation. General Mola began an attack on the Basque province of Guipúzcoa with the intention of capturing Irún and San Sebastian and cutting off the province from France. Irún was attacked daily by Italian bombers. Its poorly armed and untrained militia defenders fought bravely but were overwhelmed on 3 September. Meanwhile, Franco's Army of Africa advanced northwards to Madrid, commanded in the field by Colonel Juan de Yagüe, a hardened veteran of the Moroccan wars and the most influential military supporter of the Falange. Heading out of Seville the African army took village after village, leaving a horrific trail of slaughter in its wake. On August 10 they reached Mérida, an old Roman town near Cáceres, which had fallen at the beginning of the rising. Thus the two halves of Nationalist Spain were joined. Yagüe's troops then turned back to capture Badajoz, the capital of Extremadura, still in left-wing hands. After the walls were breached, a savage repression began during which nearly 2,000 leftists were shot.

Jay Allen, an American journalist writing for the *Chicago Tribune*, arrived shortly afterwards. He saw Falangist patrols stop workmen in the streets and check if they had fought to defend the city by ripping back their shirts in order to see if their shoulders bore the tell-tale bruises of recoiling rifles. Those who did were carted off to the bullring where Allen saw files of men, arms in the air, being brought in:

> At four o'clock in the morning they are turned out into the ring through the gate by which the initial parade of the bullfight enters. There machine guns await them. After the first night the blood was supposed to be palm deep on the far side of the lane. I don't doubt it. Eighteen hundred men – there were women, too – were mowed down there in some twelve hours. There is more blood than you would think in 1,800 bodies.

Although the massacre was also witnessed by French and Portuguese journalists, it was fiercely denied by the Nationalist press service. Speakers were paid in the United States to denigrate Jay Allen. Colonel Yagüe, however, laughed at these denials. He told Allen, 'Of course we shot them. What do you expect? Was I supposed to take 4,000 reds with me as my column advanced, racing against time? Was I supposed to turn them loose in my rear and let them make Badajoz red again?' Bodies were left for days in the streets to terrorize the population.

The terror which surrounded the advance of the Moors and the Legionnaires was one of the Nationalists' greatest weapons in the drive on Madrid. It explains why Franco's troops were initially so much more successful than those of Mola. The scratch Republican militia would fight desperately as long as they enjoyed the cover of buildings or trees, but even the rumoured threat of being outflanked by the Moors would send them fleeing, abandoning their weapons as they ran. This was made apparent during the Nationalist advance which was now begun up the valley of the Tagus towards Toledo and Madrid. The last town of importance in their way, Talavera de la Reina, fell on 2 September. Another American journalist accompanying the Nationalist army, John Whitaker, recalled later,

> I never passed a night in Talavera without being awakened at dawn by the volleys of the firing squads. There seemed no end to the killing. They were shooting as many at the end of the second month as in my first days there. They averaged perhaps thirty a day. They were simple peasants and workers. It was sufficient to have carried a trade-union card, to have been a free-mason, to have voted for the Republic.

It was not just the Army of Africa which executed the conquered population. Georges Bernanos, the French Catholic novelist, was horrified by what took place in Mallorca. He saw truckloads of men being carried to their deaths:

> The lorries were grey with road-dust, the men too were grey, sitting four by four, grey caps slung crosswise, hands spread over their tent-cloth trousers, patiently. They were kidnapping

them every day from lost villages, at the time when they came in from the fields. They set off for their last journey, shirts still clinging to their shoulders with perspiration, arms still full of the day's toil, leaving the soup untouched on the table, and a woman, breathless, a minute too late, at the garden wall, with a little bundle of belongings hastily twisted into a bright new napkin.

On 21 September Yagüe's army captured the town of Santa Olalla on the road to Madrid. John Whitaker was appalled by the mass execution of six hundred captured militiamen which took place in the main street of Santa Olalla: 'They were unloaded and herded together. They had the listless, exhausted, beaten look of troops who can no longer stand out against the pounding of German bombs.' As they clustered together, Moorish troops set up two machine-guns and, firing short lazy bursts, mowed down the prisoners.

Of course, the atrocities were not confined to the rebel zone. At the beginning of the war, particularly, there were waves of assassinations of priests and suspected fascist sympathizers. Militia units set themselves up to purge their towns of known rightists and especially churchmen. Churches and religious monuments were destroyed. Over 6,000 priests and religious were estimated to have been murdered. Falangists and members of yellow (scab) unions were favourite targets of the spontaneous *checas* or pseudo-secret police units set up by various left-wing groups, particularly the anarchists. Their frenzied activities derived justification from a boastful remark made by General Mola. Pointing at a map depicting four Nationalist columns poised to swoop on the capital, he told war correspondents about his 'fifth column' of hidden sympathizers ready to come out into the open. This merely fanned existing rumours of militiamen having been shot by snipers on balconies and rooftops. Patrols began nightly searches for the 'fifth columnists'.

However, if there was a difference in the killings in the two zones, it lay in the fact that the Republican atrocities tended to be the work of uncontrollable elements at a time when the forces of order had rebelled, while those committed by the Nationalists were officially condoned by those who claimed to be fighting in the name of Christian civilization. Nationalist propaganda naturally tried to present the killings in the Republican zone as part of official government policy. This, it was claimed, was bolshevism in action. Indeed, there were many on the Republican side who were intensely aware of the damage being done to their cause by indiscriminate killing. The attacks on priests and the wanton destruction of churches were of considerable service to the rebels. Eventually, the popular perception of this unwitting co-operation with the Nationalist cause led to it being suppressed.

The rebels consolidated their position considerably during August and September. The African veteran and Carlist sympathizer General José Enrique Varela was connecting up Seville, Cordoba, Granada and Cadiz. For the Republicans there were no such spectacular advances. In Oviedo, the outraged miners had returned and were besieging Colonel Aranda who had taken their city by trickery. The rebel garrison of Toledo was still under siege in the fortress of the Alcázar. On 23 July, anarchist militia columns had set out from Barcelona in an attempt to recapture Zaragoza. Like Seville, the Aragonese capital was a CNT stronghold and had also fallen quickly to the rebels. It thus became a futile point of honour for the CNT to take Zaragoza. Its militia set off in a frenzy of enthusiasm, got within striking distance and then halted. In a small-scale parody of the Nationalist siege of Madrid, they were to remain bogged down for eighteen months. Only twelve miles away from their lines, they could see Zaragoza at night, 'a thin string of lights like the lighted portholes of a ship', wrote Orwell. Thus, for the Republic, the war was turning into an unending cycle of losses or, at best, stalemates. Moreover, Republican attempts to gain foreign aid had been less successful than those of the rebels.

On 19 July Giral had sent a telegram appealing for assistance to Léon Blum, Prime Minister in the French Popular Front government. It read: 'SURPRISED BY DANGEROUS MILITARY COUP STOP BEG YOU TO HELP US IMMEDIATELY WITH ARMS AND AERO- PLANES STOP FRATERNALLY YOURS GIRAL.' Since a Nationalist victory would mean a third fascist state on France's borders Blum, encouraged by his Air Minister, Pierre Cot, decided in favour of sending help. Moreover, as leader of a sister regime himself, he was moved by the appeal. However, his shaky coalition cabinet was split over the issue with the Defence Minister, Yvon Delbos, especially hostile to the Spanish Popular Front. The right-wing press was already raging about the threat to French investments from Spanish revolutionaries. As Blum wavered, he was made aware during a visit to London on 23 and 24 July that the British were against his sending aid. In the lobby of Claridge's Hotel, Sir Anthony Eden warned him, 'Be prudent.' Ostensibly British caution arose from fears that French assistance to the Republic might provoke a widening of hostilities, but it also reflected the fact that British commercial interests in Spain inclined the Baldwin government towards the Nationalists.

While the French Premier was absent in London, the Spanish Military Attaché in Paris leaked the story that a decision had been made to help the Republic. The rightist press went on the rampage and the Radical ministers in the Popular Front coalition declared that they would back Blum only if he got assurances of British approval. Faced by the storm in the press and fearful of losing British support, Blum drew back from his earlier commitment to aid, and proposed instead that the principal European powers agree not to intervene in Spain. On 6 August, however, the Spanish Republic did receive some aircraft from France, though not as many as were needed. Blum hoped vainly that by preventing the international participation which would favour the rebels, he could give the Spanish Popular Front government a reasonable chance to suppress the military rising. Since this 'non-intervention' was to be an empty farce, cynically exploited by Germany and Italy, and later by the Soviet Union, the Spanish Republic was in fact doomed.

In the heat of the Spanish summer of 1936, that was far from clear. The Nationalists were occupied by the need to take a major decision concerning the route to be taken by the Army of Africa. It could either press on towards Madrid or else turn to Toledo to relieve the Nationalist garrison there, besieged by Republican militiamen. The 1,000 Civil Guards and Falangists who had retreated into the Alcázar in the early days of the rising had taken with them as hostages many women and children, the families of known leftists. The militia had wasted vast amounts of time, energy and ammunition in trying to capture this strategically unimportant fortress. The resistance of the besieged garrison had thus become the great symbol of Nationalist heroism. Naturally, the existence, and later disappearance, of the hostages was entirely forgotten. A story about the siege propagated by both Spanish and English supporters of the Nationalist cause remained current throughout the civil war and for many years after. It was claimed that, on 23 July, the Republican militia commander in charge of the siege had telephoned Colonel Moscardó, the garrison's senior officer, and told him that if he did not surrender, his son would be executed.

Above left: At a village on the Extremadura front, taken by Nationalist troops en route to Mérida and Badajoz, Moroccan *regulares* have set up a stall selling tobacco and brandy, both scarce commodities at the front and much appreciated by their comrades in arms.

Above right: Legionnaires on a road in Extremadura in August 1936. For their northward advance from Seville, the Army of Africa simply followed the main roads and used the Michelin road maps as their guide.

Left: For the soldiers at the front, the war was not all gunfire, bombs and resistance at all costs. It also consisted of other, less warlike activities which, nevertheless, constituted an important part of the soldier's life. Even the harshest campaigns had their moments of relaxation, like the arrival of the newspapers, photographed here on the Talavera front in August 1936.

The *Alcázar* stands high above the rooftops of Toledo. One corner has been entirely destroyed by gunfire and dynamiting, but the Nationalists inside refuse to surrender.

In the main square of Toledo – famous then and now for a sweetmeat of arabic origin, *mazapán* – Republican loyalists return the insurgents' fire from behind a parapet of sandbags. Perhaps anticipating a long battle, some have taken rocking chairs along, to make the siege more comfortable . . .

Moscardó reputedly told his son to commend his soul to God and to die bravely. Allegedly, he then heard over the phone the shot which took his son's life. The story is almost certainly apocryphal for a variety of reasons, but not least because of its suspicious resemblance to the legend of Guzmán el Bueno who bravely sacrificed the life of his son during the thirteenth-century siege of Tarifa by the Moors. It fitted all too conveniently into the Nationalist effort to link the civil war against other Spaniards with the *Reconquista* of Spain from the infidel. Moscardó's son was in fact shot on 23 August, and not because of the threat supposedly made against his father. He was executed, along with other prisoners, as a reprisal for a Nationalist air raid on Toledo. It is odd that, if the telephone link with the Alcázar was functioning on 23 July, further contact was never attempted. Such details hardly mattered. The Alcázar and heroic anecdotes linked to it were of immense propaganda value to the Nationalists.

The decision about whether or not to relieve the Alcázar was closely related to the power struggle which had begun to unfold in the Nationalist camp. An obvious advantage enjoyed by the Nationalists over the Republic was their unity, symbolized by the establishment on 24 July of the Burgos Junta under the symbolic presidency of General Miguel Cabanellas. However, despite the existence of the Burgos Junta, Nationalist Spain was effectively divided into three power blocks. In the power stakes, one of them, the almost medieval fief of General Queipo de Llano in Seville, did not count. The others were dominated by General Mola in Burgos and by General Franco, moving on to Madrid with his African Army. Although younger at forty-three, Franco was the senior officer, a Major-General while the forty-nine-year-old Mola was only a Brigadier-General. In addition, Franco's early hesitations had been more than redeemed by the spectacular way in which his troops had swept northwards. Furthermore, through General Alfredo Kindelán and Colonel Juan de Yagüe, Franco had let both monarchists and Falangists think that he would further their aims. Kindelán organized a meeting of the ranking Nationalist generals on 21 September at an airfield near Salamanca. All the leading generals, except Cabanellas, agreed that a commander-in-chief should be nominated to replace Sanjurjo. Not only were there sound military reasons for this, but it would also facilitate the current negotiations for aid from Hitler and Mussolini.

At the Salamanca meeting, Franco was chosen as single commander. On the same day, he decided to divert his advance against Madrid in order to relieve the Alcázar. By diverting his troops to Toledo, he lost an unrepeatable chance to sweep on to the Spanish capital before its defences were ready. Malicious tongues spread the rumour that he was trying to influence the power struggle with an emotional victory and a great journalistic coup. The delay certainly gave Madrid the breathing space in which to organize its defences. It was, militarily speaking, an unnecessary gesture since an uninterrupted push on the capital would in itself have been likely to provoke the abandonment of the siege of the Alcázar. Whatever Franco's motives, his decision did him little harm. By 26 September Nationalist forces were in Toledo and able to liberate their besieged comrades. A bloodbath ensued. As John Whitaker reported, 'The men who commanded them never denied that the Moors killed the wounded in the Republican hospital at Toledo. They boasted of how grenades were thrown in among two hundred screaming and helpless men.' Whatever the military efficacy of his action, the political benefits to Franco were enormous. The liberation was re-staged on the following day for newsreel cameras. Cinema audiences throughout the world saw Franco touring the rubble of the Alcázar with

Left: It is difficult to say whether the small boys are more startled by the photographer or by the white beard of General Cabánellas and the severe look of the members of the *Junta de Defensa Nacional*, seen here during a visit to a school in Burgos.

Below: The members of the Nationalist *Junta de Defensa* arrive at the airfield of San Fernando, near Salamanca, for the meeting to elect a supreme commander. In the centre of the picture, from left to right, Generals Kindelán, Cabanellas, Franco, Queipo de Llano and Mola.

Right: Burgos, 1 October 1936. General Franco, accompanied by Generals Mola (on his left) and Cavalcanti, walks to Military Headquarters, where he is to be appointed *Generalísimo* of the Nationalist armed forces.

Undaunted by their lack of arms and tanks, the Barcelona militias requisitioned and armour-plated all kinds of civilian vehicles. Armoured cars like this one, made by anarchists, appear to have been surprisingly resistant, in spite of their 'D.I.Y.' character.

A group of Barcelona Assault Guards, in cheerful and defiant mood, salute with clenched fists from a truck hastily inscribed with the initials 'UHP' and the title of the Catalan Communist party, *Socialistes Unificats* (United Socialists).

The militants of left-wing organizations also answered the call to enlist although they, unlike the Carlists and Falangists, had few arms and little ammunition at their disposal. The photograph shows a group of volunteers in the doorway of a Socialist recruiting post.

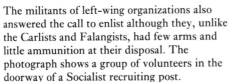

People were frequently stopped and searched by armed militiamen or police and it became essential always to carry a safe-conduct or a party or union card issued by one of the Republican organizations. Even if one travelled by public transport, such as the taxi in the photograph, one was not necessarily exempt from interrogation at gunpoint.

Two images of the regular Republican army on the Guadarrama front. In the first, troops rest amid a certain confusion of vehicles and equipment during a lull in the fighting. In the second, a column mounted on mules salutes as it patrols through the pine-covered slopes of the *sierra*.

a gaunt and bearded Moscardó. Franco thereby came to symbolize the Nationalist war effort. Inside Spain and out, he was emerging as the leader on whom rightist hopes were focused. With a little chicanery by General Kindelán and Franco's brother, Nicolás, the diminutive Galician general was able to press his advantage to become on 28 September not only sole commander but also Chief of State. He was soon being hailed as 'Caudillo' (the nearest Spanish equivalent to *Führer*) by ecstatic Nationalist crowds.

In contrast to the joy in the Nationalist ranks, the situation for the Republic looked bleak. San Sebastian had surrendered on 13 September because the Basques did not want to risk the destruction of their elegant city. General Varela continued his march into Andalusia, advancing eastwards from Seville. It was an offensive of little military importance but one which clearly underlined the socio-economic motives of the Nationalist war effort. The Nationalist army was accompanied by the sons of *latifundistas* who had formed a volunteer cavalry unit. Throughout August, defended only by peasants armed with pitchforks, shotguns and old blunderbusses, village after village fell. Swarms of terrified refugees clutching their few possessions fled before the looting Moorish mercenaries and Carlist *Requetés*. Cruel acts of revenge against the *braceros* who had collectivized the land were then often supervized by the very landowners who had fled in the spring. In the small town of Lora del Río in the province of Seville, where the only victim of the left had been the particularly despotic *cacique*, the Nationalists shot three hundred citizens as a reprisal. In nearby Palma del Río in the neighbouring province of Cordoba, Civil Guards and Falangists smashed down doors and drove out those villagers who had not managed to flee. Under the supervision of the local *cacique*, they were lined up and he marched along the lines picking out those who were to be shot in atonement for the killing of his bulls. More than two hundred were herded into the estate yard and machine-gunned down. Elsewhere, the prisoners underwent a rudimentary trial and were shot for crimes such as failing to go to mass, reading Rousseau and Kant, criticizing Hitler and Mussolini or admiring Roosevelt.

On 16 September, Varela's troops captured Ronda in the province of Malaga. Mola's forces were heading towards Madrid once again, and on 7 October the Army of Africa resumed its northward march. Supplies of arms had been collected and they were augmented by the arrival of Italian artillery and armoured cars. Already the Nationalists occupied most towns within fifteen miles of Madrid, so the capital was inundated with refugees and had major problems of food and water distribution. Now the militia columns were also falling back on Madrid in total disarray. Franco had announced to newspaper correspondents that he would take the capital on 20 October. Nationalist radio stations broadcast the news that Mola was preparing to enter Madrid's Puerta del Sol on a white horse. He even offered to meet the *Daily Express* correspondent there for coffee, and wags set up a table to await him. Telegrams addressed to Franco congratulating him on his victory were piling up at the Telefónica building. There seemed little hope for Madrid. Then on 15 October, the first arms began to arrive from the Soviet Union. There would now be no easy victory for the Nationalists.

5

'Behind The Gentleman's Agreement':
The Great Powers Betray Spain

To a large extent, the reaction of foreign powers dictated both the course and the outcome of the Civil War. That was hardly surprising for the Spanish conflict was only the latest and fiercest battle in a European civil war which had been raging intermittently for the previous twenty years. The Russian revolution of October 1917 had provided a dream and an aspiration for the left throughout Europe. Ever since, the right in Europe had been trying both internationally and domestically to build barriers against real and supposed revolutionary threats. The savage repression of revolution in Germany and Hungary after the First World War, the destruction of the left in Italy by Mussolini, the establishment of dictatorships in Spain and Portugal and even the defeat of the general strike in Great Britain had been part of this process. The crushing of the German left in 1933 and of the Austrian in 1934 were its continuation. On a wider canvas, fear and suspicion of the Soviet Union had been a major determinant of the international diplomacy of the Western powers throughout the 1920s, and even more so in the 1930s. The early tolerance shown to both Hitler and Mussolini in the international arena was a tacit sign of approval of their policies towards the left in general and towards communism in particular. Gradually, it became apparent that the corollary of the rearrangement of the domestic power balance in Italy and Germany in favour of capitalism was to be an effort to alter the balance of foreign competition by policies of imperialist aggression. Yet, even then, the residual sympathy of the policy makers of the Great Powers for fascism ensured that their first response would be simply to try to divert such ambitions in an anti-communist, and therefore eastward, direction.

Throughout the Republican period, the Spanish right and the left had both been intensely aware of their part in that wider European process. Gil Robles attended a Nuremberg rally and based much CEDA propaganda on techniques learnt on a study tour of Nazi Germany. Both Renovación Española and the Carlists had close relations with the Italian Fascists. The Falange was actually subsidized by the Italian government. 'Accidentalists' and 'catastrophists' never tired of expressing admiration and a determination to emulate both Hitler and Mussolini. The left was equally sensitive to European parallels, its daily press full of horror stories of fascism. German, Italian and Austrian exiles wrote dire warnings in Spanish leftist periodicals of the need to fight fascism.

The only power to establish diplomatic relations with the Republic during the war was the Soviet Union, whose Ambassador, Marcel Rosenberg (first left) is seen here after presenting his credentials to President Azaña.

Above: Portugal assisted the rebels by, for example, acting as a clearing centre for war material bought in Germany or surrendering Republican refugees to the Nationalists. In the photograph, a group of Portuguese officers in Salamanca at the end of the war.

Right: The smiling faces of the sailors do not seem to reassure this small girl, who is being put aboard a British ship as a refugee bound for England.

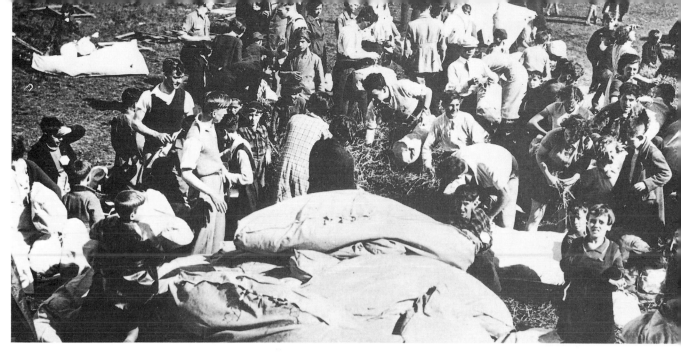

Above: A total of 4,000 Basque children found refuge in Great Britain. Here, refugees recently arrived at a camp in North Stoneham, near Southampton, put straw into the sacks which are to serve as their mattresses.

Left: About 70,000 Italian regular soldiers were sent by Mussolini to Nationalist Spain between 1936 and 1939. Many of the so-called 'volunteers' had, in fact, been recruited under threat of reprisals from their commanding officers. In the photograph, a group of Italians taken prisoner during the battle of Guadalajara in March 1937.

Below: Not all the Italians who came to Spain fought on the Nationalist side. The 'Garibaldi Battalion', posing here for a group photograph, had fought for the Republic on the Madrid and Jarama fronts before participating in the battle of Guadalajara.

Accordingly, when the war broke out in Spain, both sides were aware of taking part in a conflict with wide international ramifications. Without German and Italian aircraft, the rebel generals would not have been able to transport their best troops for use on the Spanish mainland. Similarly, Soviet arms played a crucial part in the defence of Madrid. Indeed, in the last resort, the availability of international credit and arms supplies were of sufficiently crucial importance to make it seem that the outcome of the war was determined in the chancelleries of Europe rather than on the battlefields of Spain.

Nonetheless, the official international line on the Spanish crisis was that of non-intervention. This institutionalized hypocrisy originated in a suggestion by the French. At first in favour of aiding the Republic, the French premier, Léon Blum, had been virtually told by the British that if, as a consequence of their assistance to Spain, war resulted (presumably with Germany or Italy), then Britain would not help France. It was hoped that if this could be imposed, the Spanish war would peter out for lack of arms and ammunition. None of the great powers had a policy ready when the Spanish crisis broke on them in the summer of 1936. Each responded to non-intervention in the way that best agreed with the policy it was already following: the fascist powers with instinctive aggression, the democracies with caution. This was particularly the case with Britain. By tradition and as a reaction against the horrors of the First World War, the British were determined to avoid a general war. The Spanish Republicans, however, found it hard to believe that this could outweigh an awareness of the need to avoid strengthening the position of Nazi Germany. After the Civil War had come to an end, the Republican Minister of Foreign Affairs in both the Largo Caballero and Negrín cabinets, the Socialist Julio Alvarez del Vayo, wrote, 'Not a day passed until almost the end, when we did not have fresh reasons to hope that the Western democracies would come to their senses and restore us our rights to buy from them. And always our hopes proved illusory.' The British, however, saw the Spanish conflict in the context of a wider foreign policy which involved issues far more complex than the Republic's rights to buy arms. Like the French, the British government was committed at all costs to diminishing the risks of a European conflagration. In addition, an implicit goal of British appeasement was to persuade the Germans that they should look to the east if they wished to expand. Hence the willing sacrifice of Austria and Czechoslovakia; hence the attempts by Chamberlain to extricate Britain from her agreement to go to Poland's aid in the event of attack. This was the logical concomitant of British policy since 1935, during which period a blind eye had been turned to Germany's open rearmament.

Besides their concern about the overall left-right balance in Europe, the British were inclined by their considerable commercial interests in Spain, with substantial investments in mines, sherry, textiles, olive oil and cork, to be anything but sympathetic to the Republic. The business community inevitably tended towards the Nationalist side since it was believed that the anarchists and other Spanish revolutionaries were liable to seize and collectivize British holdings. Equally, members of the British government, for reasons of class and education, sympathized with the anti-revolutionary aims of the Nationalists as they did with those of Hitler and Mussolini. Added to the determination to avoid war, these factors made the adoption of a policy of non-intervention a logical step. Above all, it would serve to neutralize and localize the Spanish war. But it had a further advantage for the British Conservatives. Non-intervention treated both sides in the Civil War as equally reprehensible, although one was the legal government and the other a group of rebellious generals. Both sides were denied aid, although the Republic had a right at international law to buy arms and supplies. By denying the Republic this right, non-intervention absolved the British from any fear that they might be helping the forces of revolution.

It is not the case, though, that either the Conservative or the Labour Party was undivided on the issue of Spain. Atrocity stories about sex-crazed, looting Spanish anarchists were spread by British Catholic supporters of the Nationalists. Through the Right Book Club and the conservative press, they had considerable impact on the middle classes. Even without their efforts, the majority of Conservatives accepted Chamberlain's policy of appeasement at virtually any price. Nevertheless, he was opposed by a significant minority. Anthony Eden, for instance, came increasingly to distrust Italian motives. Churchill, despite his open hostility to the Spanish left, concluded that Britain would be risking its Great Power status in the Mediterranean if it helped create a fascist Spain. In the Labour Party, division rested on less imperialistic considerations. Sympathy for Spanish democracy was balanced by much hostility, particularly amongst trade unionists, to the Communists, who had only recently been instructed by the Comintern to abandon their denunciation of reformist social democratic parties as 'social fascists'. Ernest Bevin argued that in any case Britain was not in a position to help Spain. Leaders such as Aneurin Bevan and Stafford Cripps, however, called for positive assistance, although in general they remained opposed to rearmament. The contradictions in their position were exploited by Bevin and led to their defeat when they attempted at the 1936 Party Conference in Edinburgh to commit the party to supporting the Republic. At an individual level, though, rank-and-file members of the Labour Party worked hard to help Spain in many ways, including donations of money and service in the International Brigades.

Non-intervention was equally convenient for the French. Although Léon Blum was anxious to help the Spanish Republic, even he could see positive benefits in the policy of non-intervention. Certainly he had to contend with intense pressure against aid for Spain, both from Britain and from within his own country. Among those opposed to any French involvement in the Spanish conflict were the French President, Radical Party ministers in Blum's Popular Front cabinet, and the combined forces of the French Right. The British attitude was also crucial. Since 1918 the French had been haunted by the memory of their casualties in the First World War and hence obsessed with an unending quest for security. When the Nazi-Polish non-aggression pact of January 1934 broke the French network of alliances in Eastern Europe, France was forced to rely almost totally on British support. Dread of losing this support was enough to incline France towards non-intervention once the official British position became clear. In any case, Blum's domestic problems precluded international tightrope walking. Large sections of French society sympathized with the Spanish Nationalists at the same time as they bitterly resented Blum's Popular Front government. Caught between this right-wing opposition and a rash of left-wing strikes and riots, the French government understandably took the line of least resistance in foreign affairs. Fears of provoking civil war in France played a not inconsiderable role in Blum's decision to adopt non-intervention. Had he intervened on the side of the Spanish Popular Front, he believed, there would have been a fascist rising in France with the consequence that 'Spain could not have been saved, but France would have gone Fascist.'

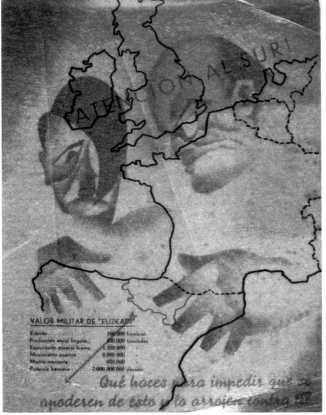

VALOR MILITAR DE "EUZKADI"

Ejército .... 100,000 hombres
Producción anual lingote.. 400,000 toneladas
Exportación mineral hierro.. 1,500,000 -
Movimiento puertos.......... 8,000,000 -
Marina mercante............. 600,000 -
Potencia bancaria........... 7,000,000,000 pesetas

Qué haces para impedir que se
apoderen de esto y lo arrojen contra tí?

Above: The British Prime Minister, Neville Chamberlain, on his return from Munich in September 1938. In Germany, Chamberlain had suggested that the four signatories to the agreement on Czechoslovakia might also try to find a solution to the Spanish conflict. His proposal was not taken up.

Left: The autonomous government of the Basque Country was anxious to make the Western democracies aware that, if Franco triumphed with the help of Hitler and Mussolini, Europe would have a fascist-backed régime on its south-western flank. The cover of a pamphlet published to explain the gravity of the Nazi-fascist threat in Spain.

Opposite above: Some time after the relief of the *Alcázar*, José Moscardó (by then promoted to the rank of General) revisited the ruins. In his arms, he holds a child born during the siege, Restituto Valero. Ironically, in the 1970s Valero was expelled from the Army on account of his belonging to a clandestine military organization, the Democratic Military Union.

Opposite below: In the course of the war, Germany sent approximately 15,000 men to fight with the Nationalists. Perhaps the most important part of this contribution was the 'Condor Legion', composed mainly of planes and air force troops, created in November 1936 specifically to strengthen Franco's armies. The 'Condor Legion' remained in Spain throughout the war and on its departure in 1939 was enthusiastically cheered by crowds of Francoist Spaniards.

The United States was too wrapped up in its New Deal isolationism to be overly preoccupied by what was happening in Spain. American strategic interests in Spain were insignificant. However, US investments in Spain amounted to 80 million dollars in 1936. That part of politically influential opinion which followed events in Europe was bitterly divided over Spain. Liberal, Protestant and left-wing groups favoured the Republic. The right, business and the bulk of the Catholic Church supported the rebels. The Hearst press chain was unequivocally behind Franco. A typical headline carried by its paper, the *Journal*, on 3 August 1936 declared: 'Red Madrid Ruled By Trotsky'. President Roosevelt bowed to the power of the rightist-Catholic lobby, and on 7 August his acting Secretary of State, William Phillips, announced that the United States would 'scrupulously refrain from any interference whatsoever in the unfortunate Spanish situation'. Seven days later, speaking at Chautauqua in New York State, the President himself presented the formula of a 'moral embargo' on arms sales to Spain as a way of maintaining international peace.

Without taking specific legislative action, the US government was effectively extending the 1935 Neutrality Act. The liberal weekly *The Nation* protested that this meant taking sides against the Republic. The embargo certainly hurt Franco far less than it did the Republic. The pro-Nazi President of the Texaco oil company, Thorkild Rieber, for instance, risked six million dollars by supplying the Nationalists with a substantial proportion of their oil needs on credit. He was penalized with a small fine. The Glenn A. Martin Aircraft Corporation of Baltimore and Robert Cuse, a businessman specializing in aircraft parts, were refused export licences for the shipment of long-standing orders to the Spanish Republic. Protestants were appalled at the Nationalists' attitudes to democracy and freedom of worship. They filled the press with letters expressing disquiet at the use of religious arguments to justify atrocities. The US ambassador to Spain, the historian Claude Bowers, bombarded the President with detailed letters urging him to help the Republic. Roosevelt replied nonchalantly, 'Do write me some more marvellous letters like that last one.' In 1939, when Bowers returned to Washington, Roosevelt told him, 'We have made a mistake; you have been right all along.' The distinguished American diplomat Sumner Welles, Under-Secretary of State from 1937 to 1943, wrote later, 'Of all our blind isolationist policies, the most disastrous was our attitude on the Spanish Civil War.'

The Soviet Union's attitude was complex and rather more subtle. In May 1934 the Comintern had given the signal for a radical change in Communist party tactics. No longer were social democratic parties in Europe to be excoriated as 'social fascist'. Instead, in order to facilitate the forging of alliances between the Soviet Union and the Western bourgeois states, Communist parties were to propose joint action with Socialist parties. This represented a fundamental shift in Comintern tactics, bringing to an end ten years of isolationist and sectarian rigidity. The reasons for the shift lay in Stalin's altered assessment of the foreign policy interests of the Soviet Union. The rise of Fascism in Italy and even more so of Nazism in Germany had convinced the Soviet leader of the need to seek alliances with the democratic capitalist states, France and Britain. Thus *L'Humanité*, the French Communist newspaper, called for a united front with the French Socialists. The corollary of this was a diplomatic effort to revive the traditional anti-German defensive alliance between Russia and France. On 2 May 1935 a Franco-Soviet Pact of Mutual Assistance was signed in Paris.

Shortly after the signing of this Pact, the Seventh Congress of the Comintern opened in Moscow, and the policy of the 'People's Front' was officially adopted. The main concern of the Comintern Congress was to formulate a strategy to safeguard the Soviet Union from external attack. The central slogan chosen for the Communist parties was 'The fight for peace and for the defence of the USSR'. Palmiro Togliatti, who was to be a Comintern representative in Spain during the Civil War, spelled things out clearly during the Congress when he stated:

> For us it is absolutely indisputable that there is complete identity of aim between the peace policy of the Soviet Union and the policy of the working class and the Communist parties of the capitalist countries. There is not, and cannot be, any doubt in our ranks on this score. We not only defend the Soviet Union in general. We defend concretely its whole policy and each of its acts.

Comintern policy, like that of the Russian Foreign Ministry, was a response to Hitler's well-advertised designs on Soviet territory. Defence of Russian territory would take precedence over the encouragement of revolution. In Spain it was to be made starkly clear that the agents of the Comintern were not the general staff of world revolution but the frontier guards of the Soviet Union.

Beyond seeking alliances with Britain and France, Stalin also wished to avoid doing anything which might provoke Germany. Conscious of the Soviet Union's unpreparedness for war, which was soon to be exacerbated by his own purges of the officer corps of the Red Army, he had been virtually silent concerning the new Nazi regime. Indeed, he had gone to great lengths to ensure that Russia would remain for as long as possible on the same terms with the Third Reich as it had been with the Weimar Republic. The Spanish conflict thus came as a profound embarrassment to Stalin. There was animated debate in the Comintern about how to react. Enthusiastic revolutionaries were all for aiding the Spanish Republic, but Stalin crucially sided with the more thoughtful moderates. Accordingly, by 29 July when Dolores Ibárruri, the Spanish Communist parliamentary deputy, appealed to the countries of the world to save Spanish democracy, there had been no overt reaction from the Soviet Union. Stalin's dilemma was obvious. On one hand, he could not stand back and let the Spanish Republic go under, for a further fascist state on the borders of France would so strengthen the French right and weaken the left as to increase the probability of the Franco-Soviet Pact being abrogated. On the other hand, victory for the Spanish left could lead to an all-out social revolution in the Iberian peninsula, which would alienate the conservative Western powers that were being courted by the Soviet Union. Stalin dreaded the prospect of the democracies being driven to line up with the dictators against Soviet Spain and Soviet Russia.

Stalin's mind was made up for him by the news that two of the three Italian bombers lost *en route* to Spanish Morocco had crash-landed in French North Africa. The initial Soviet reaction to this evidence of fascist intervention in Spain was cautious. On 3 August a crowd of 150,000 people gathered in Red Square in Moscow to express solidarity with the Spanish Republic. Collections for Spain were held in Soviet factories and Russian workers allegedly voted unanimously to donate 0.5 per cent of their salaries to help the Republic. These were clear indications of official policy. On 18 September the first shipment of food left Russia for Spain. Although Stalin was never particularly sensitive to the views of the workers of other countries, he was aware that it would be immensely damaging in propaganda terms if the Soviet Union, the 'First Workers' State', failed to come to the aid of a beleagured Popular Front government. Untrammelled success for the Nationalists in Spain would, in turn, strengthen the international positions of Hitler and Mussolini to the detriment of that of Stalin.

Stalin's policy towards the Spanish conflict was therefore conditioned by the need to resolve an appalling dilemma. He had to attain a balance whereby Soviet aid to Spain would prevent a major alteration in the international balance of power in favour of Germany, yet at the same time not provoke the conservative reflexes of Chamberlain or the French right. Essentially, he needed to prevent the Republic being defeated, but he also wished to avoid an outright victory for the Spanish revolutionary left. Thus, his reaction to the proposal of a non-intervention agreement was one of unalloyed relief. It seemed to free him from the decision of whether to abandon the Spanish left or risk an international war for which the Soviet Union was not ready. Arms supplies to Spain began only when it became unavoidably clear that Germany and Italy were merely using non-intervention as a convenient front for their aid to the Nationalists. The first Soviet ship containing arms, the *Komsomol*, docked in Cartegena on 15 October.

Stalin had decided to supply enough arms to keep the Republic alive, while instructing his agents in Spain to make every effort to ensure that the revolutionary aspects of the struggle were silenced. Accordingly, aid for Spain came with a condition attached, which was effectively that the Spanish proletariat should go no further than was acceptable to French and British policy makers. Stalin helped the Spanish Republic not in order to hasten its victory but rather to prolong its existence sufficiently to keep Hitler bogged down in an expensive venture. The most that Stalin wished for the Republic was that there might be a compromise solution acceptable to the Western democracies. He was less concerned about the fate of the Spanish people than that his co-operation with the democracies in the fight against fascist aggression should be sealed by an ostentatious Soviet readiness to keep social revolution in check. Thus, through an irony of history, the revolutionary elements in the Republican zone – the anarchists and the quasi-Trotskyists of the POUM – would face the most determined opposition not from the fascist forces of Franco, but from the Moscow-dominated Communists.

There exists less consensus on the reasons for Nazi involvement in the Spanish Civil War. Recent research by Professor Denis Smyth suggests that German support to the rebel generals came about as a result of a deliberate decision by Hitler, who saw aid to Franco as serving essential foreign policy interests of the Third Reich. This remained the case throughout the duration of the war. Hitler was well aware of British fears of the Communist threat, and quite consciously played on these. In the words of the then French Ambassador in Berlin, André François-Poncet,

> Rarely have I seen so strong an effort made by the National Socialist Government to influence Great Britain. It believes that the events in Spain will impress English conservatives and, by opening their eyes to the reality of the Bolshevik peril and the dangers of an over close friendship with an already contaminated France, will detach them from our country. It is lavishing attentions upon Sir Robert Vansittart who is in Berlin on a visit. Its hope that circumstances are working for an Anglo-German rapprochement keeps on growing.

Hitler himself talked to Count Ciano about what he referred to as 'the tactical field' of anti-Bolshevism, by which he meant that Axis intervention in Spain should be presented to the democracies as disinterested anti-Communism. Nonetheless, Hitler also had a genuine and extreme ideological antipathy towards Bolshevism and the Soviet Union. This was reflected in the attempts by the Nazis to argue that the anarchy and disorder associated with the Spanish conflict had in fact been planned by the Kremlin, despite the obvious fact that the Soviet Union had been taken by surprise by the events in Spain.

However, the German response to the Spanish Civil War was like that of the Soviet Union, determined by its broad strategic assessment of the international situation. Hitler was as fearful of the idea of a Communist Spain as Stalin was of the idea of a Fascist Spain. The reason for this was that for both Germany and the Soviet Union, the position of France in the mid-1930s was crucial, and the French situation was seen as intimately related to events in Spain. As the British Ambassador in Moscow, Viscount Chilston, commented, 'Any danger to France is a danger to the Soviet Union.' In Hitler's calculation a victory for the Popular Front forces in Spain would go some way towards creating a leftist bloc in Europe, which would stand in the way of the Third Reich's plans for imperialist expansion into Central and Eastern Europe. The quest for *Lebensraum* was dependent on a prior defeat of France, and that defeat would be endangered if the Spanish Popular Front were not first eliminated.

Suggestions that Hitler's intervention in Spain was motivated by the possibilities of economic advantage have been overplayed. Although Spain's mineral resources were tempting to a Germany bent on rearmament, this was not the main attraction for Hitler. Spanish iron ore constituted only 6.6 per cent of German consumption in 1935. Although in the same year Spanish pyrites (copper ore) made up 46 per cent of total German pyrites imports, in neither case was there any threat to supplies through normal channels. Indeed, even at the time of the Third Reich's great foreign exchange crisis in early 1936 imports of Spanish ores were unaffected, owing to Germany's extremely favourable balance of trade with Spain. Rather, the German position in some ways was the mirror image of that of the Soviet Union. Hitler wished to avoid the creation of a 'Soviet Spain', but he was not yet ready to provoke a European conflict through excessive involvement in Spanish affairs. Just as Stalin wanted a Republican victory without any revolutionary overtones, so Hitler supported a victory for the rebel forces, but did not want to alarm or antagonize the Western powers.

Instead, he used the Spanish conflict as a form of preparation for the struggle in Europe which would inevitably break out in due course. This much was admitted by Hermann Goering, Commissioner for Air during the Third Reich, at the Nuremberg trials:

> When the civil war broke out in Spain, Franco sent a call for help to Germany and asked for support, particularly in the air. One should not forget that Franco with his troops was stationed in Africa and that he could not get the troops across, as the fleet was in the hands of the Communists. . . . The decisive factor was, first of all, to get his troops over to Spain.
>
> The Führer thought the matter over. I urged him to give support under all circumstances, firstly, in order to prevent the further spread of communism in that theatre and, secondly, to test my young Luftwaffe at this opportunity in this or that technical respect.
>
> With the permission of the Führer, I sent a large part of my transport fleet and a number of experimental fighter units, bombers, and anti-aircraft guns; and in that way I had an opportunity to ascertain, under combat conditions, whether the material was equal to the task. In order that the personnel, too, might gather a certain amount of experience, I saw to it that there was a continuous flow, that is, that new people were constantly being sent and others recalled.

Goering had clearly forgotten that nine years before he had been initially less enthusiastic to help Franco than had Hitler. None the less, once the decision was taken, his commitment to using Spain as a testing ground was unquestionable. The volunteer members of the crack Condor Legion, private soldiers as well as officers, were paid executive salaries to fight in Spain.

Italy was the European power whose policy most lacked consistency and rationality. Her geographical position and lack of strategic raw materials dictated that she follow a modest and realistic policy of alignment with England, the dominant naval power in the Mediterranean. Mussolini's policy, however, was always dominated by the restless desire to redress what he saw as the injustices of the Versailles peace settlement. By striking out at random, whether in Corfu or Abyssinia, Mussolini hoped 'to make Italy great, respected and feared'. A desire for a dynamic restructuring of the world order in favour of fascism led eventually to alignment with Nazi Germany and the Rome-Berlin Axis. Mussolini took his position as the founder of fascism immensely seriously and, given that the Spanish war was widely seen as the beginning of a world counter-offensive against fascism, he was unable to resist the urge to intervene. The defeat of the Spanish Nationalists would be a defeat for what he saw as a sister movement, and the *Duce* could not contemplate that. In any case he was always looking for an arena in which to flex the muscles of his armed forces. To a certain extent Spain was seen by the Italians, as by the Germans, as a possible testing ground for men and equipment. More crucially, however, Mussolini believed that immersion in blood and violence was the only way to forge the spirit of the new Fascist man.

Economic factors were of even less importance in Mussolini's decision to help the Spanish rebels than they had been in Hitler's. The position of France was the key factor. Indeed, his decision to help the Nationalists had been precipitated to a very large extent by the release of the news that Blum planned to aid the Spanish Republic. The possibility that Spain and France would thereby be drawn together, to the detriment of Italian ambitions in the Mediterranean, was alone sufficient to persuade Mussolini to intervene. By helping the Nationalists he was not only defending the vague interests of world fascism, but also likely to boost Italian power in the Mediterranean. A Nationalist victory might lead to the expulsion of the British from Gibraltar. It would probably give Italy access to bases in the Balearic Islands. In either eventuality it was an excellent opportunity to weaken Britain's communications with Suez. At the time, the idea was current that Mussolini's decision was the logical conclusion to the agreements made with Goicoechea and the Carlists in Rome in 1934. A pamphlet published in 1938, *How Mussolini Provoked The Spanish Civil War*, reprinted those agreements and thereby substantiated the idea of continuity. Recent research, however, has suggested that like Hitler, Mussolini made his mind up on the spur of the moment. Intervention in Spain was a continuation of his headlong search for prestige.

The extent to which Italian intervention in Spain suited Hitler's foreign policy interests and damaged those of the democracies was shrewdly perceived by Ulrich von Hassell, the German Ambassador in Rome. In a report sent to Berlin on 18 December 1936, he wrote enthusiastically that:

> Germany has in my opinion every reason for being gratified if Italy continues to interest herself deeply in the Spanish affair. The role played by the Spanish conflict as regards Italy's relations with France and England could be similar to that of the Abyssinian conflict, bringing out clearly the actual, opposing interests of the powers and thus preventing Italy from being drawn into

the net of the Western powers and used for their machinations. The struggle for dominant political influence in Spain lays bare the natural opposition between Italy and France; at the same time the position of Italy as a power in the Western Mediterranean comes into competition with that of Britain. All the more clearly will Italy recognize the advisability of confronting the Western powers shoulder to shoulder with Germany.

For Mussolini, then, Spain provided a splendid opportunity to try to impress the Germans of Italy's claims to be an indispensable ally. Unfortunately, the desire to show off Italy's 'iron military strength' would end in the humiliation of the battle of Guadalajara, on which Lloyd George wrote a mocking article under the heading 'The Italian Skedaddle'. In consequence, hurt vanity led to Mussolini trying to prove his mettle to Hitler by unswerving commitment to the Rome-Berlin Axis. Italy was therefore pushed ever closer to Germany and ultimately into the Second World War on Hitler's side.

It was the French, conscious of their pivotal role, who had proposed an agreement of non-intervention in the Spanish conflict. In August 1936, twenty-seven European nations formally adhered to such an agreement. In the event, it was to mean little: intervention continued as if the agreement had never existed. Thus the Non-Intervention Committee, set up on 9 September 1936, and based in London, was little more than a sham. However, it was a sham which worked in the interest of the rebel forces in Spain, and hindered the efforts of the legitimate Republican government to stage an effective defence against the insurgents. The Soviet Union, which believed in neither the legality nor the efficacy of the Non-Intervention Agreement, initially decided to adhere to its terms out of a desire to keep its relations with the West cordial. The Germans and Italians, however, openly flouted the Agreement. They found it so convenient a cloak for their activities on behalf of the Spanish Nationalists that they were to be found cynically defending its existence against the criticisms of the Russians.

Scrupulous observation of the Non-Intervention Agreement would have suited Stalin's plans. It was Italo-German arms shipments to the Nationalists that obliged him to provide support for the Republic, which he did cautiously while continuing to proclaim Soviet neutrality. Had it been possible to stop German and Italian aid to the rebels, Stalin would gladly have stopped Soviet shipments to the Republic. Yet the Non-Intervention Committee, under the chairmanship of the Conservative Lord Plymouth, consistently revealed a bias against the Soviet Union while always being extremely polite to the Fascist powers. The Soviet Ambassador to London, Ivan Maisky, commented of Lord Plymouth that:

> In this large, imposing and well-groomed body dwelt a small, slow-moving and timid mind. Nature and education had made Plymouth a practically ideal personification of English political mediocrity, nourished by the traditions of the past and by well-worn sentiments. As Chairman of the Committee Plymouth presented an entirely helpless and often comic figure.

Plymouth's daily bewilderment and his readiness to meet urgent problems by adjourning the Committee enabled both the Italians and Germans to continue openly to assist Franco's forces. The flamboyant Italian representative, Dino Grandi, and the German Ambassador in London, the bumbling ex-champagne salesman, Joachim von Ribbentrop, combined to render non-intervention a tragic mockery of the position of the Spanish Republic. Under Plymouth's chairmanship, the Committee moved with agonizing slowness, stopping for long-drawn-out discussions of such topics as whether gas masks constituted armaments but always ready to ignore hard evidence of the Agreement being breached.

In the words of Pandit Nehru, non-intervention was 'the supreme farce of our time'. It left the Republic at a clear disadvantage in comparison to the rebels and thereby confirmed the anti-revolutionary trend of international diplomacy since 1917. The Spanish democratic regime was to be as much a victim of the pusillanimity of the Western powers as were Austria and Czechoslovakia. However, it would be wrong to see the international diplomacy of the Spanish Civil War as merely a microcosm of Western appeasement, fascist aggression and Soviet duplicity. When placed in the context of the post-1917 series of defeats suffered by the European left, the abandonment of Spain to fascism assumes an iron logic. What is remarkable is that the political representatives of the Spanish Republic were so shocked by the nonchalance of the Western powers. They had witnessed fascism in action and could not believe that British and French statesmen could be so blind to its threat. Eventually, even the conservative leaders of the democracies would perceive the danger. In 1936, however, their attitude to fascism, and therefore to the Spanish conflict, was compounded of an understandable desire to avoid war and a quiet glee that they might be able to do so by turning Hitler and Mussolini against the European left. They thereby passed a death sentence on the Spanish Republic.

6

'Madrid is the Heart': The Central Epic

The inexorable advances of the Nationalists exposed the inadequacies of the Giral government. Like Casares Quiroga, Giral had been in the absurd position of presiding over a cabinet representing only a small section of the Popular Front coalition which had won the February 1936 elections. Largo Caballero, who must bear the ultimate responsibility for the crucial absence of the PSOE from the cabinet, remained committed to the idea of an exclusively workers' government. However, Largo Caballero was eventually brought round to the view of his arch-rival Indalecio Prieto that the survival of the Republic required a cabinet backed by both the working-class parties and the bourgeois Republicans. On 4 September a true Popular Front government was formed with Largo Caballero as both Prime Minister and Minister of War. It contained Communists as well as Socialists and Republicans. Two months later, on 4 November, with the Nationalists already at the gates of Madrid, four representatives of the anarcho-syndicalist CNT also joined the cabinet. It was an indication of the gravity of the situation that the CNT should thus abandon its most sacred principles in order to help defend the beleaguered democratic regime.

Already in mid-October, the artillery fire of the approaching Army of Africa had been heard in Madrid. The armies of Franco and Mola were aiming to meet in the capital. The rebels had amassed considerable supplies of arms, and these were supplemented by Italian weaponry. By 1 November 25,000 Nationalist troops under General José Varela had reached the western and southern suburbs of Madrid. Their aim was to cut through the Casa del Campo, the old royal hunting ground, and the University City. They were considerably strengthened by the arrival on 6 November of the German Condor Legion under General von Sperrle. This was a force of specialized units equipped with the latest developments in German bomber and fighter aircraft and motorized weapons which were to be tested out in Spain. Indeed, so sure was the Republican government that Madrid would fall that it left for Valencia on 6 November, and placed the protection of the city in the hands of a Defence Junta presided over by General Miaja.

The decision to move the Republican government to Valencia was divisive and controversial. The four newly incorporated anarchist ministers, Juan García Oliver (Justice), Juan López (Commerce), Federica Montseny (Health), and Juan Peiró (Industry), were reluctant to abandon Madrid. According to Indalecio Prieto the anarchists 'considered

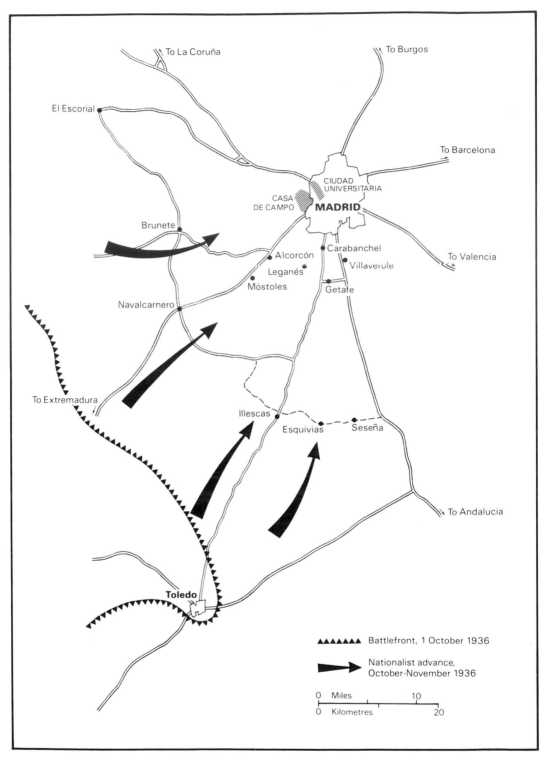

To La Coruña

To Burgos

El Escorial

To Barcelona

CIUDAD
UNIVERSITARIA

CASA
DE CAMPO

MADRID

Brunete

Carabanchel

Alcorcón

To Valencia

Villaverde

Leganés

Móstoles

Getafe

Navalcarnero

To Extremadura

Illescas

Esquivias

Seseña

To Andalucia

Toledo

▲▲▲▲▲▲▲ Battlefront, 1 October 1936

➤ Nationalist advance,
October–November 1936

| 0 | Miles | 10 |
| 0 | Kilometres | 20 |

Madrid and its hinterland. In October 1936, the Nationalists began to close in on the
capital from the West and South-west.

themselves victims of a deception, thinking that they had been made ministers only in order to implicate them in such a serious measure, and they resisted giving their approval'. The decision to leave Madrid, though, was not a last-minute act of desperation. The transfer of government headquarters had been discussed previously. Moreover, not all members of the government saw the abandonment of Madrid as an admission that the city was bound to fall to the rebels. The Communist Party representatives in Largo Caballero's cabinet, Jesús Hernández (Education) and Vicente Uribe (Agriculture), had argued in October that the defence of Madrid and the evacuation of the government were not incompatible objectives. The four anarchists, however, regarded leaving the capital as cowardice and proposed to remain in Madrid while the other members of the cabinet left. This was firmly rejected by Prieto, who was quick to perceive the political advantage that their bravery would confer upon the CNT.

Prieto, who was Navy and Air Force Minister, was, however, distressed by the manner in which the government proposed to leave. Although with characteristic pessimism Prieto, like Largo Caballero, was convinced that Madrid would swiftly fall to the insurgents, he believed the government should announce in advance its plans to leave the capital. He later claimed that some weeks earlier he had proposed that the government should leave, but with adequate publicity. Prieto was anxious that the transfer should not take place suddenly and unexpectedly at the last moment and thereby give the impression of a desperate flight. He considered it advisable that the people of Madrid should be psychologically prepared so that they would find the measure militarily justifiable, not the act of cowardly fugitives. As so often, Largo Caballero ignored the advice of Prieto.

The cabinet debate on the Prime Minister's evacuation proposal was extremely tense. After asking permission to discuss the matter privately, the four CNT ministers withdrew and only after considerable delay returned to say that they agreed. Largo Caballero announced that the new seat of government would be Valencia, not Barcelona as had originally been expected, because the President of the Republic, Manuel Azaña, had already moved there. Prieto announced that he had made two passenger aircraft available to ferry the cabinet members to Valencia, but none took him up on his offer. Largo Caballero left by the main Madrid–Valencia road which passed through the town of Tarancón, occupied by anarchist militiamen under a certain Colonel Rosal. Rosal impeded the passage of the ministers and civil servants. Julio Alvarez del Vayo, the left Socialist Foreign Minister, was jostled and insulted. Juan Peiró and Juan López, the CNT Ministers of Industry and of Commerce, were turned back to Madrid and forced to travel to Valencia by plane with Prieto.

According to Prieto, Largo had decided unilaterally that the government should go to Valencia. In his own memoirs, however, Largo states that it had been unanimously decided to go to Valencia, and that Azaña had changed his mind and gone to Barcelona on 19 October without consulting anyone. Whatever the truth of the matter, there can be little doubt that the manner in which the government left Madrid created a very poor impression and allowed the Communist Party to assume the lead in defending Madrid, and thereby to enhance its own prestige. It was an important step along the path to its ultimate take-over of the whole Republican war effort. In the meantime, the main issue was the situation in the Spanish capital, suddenly bereft of a government. The atmosphere in the city on the evening of 6 November is well conveyed by Mikhail Koltzov, the Soviet journalist and personal emissary of Stalin:

I made my way to the War Ministry, to the Commissariat of War.... Hardly anyone was there. ... I went to the offices of the Prime Minister. The building was locked. I went to the Ministry of Foreign Affairs. It was deserted.... In the Foreign Press Censorship an official... told me that the government, two hours earlier, had recognized that the situation of Madrid was hopeless ... and had already left. Largo Caballero had forbidden the publication of any news about the evacuation 'in order to avoid panic'.... I went to the Ministry of the Interior.... The building was nearly empty.... I went to the central committee of the Communist Party. A plenary meeting of the Politburo was being held.... They told me that this very day Largo Caballero had suddenly decided to evacuate. His decision had been approved by the majority of the cabinet.... The Communist ministers wanted to remain, but it was made clear to them that such a step would discredit the government and that they were obliged to leave like all the others.... Not even the most prominent leaders of the various organizations, nor the departments and agencies of the state, had been informed of the government's departure. Only at the last moment had the Minister told the Chief of the Central General Staff that the government was leaving.... The Minister of the Interior, Galarza, and his aide, the Director of Security Muñoz, had left the capital before anyone else.... The staff of General Pozas, the commander of the central front, had scurried off ... Once again I went to the War Ministry.... I climbed the stairs to the lobby. Not a soul! On the landing ... two old employees are seated, like wax figures, wearing livery and neatly shaven ... waiting to be called by the Minister at the sound of his bell. It would be just the same if the Minister were the previous one or a new one. Rows of offices! All the doors are wide open.... I enter the War Minister's office.... Not a soul! Further down, a row of offices – the Central General Staff, with its sections; the General Staff, with its sections; the General Staff of the Central Front, with its sections; the Quartermaster Corps, with its sections; the Personnel Department, with its sections. All the doors are wide open. The ceiling lamps shine brightly. On the desks there are abandoned maps, documents, communiqués, pencils, pads filled with notes. Not a soul!

There was deep confusion over how the defence of Madrid was to be organized when the government left. Moreover, there was a general sense of panic and disorder in the capital. The Socialist Arturo Barea, head of the Foreign Press and Censorship Bureau, described in his autobiography, *The Forging of a Rebel*, how he received the news of the government's departure:

When Luis Rubio Hidalgo told me that the government was leaving and that Madrid would fall the next day, I found nothing to say. What could I have said? I knew as well as anybody that the Fascists were standing in the suburbs. The streets were thronged with people who, in sheer desperation, went out to meet the enemy at the outskirts of their town. Fighting was going on in the Usera district and on the banks of the Manzanares. Our ears were forever catching the sound of bombs and mortar explosions, and sometimes we heard the cracking of rifle shots and the rattle of machine guns. But now the so-called War Government was about to leave, and the Head of its Foreign Press Department expected Franco's troops to enter ... I was stunned, while he spoke on urbanely.

The departing government had decided to entrust the defence of Madrid to General José Miaja. The hero of Madrid, as he was to become, had a chequered background. Convinced that the rebels must win against the Republic, he had refused to continue as Minister of War in the government of Giral, and was even accused of having been a member of the ultra-rightist *Unión Militar Española*. Transferred to command the Third Division in Valencia, he had then been beaten back in an attempt to take Cordoba and relieved of his command. He was thus under some suspicion when given the awesome

Above: The new campus of Madrid University, still under construction when the war began, was virtually destroyed by the three years of fighting which went on in and around its unfinished buildings. In the photograph, a shell explodes close to the remains of two shattered Faculty buildings.

Left: The popular slogan of the defence of Madrid was '*No pasarán*' ('They shall not pass'), seen here on a banner slung across a narrow street close to the Plaza Mayor. Beneath its authoritative first line, the banner continues. 'Fascism wishes to conquer Madrid. Madrid will be the tomb of fascism'.

Below: General Miaja (seated fourth from right) presides over a meeting of the somewhat heterogenous Committee for the Defence of Madrid, created on the eve of the transfer of the Republican government to Valencia.

task of organizing the defence of Madrid. Indeed, he was sure it was part of a deliberate attempt to sacrifice him in a futile gesture. According to Largo Caballero, Miaja's reaction on hearing the news of his unexpected, and probably unwanted, promotion was to turn pale, stammer and point out that, while he was at the orders of the Prime Minister, it should be remembered that his family was in prison in Nationalist-held Morocco and that he had business interests there.

On the same day Largo, in his capacity as Minister of War, had drawn up with General José Asensio Torrado, his Under-Secretary, orders for the defence of Madrid. These were handed in sealed envelopes, with further instructions that they were not to be opened until the following morning at six, to Miaja, the newly appointed commander of the Madrid military district, and to General Sebastián Pozas, commander of the Army of the Centre. Miaja and Pozas ignored orders and opened their envelopes on the evening of 6 November. It transpired that each had been given the other's orders, a mistake which remains a source of controversy. Miaja was instructed to set up a *Junta de Defensa* (Defence Council), made up of all the parties of the Popular Front, and to defend Madrid 'at all costs'. Pozas received instructions on tactical movements and for the setting up of new headquarters. Nonetheless, according to Julián Zugazagoitia, editor of *El Socialista* and supporter of Prieto, no one in the government believed that Madrid could be defended, least of all Largo Caballero who was fully conversant with the prevailing state of military confusion and disintegration. The Prime Minister left Madrid as convinced as Prieto that it would fall to the enemy within a week.

However, the arrival of rebel forces had been delayed by Franco's decision to liberate the Alcázar of Toledo. This proved to be vital for the Republicans. Not only did it allow the delivery of Soviet aid – which was paid for on 25 October by sending half of Spain's gold reserves to the Soviet Union – but also the formation of the International Brigades. These were organized and recruited by the Comintern, which had quickly recognized the existence of a spontaneous urge to help Spain among workers throughout Europe and America. Volunteers from all over the world, anxious to fight fascism, were shipped to Spain via Paris, where the organization was run by various agents including the future Marshal Tito. They began to arrive in October and were trained at Albacete under the direction of André Marty, the brutal French Communist. The first units reached Madrid on 8 November, consisting of German and Italian anti-fascists, plus some British, French and Polish left-wingers. Sprinkled among the Spanish defenders at the rate of one to four, the members of the brigade both boosted their morale and trained them in the use of machine-guns.

Known as the 'International Column' in the Republican press, the Eleventh International Brigade under the leadership of the Soviet General, Emilio Kléber, was vital to the defence of Madrid. Together with the Communist party's Fifth Regiment, the most highly organized and disciplined force in the central zone, the Eleventh Brigade enabled Miaja to lead the entire population of Madrid in a desperate and remarkable defence. By early November there was hand-to-hand fighting between militiamen and Moors in the University buildings. Yet the people fought on, under banners which proclaimed 'They Shall Not Pass' and 'Madrid Will Be The Tomb Of Fascism'. The fiery Communist orator, Dolores Ibárruri, 'La Pasionaria', rallied the defenders with ringing oratory: 'It is better to die on your feet than to live on your knees.' She harangued the women of Madrid: 'It is better to be the widow of a hero than the wife of a coward.' A women's

Top left: Among the tens of thousands of men and women who fought for the Republic in the International Brigades was a group of Britons who formed the 'Tom Mann' centurion, seen here with their standard. The group took its name from an English Communist.

Top right: In addition to strengthening the Popular Army in military terms, the International Brigades were a source of other kinds of crucial support, like this ambulance, provided through members of the Abraham Lincoln battalion.

Centre left: 'An army marches on its stomach'. Rations were never over-abundant on either side, but the problem was particularly serious for the Republicans, whose armies did not control the main food-producing areas of the country.

Left: Although the Republicans were retreating all the way, their defence of the southern suburbs of Madrid prevented the Nationalists from occupying the capital in the Autumn of 1936. The use of Russian fighter planes and artillery, such as that seen in action here near the village of Alcorcón, inflicted considerable, if not decisive, damage on the Nationalist forces.

brigade was in fact involved in the fighting. Working-class districts were shelled and bombed, although Franco was careful to spare the plush Barrio de Salamanca, the residential districts where his fifth columnists lived. Those of them that were caught were slaughtered by the desperate militiamen.

Volunteers from all over the world flocked to fight for the Republic. Some were out of work, others were adventurers, but the majority had a clear idea of why they had come: to fight fascism. For the victims of the fascist regimes of Mussolini and Hitler, it was a chance to fight back against an enemy whose bestiality they knew only too well. Forced out of their own countries, they had nothing to lose but their exile and were fighting to go back to their homes. One of the battalions which saw its first action in Madrid, and which was to suffer enormous casualties, was the Thaelmann, consisting mainly of German, and some British, Communists. Esmond Romilly was a British member of the Thaelmann Battalion. He later wrote of his comrades-in-arms:

> For them, indeed, there could be no surrender, no return; they were fighting for their cause and they were fighting as well for a home to live in. I remembered what I had heard from them of the exile's life, scraping an existence in Antwerp or Toulouse, pursued by immigration laws, pursued relentlessly – even in England – by the Nazi Secret Police. And they had staked everything on this war.

Indeed, when the Republic finally fell in 1939, many German, as well as Italian, anti-fascists were still fighting in Spain. They ended up in French camps, and many fell into the hands of the SS and died in the gas chambers.

For the British and American volunteers, the need to fight in Spain was somewhat different. They made more of a conscious choice. The hazardous journey to Spain was undertaken out of the awful presentiment of what defeat for the Spanish Republic might mean for the rest of the world. One who made such a choice was Jason Gurney, a sculptor living in Chelsea, who went to fight and received a wound which would prevent him from ever being able to sculpt again: 'The Spanish Civil War seemed to provide the chance for a single individual to take a positive and effective stand on an issue which appeared to be absolutely clear. Either you were opposed to the growth of Fascism and went out to fight against it, or you acquiesced in its crimes and were guilty of permitting its growth.' Gurney was typical of the volunteers who believed that, by combating fascism in Spain, they would be fighting against the threat of fascism in their own countries. They were offered nothing in the way of pay or even insurance. One man who asked the British recruiters about conditions of service was told, 'You're not the kind of bloke we want in Spain. So get out.' All they were offered, and all most of them wanted, was the chance to fight fascism.

In contrast, and despite being described as volunteers, the Germans and Italians who fought with the rebels were properly trained regular soldiers. However, there were also some genuine volunteers on the Francoist side. These included at least half a dozen Englishmen and an American. One of the Englishmen, Peter Kemp, became an officer first with the Carlists, and then with the ferocious Spanish Foreign Legion. However, the most well-known foreign volunteers for Franco were the Irish brigade under General Eoin O'Duffy. For them, this was no more nor less than a religious crusade, as evidenced by the following extract from O'Duffy's *Crusade in Spain*, published in 1938:

> Before leaving, the volunteers were presented with Rosaries, Agnus Deis and other religious emblems, the gift of the Right Rev. Monsignor Byrne, Clonmel, Dean of Waterford.

Seventeen counties were represented in this party, the largest contingent coming from Tipperary. Referring to their departure, the Right Rev. Monsignor Ryan, Dean of the Archdiocese of Cashel, preaching after Mass the following Sunday, said: 'They have gone to fight the battle of Christianity against Communism. There are hosts of difficulties facing the men whom General O'Duffy is leading, and only heroes can fight such a battle. Those at home can help the cause with their prayers. The Rosary is more powerful than weapons of war. In the presence of Our Lord Jesus Christ let us promise that we will offer one decade of the family Rosary daily for poor suffering Spain; for the Irish boys who have gone out to fight the desperate battle that is threatening desolation all over the world. Let us pray that the destruction of civilization may be averted, that Christ may live and reign, and that Communism and the power of Satan on earth may be brought to naught.'

O'Duffy, in fact, was head of the Irish fascist Blue Shirt movement, and hoped that success in Spain would further his own dictatorial ambitions in Ireland. In the event, the Irish brigade did not find the glory which might have facilitated a fascist coup in Ireland. O'Duffy diminished the military efficacy of his brigade by giving the most responsible appointments to his own political supporters, regardless of their experience. Disaster followed; and their first casualties were inadvertently at the hands of the Francoists. At the Jarama, one of their companies was fired on by a Falangist unit which mistook them for International Brigaders and a minor skirmish ensued. During the actual battle at Jarama, the Irish brigade suffered heavy casualties while contributing little to the rebel cause. In the summer of 1937 they went home, thoroughly disillusioned.

The recruitment of the Republican volunteers was organized largely by the Communist Party. That does not mean that they were all Communists, although a fair proportion of them were. Hindsight about the awful crimes of Stalin or about the sordid power struggles within the Republican zone cannot diminish the idealism and heroism of those who sacrificed their comfort, their security and often their lives in the anti-fascist struggle. Francoists and anti-Communist historians in the United States have presented the International Brigaders as the dupes of Moscow. This tendency reached its peak in a recent work which, somewhat bizarrely, drew much of its evidence from the records of the US Congress House Committee on Un-American Activities and of the hearings of the US Subversive Activities Control Board. The fact that the Brigades were largely Communist-organized should not be allowed to obscure the fact that the volunteers went to Spain to fight Hitlerism. They perceived, as democratic politicians evidently did not, what the poet Edgell Rickword vividly expressed in his satirical lines:

> In Hitler's frantic mental haze
> Already Hull and Cardiff blaze,
> And Paul's grey dome rocks to the blast
> Of air torpedoes screaming past.

It was, nevertheless, left to the Communists to sneak the volunteers across the French border, either on foot or in buses. Some even crossed the Pyrenees, wearing rope-soled sandals or *alpargatas*. On the bus carrying Jason Gurney, one man began to scream, 'I don't want to go.' To prevent him alerting the French authorities to their illegal crossing, Gurney hit him. He wrote later that the man 'cried a lot that night at Figueras but seemed quite content thereafter and never held it against me. But when I saw his body lying dead, two months later, on the Jarama fields, I felt like a murderer.' As the recruiters had warned, it was 'a bastard of a war'. When the volunteers arrived at Barcelona, they were greeted by huge welcoming crowds. Most of them had no experience of warfare, and they had to be organized quickly into units and given a few hours' rudimentary training. Often with inadequate equipment, they were then sent out to do battle with the fascist forces. The first units reached Madrid on 8 November. Geoffrey Cox, *News Chronicle* correspondent, was in the Spanish capital when they arrived:

> The few people who were about lined the roadway, shouting almost hysterically, '¡Salud! ¡Salud!', holding up their fists in salute, or clapping vigorously. An old woman with tears streaming down her face, returning from a long wait in a queue, held up a baby girl, who saluted with her tiny fist.
>
> The troops in reply held up their fists and copied the call of '¡Salud!' We did not know who they were. The crowd took them for Russians. The barman turned to me saying 'The Rusos have come. The Rusos have come.' But when I heard a clipped Prussian voice shout an order in German, followed by other shouts in French and Italian, I knew they were not Russians. The International Column of Anti-Fascists had arrived in Madrid.

The boost to the morale of the *Madrileños* was incalculable.

Nevertheless, the role of the International Brigades in the defence of Madrid should not be exaggerated. They were one component of a heroic effort which involved the whole population. Women and children helped with food, communications and medical supplies. On 14 November the column of the legendary anarchist fighter, Buenaventura Durruti, arrived. Durruti himself was to die within a week, killed in circumstances which remain the source of dispute. His death occurred near the University City but away from the thick of action, and was almost certainly the result of a gun accidentally going off in his car. A story was issued that he had been shot by a Nationalist sniper. Many anarchists were unable to accept this, and accused the Communists of having assassinated their heroic leader. The Communists countered with an assertion that Durruti had been killed by his own men resentful of his efforts to impose discipline. A gigantic funeral procession followed Durruti to his final resting place on 22 November. The hundreds of thousands of mourners who edged slowly through Barcelona constituted the last public demonstration of the CNT's mass strength. Thereafter, recriminations over his death provided a focus for bitter confrontation born of contradictory interpretations of how the struggle against the rebels should be carried out. The anarchists accused the Communists of imposing the authoritarian rigidity of Soviet Communism over the spontaneity of the libertarian social revolution. The Communists responded with severe criticisms of the way anarchist inefficiency impeded the job of feeding the refugees crammed into the besieged city, and mocked the performance of the Durruti column in defending the University City.

It is true that the Nationalists, in the form of Moorish troops, had been able to make significant advances and had crossed the Manzanares river. In the end, though, their surge forward was contained. In fact, Durruti's men had gone into action with some reluctance. The anarchist leader had insisted on his arrival in Madrid that his men needed to rest and reorganize. However, Durruti was subjected to enormous pressure by the recently-formed Madrid *Junta de Defensa*, under Miaja, which had debated in its session of 14 November the placing of the anarchist column under its direct orders. This turned out to be unnecessary, for Durruti had agreed at the last moment to go to the Republican

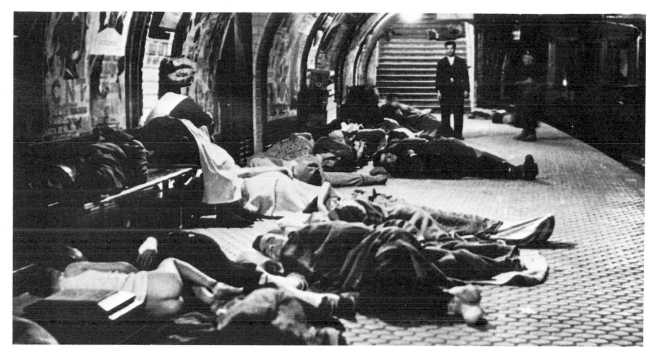

The mass of the civilian population in Madrid endured with stoicism the privations of the war. These two photographs show two aspects of life in the Republican rearguard. (*Top*) the tube stations doubled as air-raid shelters, where people frequently had to sleep crowded together on the platforms. (*Bottom*) women queue, probably for food.

lines straight away. His militiamen, however, were both ill-equipped and exhausted after two months of uninterrupted fighting on the Aragon front, and many of them fled in the face of Moorish attacks. The Moors almost reached the city centre, but they were driven back after a heroic struggle by the people of Madrid. By 23 November the Nationalist attack was spent. For the moment the city was saved.

The great popular hero of the defence of Madrid was General Miaja. His success in holding off the rebel forces owed an enormous amount to the immediate offer of support to the *Junta de Defensa* by the Communist Party, its Fifth Regiment, and the Communist-dominated united Socialist youth movement, the Juventudes Socialistas Unificadas (JSU). Nonetheless, he was later to be vilified by the Communists after having been built up by them to the Status of a living legend. This has been seen by some as part of a deliberate policy by the Communists in order to gain access to the leading positions in the *Junta de Defensa*. Having been abandoned by the Republican government and convinced that he had been chosen as a sacrificial scapegoat, it was not surprising that Miaja looked to the Communists. They in turn perceived that the battered spirits of the *Madrileños* needed a hero. Miaja was therefore put on a pedestal and became intoxicated by the praise lavished upon him. He told Julián Zugazagoitia, 'When I am in my car women call out to me, "Miaja!" "Miaja!" And they scream to each other, "There goes Miaja! There goes Miaja!" ... and I greet them and they greet me. They are happy and so am I'. To many, though, Miaja was an unimpressive figure.

Herbert L. Matthews, the *New York Times* correspondent in Madrid, described Miaja as the very reverse of his image as the loyal, dogged, courageous defender of Madrid. Unlike the hero of the myth, he was weak, unintelligent, unprincipled. Mikhail Koltzov, meanwhile, always maintained that the real director of operations in Madrid was General Vicente Rojo, appointed Miaja's chief of staff by Largo Caballero just before the government left for Valencia. The Soviet journalist noted in his diary:

> Miaja is very little involved in operational details; he even knows little about them. These are matters he leaves to his Chief of Staff and to the commanders of columns and sectors. Rojo wins the confidence of the men by his modesty, which conceals his great practical knowledge and unusual capacity for work. This is the fourth day that he has remained bent over the map of Madrid. In an endless chain, commanders and commissars come to see him, and to all of them, in a low, calm voice, patiently, as though in a railroad information office, sometimes repeating himself twenty times, he explains, teaches, indicates, annotates papers, and frequently draws sketches.

The average citizen of Madrid, however, knew little of the political intrigues within the *Junta de Defensa*.

The siege of the capital went on, with intermittent bombing and shelling, for nearly three years. Esmond Romilly was once caught in a Metro station during an air raid. His description gives an indication of the horrors undergone by the Madrid population:

> We tried to get out on to the street, but a panic-stricken crowd made it impossible to move. The fear of suffocation was stronger than that of the bombs – women screamed and on the steps men were fighting to get into the shelter.
> As we heard the roar of the aero-engines overhead, I remembered the crowds gathered around the Metro station on our first day – bodies were still being excavated; two hundred people had been killed when an incendiary bomb burst over a 'bomb-proof' shelter.

Yet the horrors of the siege were not confined to the loyalist inhabitants of the city. Many Nationalist sympathizers lived through the siege in fear of their lives, hiding in the homes of friends and at foreign embassies, terrified of falling into the hands of the *checas*. Many rightists had in fact been rounded up at the beginning of the war. Large numbers of them were to die in the course of the so-called *sacas*, or removals, of prisoners from Madrid's jails, the Carcel Modelo, Porlier, Ventas and San Anton. Before the siege the murder of imprisoned rightists had been the work of uncontrolled militia patrols. However, from 4 to 8 November the *sacas* were officially organized and on an appallingly large scale.

With popular panic and serious military trepidation intensifying, a decision was made to remove the prisoners. It was feared that the hundreds of army officers among them could form the basis of new columns for the Nationalist army which seemed on the point of taking the capital. The responsibility for the prisoners lay with the young Communist Secretary-General of the JSU, Santiago Carrillo, who was Councillor for Public Order in the *Junta de Defensa*. The fact that he held such an important position at the age of twenty-one indicated his special relations with the Russians. Koltsov, whose apparent status as a journalist was belied by the enormous influence he wielded, insisted that dangerous prisoners be evacuated. About 2,000 of them were taken by bus and shot at the villages of Paracuellos del Jarama and Torrejón de Ardoz. Communist claims that the buses had been waylaid at anarchist control posts on the outskirts of Madrid were unconvincing. It was a deliberate military decision, and Nationalist propaganda built on it to create a picture of *la barbarie roja* (red barbarism). The Francoists consistently claimed that 12,000 had been murdered and never lost an opportunity to use Paracuellos to denigrate Santiago Carrillo when he was Secretary-General of the Communist Party.

The prisoners of Paracuellos were not the only Nationalist victims of the panic provoked by the advance on Madrid. The most celebrated was José Antonio Primo de Rivera. Although the Falangist leader was in a Republican jail in Alicante, an escape bid or a prisoner exchange was not inconceivable. Several prominent Nationalists had crossed the lines in these ways, including such important Falangists as Raimundo Fernández Cuesta who was officially exchanged, and Ramón Serrano Suñer who escaped. Obviously, given the pre-eminence of José Antonio Primo de Rivera, his release or escape would be far from easy. Yet there were attempts to liberate him. The first had been the work of isolated groups of Falangists in Alicante. Then in early September, when the Germans had come to see the Falange as the Spanish component of a future world political order, more serious efforts were made, largely under the auspices of their Consul in Alicante, Joachim von Knobloch. A band of Falangists led by Agustín Aznar arrived on a German torpedo boat on 17 September. However, their plans for a *coup de main* were changed into an attempt to get Primo de Rivera out by bribery, which failed when Aznar was caught and only narrowly escaped himself.

In October von Knobloch and Aznar continued their efforts, but came up against a less than enthusiastic backing from the newly elevated Head of State. This was entirely understandable. Franco needed the Falange both as a mechanism for the political mobilization of the civilian population and as a way of creating a spurious identification with the ideals of his German allies. If the charismatic José Antonio Primo de Rivera were to have turned up at Salamanca, Franco could never have dominated and manipulated the Falange as he was later to do. After all, since before the war, José Antonio had been wary about too great a co-operation with the army for fear that the Falange would simply be used as cannon-fodder and political trimming for the defence of the old order. In his last ever interview, with Jay Allen, published in the *Chicago Daily Tribune*, the Falangist leader had expressed his dismay that the defence of traditional interests was taking precedence over his party's rhetorical ambitions for sweeping social change. Even taking into account the possibility that José Antonio was exaggerating his revolutionary aims to curry favour with his jailers, the implied clash with the political plans of Franco was clear.

On 6 October Franco had been visited in Salamanca by Count Du Moulin-Eckart, Counsellor at the German Legation in Portugal. The new Head of State informed his first diplomatic visitor that his main preoccupation was the 'unification of ideas' and the establishment of a 'common ideology' among the Army, the Falange, the monarchists and the CEDA. Given the links of most of those groups with the old order, such a unification could be carried out only at the cost of the political annihilation of the Falange, something hardly likely to be approved of by its leader. Accordingly, the plans of Knobloch and Aznar were not pressed forward with any urgency. A further possibility for Primo de Rivera's release arose from a suggestion by Ramón Cañazas, Falangist *Jefe* (chief) in Morocco. He proposed that an exchange be arranged for General Miaja's wife and daughters who were imprisoned in Melilla. Franco apparently refused safe conducts for the negotiators, although the family of General Miaja was later exchanged for the family of the Carlist, Joaquín Bau. Similarly, the *Caudillo* refused permission for another Falangist, Maximiano García Venero, to drum up an international campaign to save José Antonio's life.

José Antonio Primo de Rivera was shot in Alicante prison on 20 November 1936. Franco made full use of the propaganda opportunities thereby provided. At first, he chose, at least publicly, to refuse to believe that José Antonio was dead. The Falangist leader was more use 'alive' while Franco made his political arrangements. Franco's immediate response to the news of the execution was enormously revealing of his peculiarly repressed way of thinking. 'Probably,' he told Serrano Suñer, 'they've handed him over to the Russians and it is possible that they've castrated him.' Once the death was officially accepted, Franco used the cult of *el ausente* (the absent one) to take over the Falange. All its external symbols and paraphernalia were used to mask its real ideological disarmament. Even certain of Primo de Rivera's writings were suppressed and his designated successor, Manuel Hedilla, was imprisoned under sentence of death.

In Madrid the rebel advance under Varela had finally been halted. Both sides dug in and for a month things were relatively quiet. However, the consequent depression of the rebels, who had expected a rapid triumph, was somewhat relieved by the joint Italian and German announcement of their recognition of the Nationalist Junta at Burgos as Spain's legitimate government. In October, the Asturian capital Oviedo had been 'liberated' from the miners who were besieging it. *ABC* of Seville commented with joy on 18 October that the victorious Nationalist columns had entered the Asturian capital after a 'real butchery' of the miners. Further good news from the north came at the end of November with the defeat of a Basque offensive. Madrid, of course, remained the principal front. On 13 December the Nationalists began an attempt to cut the Madrid–La Coruña road to the north-west. After crippling losses in fighting around the village of Boadilla del Monte, the attack was called off. On 5 January the assault was renewed with increased ferocity. A slow tank advance was met by Republican forces. In four days, only ten kilometres of road had been taken and at enormous cost, each side having lost in the region of 15,000 men. Casualties among the International Brigades were particularly high.

Meanwhile, the farcical and somewhat dishonest attempts of the British and French to impose the policy of non-intervention could do nothing to stop the flow of foreign fascist assistance to Franco. In response the legitimate Republican government, refused arms by the Western democracies, had been forced to turn to the Soviet Union. Largo Caballero had sent a letter to the Soviet ambassador on 17 October requesting him to ask his government if it would 'agree to the deposit of approximately 500 metric tons of gold, the exact weight to be determined at the time of delivery'. The role of the moderate Socialist Finance Minister, Dr Juan Negrín, was crucial in the transfer of the gold. In September Negrín had taken the decision to transfer the gold reserves of the Bank of Spain to a more secure deposit in the caves used as ammunition dumps at the naval base of Cartagena. In October, along with Largo Caballero, he decided to send the gold to Moscow to be held there as credit for future arms purchases. In consequence, he has been accused of being the stooge of the Russians.

Numerous accounts of the transactions between Madrid and Moscow imply that Spain was somehow cheated by the Soviet Union. However, the leading expert on the financing of the Civil War, Professor Angel Viñas, has demonstrated that out of over four hundred tonnes of fine gold transferred to the Soviet Union, there exists an accounting gap of only 0.4 tonnes, equivalent to some 450,000 dollars. In any case, it is hard to see that Negrín had any real option but to buy arms from the Soviet Union with Spanish gold. Even Largo Caballero, who was later to turn against Negrín, asserted that the Finance Minister's request for authority to transfer the gold to an unnamed safe hiding place was entirely reasonable given the proximity of the rebel forces. If the gold had fallen into Nationalist hands, there would have been no more arms for the Republic and defeat would have been inevitable. According to Largo Caballero, once the gold had been transferred to Cartagena, fears of a Nationalist landing led Negrín to send it abroad. Since banking circles in England and France had already shown their hostility to the Republic by freezing Spanish assets, there was little alternative but Russia, where Republican funds were anyway destined in order to pay for arms and food.

In contrast, the Nationalists, despite the fact that the Spanish gold reserves remained in Republican hands, did not encounter so much difficulty in financing their war effort. The insurgents aimed from the outset to obtain as much aid in war *matériel* as the fascist powers were prepared to provide. While the Italians were particularly generous, or irresponsible, the Germans sought to derive some financial benefit from arms supplies to the rebels. To this end a firm was set up in Spain, the *Compañía Hispano-Marroquí de Transportes* (HISMA), to handle transactions between Spain and Germany. From September 1936 HISMA conducted German-Spanish trade on the basis of bartering goods, thereby avoiding the use of foreign currency, of which the Nationalists were very short. In October 1936 a counterpart to HISMA, the *Rohstoffe- und Waren-Einkaufsgesellschaft* (ROWAK), was set up in Berlin. These two companies established for the Nazis a virtual monopoly of Nationalist commerce with the outside world. They also played an important role in placing the Nationalist economy on a war footing. In addition, the HISMA/ROWAK system had far-reaching long-term effects on the Nationalist economy. Those Spanish exports of most value to the German war economy were diverted to the Third Reich, thereby reducing the Nationalists' capacity to raise foreign currency elsewhere.

Some money was raised by a 'National Subscription' whereby people in the Nationalist zone handed over their jewellery, watches and gold coins; but the basic mechanism relied upon by Franco was credit. Angel Viñas has estimated that the Nationalists received approximately 700 million dollars' worth of resources and services on credit during the Civil War. Much aid, though, particularly from Italy, was given free of charge. Between December 1936 and April 1937, the Italians sent nearly 100,000 troops. They were given their first action in the south. To offset the stalemate in Madrid, the campaign to mop up the rest of Andalusia had been continued. It was a campaign almost as bloodthirsty as the march on Madrid had been. Under the extraordinary General Queipo de Llano, troops began to advance on Malaga from Marbella and Granada. Known as the 'Radio General', Queipo would broadcast nightly on the airwaves of Spain, telling tales full of sexual innuendo about 'the Jew Blum', 'Doña Manolita' (Azaña), Miaja and Prieto, as well as relishing what his Moorish mercenaries would do to Republican women. A typical broadcast bristled with pride because 'Our valiant legionaries and *Regulares* have shown what it is to be a man to the reds, and to their women who have finally known real men and not impotent militiamen.' For all his obscene humour, Queipo was a ruthless and vengeful leader.

On 3 February 1937 a force of Moors and Italians reached Malaga, which collapsed easily. The Republican defences were in some disarray from the outset, largely because of an absence of military discipline and organization, as well as a shortage of arms. None the less, the Nationalists under Queipo showed no mercy. After the battle, refugees escaping along the coast road were bombarded by the navy and air force, and within the city itself nearly 4,000 Republicans were shot. T. C. Worsley was an English volunteer ambulance driver on the road from Malaga to Almeria along which the refugees were fleeing. His description is harrowing:

> The refugees still filled the road and the further we got the worse was their condition. A few of them were wearing rubber shoes, but most feet were bound round with rags, many were bare, nearly all were bleeding. There were seventy miles of people desperate with hunger and exhaustion and still the streams showed no signs of diminishing. Then the faint hum of bombers.
>
> The sides of the road, the rocks and the shore were dotted with the refugees, pressed down on their faces burrowing into holes. Children lay flat, with one frightened eye turned upwards towards the sky, with their hands pressed tight over their ears or folded backwards to protect their vulnerable necks. Huddled groups crouched everywhere, mothers already on the brink of exhaustion, held down their children pushing them into every cranny and hollow, flattening themselves into the hard earth, while the planes droned nearer. They had been bombed before and knew only too well what to do. We decided to fill the lorry with kids. Instantly we were the centre of a mob of raving shouting people, entreating and begging, at this sudden miraculous apparition. The scene was fantastic, of the shouting faces of the women holding up naked babies above their heads, pleading, crying and sobbing with gratitude or disappointment.

The crowds of refugees who blocked the road out of Malaga had been in an inferno. They were shelled from the sea, bombed from the air and then machine-gunned. The scale of the repression inside the fallen city explained why they were ready to run the gauntlet.

Encouraged by their success in the south, the rebels renewed their efforts to take Madrid. While the Republicans were preparing a counter-attack the Nationalist forces, under the direction of General Orgaz, launched a huge attack through the Jarama valley

Left: Republican soldiers in the main square of the village of Morata de Tajuña, on the Jarama front. Close to here, on 12 February 1937, a battalion of British International Brigaders formed the vanguard of the Republican defence in one of the fiercest clashes of the battle.

Above: With arms, ammunition and spare parts in desperately short supply and existing material in constant use, wear and tear was a serious problem for the Republican Army. Here, some soldiers check a field gun during the battle of the Jarama, whilst others take advantage of the pause to roll a cigarette.

Right: An expressive image of weary troops as they walk down a seemingly endless road in the desolate landscape of Guadalajara in March 1937. Many more lay dead on the battlefield.

on the Madrid–Valencia highway to the east of the capital. This was defended fiercely by Republican troops reinforced by the International Brigades. They were unprepared for the intensity of the Nationalist artillery fire or the special ability of the Moorish mercenaries to move across country without being seen. The outcome of the battle of the Jarama Valley was similar to that which took place for the La Coruña road. The Nationalist front advanced a few miles, but no strategic gain was made. The Republican forces had again demonstrated that while they were heroically brave in defence, they had little left for a counter-attack. Again the casualties were enormous. The Republicans lost 25,000 including some of the best British and American members of the Brigades, and the Nationalists about 20,000. The Republican efforts had not been helped by disputes between General Miaja and General Pozas, head of the Army of the Centre. Since the Jarama Valley fell within Pozas' area of command, Miaja refused to send troops until the government made him commander of the whole zone. Nonetheless, it was the International Brigades which bore the brunt of the fighting. The British contingent was almost wiped out in one afternoon.

After these various stalemates, Franco came under pressure from the Germans and Italians to seek a rapid victory. It was decided to make an attack on Guadalajara, forty miles north-east of Madrid. Fifty thousand troops were gathered: 30,000 Italians and 20,000 legionnaires, Moors and *Requetés*, under General Moscardó, the hero of the Alcázar. With 250 tanks, 180 pieces of heavy artillery, seventy planes and ample trucks, it was the best-equipped and most heavily armed force yet to go into action in the war. On 8 March Italian troops broke through but, moving rapidly towards Madrid, they over-extended their lines of communication. While Republican reinforcements moved up, the Italians were caught in a heavy snowstorm. Their aeroplanes stranded, they made excellent targets for the antique Republican air force. On 12 March Republican troops, with the Garibaldi Battalion of the International Brigade and Soviet tanks, counter-attacked. Within five days the Italians had been routed.

Militarily, Guadalajara was only a minor defensive victory, but in terms of morale it was a huge Republican triumph. Much valuable equipment was captured, and also documents which proved that the Italians were regular soldiers and not volunteers. However, the Non-Intervention Committee refused to accept this evidence because it was not presented by a country represented on the Committee. And to emphasize that the Republic could expect no help from the Committee, the Italian representative, Grandi, announced on 23 March that no Italian soldiers would be withdrawn until the Nationalist victory was secure. The Republicans were hanging on, but it was an increasingly desperate struggle merely to survive. What made their plight even more desperate was the extent of the growing bitterness of the vicious political conflicts raging within the Republican camp as to how the struggle should be conducted. The intensity of these divisions would soon reach a point at which a civil war within the Civil War would break out.

7

Politics Behind the Lines: Reaction and Terror in the City of God

If Stalin was cautious in helping the Spanish Republic, Hitler and Mussolini were by comparison unstinting in their aid to Franco. Stalin's attitude was summed up in his admonition to the high-ranking Soviet advisers sent to Spain, 'Stay out of range of artillery fire.' However, as important as the scale and enthusiasm of foreign assistance were to be the strings attached to it. Unlike the Soviet Union, the fascist powers did not exact the right to intervene in Spanish internal affairs as an additional levy on their aid. The way dependence on Soviet assistance was manipulated to inflate the influence of the Spanish Communist Party exacerbated the Republic's greatest weakness; the interminable and violent polemics between its various factions as to how the war should be fought. Axis help, in contrast, was less complicated. The trappings and symbols of the Falange provided the necessary veneer of international fascist solidarity. However, the German and Italian regular army officers in Spain tended to sympathize much more with the traditional values of their Spanish brothers-in-arms than with the anti-oligarchical rhetoric of Falangism. Thus, in the competition for power in the Nationalist zone, the Falange was not boosted by the Germans and Italians in the way that the Communist Party was elevated to a dominant position by the committed backing of the Russians. In consequence, the Nationalists enjoyed a dramatically higher level of unity behind their lines than did the Republicans.

This unity derived largely from the pre-eminence of the military. Virtually all other questions were relegated while the soldiers got on with the job of winning the war. Thus, despite the existence during the Second Republic of competing rightist political groups – the CEDA, Falangists, Carlists and Alfonsine monarchists – there was effectively a moratorium on political activity once the war had broken out. This was not especially difficult in view of the level of co-operation between them that had existed before 1936. Falangist terror squads had been financed by the monarchists of Renovación Española, and their activities used by the CEDA to present the Republic as a regime of chaos and disorder. All owed a large part of their ideology to Carlism, the fountainhead of indigenous Spanish reactionary thought. The left regarded the tactical and rhetorical divisions of the various rightist groups as a smokescreen of trivia behind which they pursued their shared interests as specialist units in the same army. They shared a determination to establish an authoritarian corporative state, to destroy the organizations of the working class and to dismantle the institutions of democracy. They addressed each others' meetings and wrote in each others' newspapers. They had been united in parliament and at elections. Now, during the Civil War, they accepted with alacrity that their future survival depended on the success of the military rising. Accordingly, the generals faced relatively few problems in imposing unity within the rightist ranks.

For those who did not share the values and aspirations of the 'Movement' and were unfortunate enough to find themselves in the Nationalist zone, unity was imposed by means of a vicious terror. Members of the Popular Front parties and the trades unions were shot in their thousands as the Nationalists conquered each new piece of territory. In Old Castile and Galicia the Falange was allowed to purge its old enemies; and in their religious fervour the Carlist *Requetés* were often guilty of barbaric excesses. Details of appalling atrocities committed by Nationalist troops against women and men were published by the Madrid College of Lawyers. What made the horrors seem worse was that they were carried out under the watchful gaze of the forces of law and order: the army, the Civil Guard and the police. At least 200,000 liberals and leftists lost their lives in this way, although there is considerable controversy over exact figures. Francoists continue to produce spurious computations which diminish the number of leftist victims. However, in recent years, there have been a number of detailed local studies which suggest that, if some of the older estimates are exaggerated, the real figures are still horrifying.

Three examples, Seville, Cordoba and Navarre, will suffice. Queipo de Llano's chief propaganda officer, Antonio Bahamonde, who fled to the Republican zone, claimed that 150,000 had been executed in Andalusia and 20,000 in Seville alone before the end of 1938. Count Ciano complained in July 1939 that eighty people per day were still being shot in Seville, although Bahamonde reckoned in 1938 that the figure then was between twenty and twenty-five per day. In 1946, an ex-CEDA notary estimated the total executed in the province of Cordoba as 32,000. The exhaustive investigations of Francisco Moreno Gómez produced in 1985 definite proof of the executions of 2,543 persons in the provincial capital and of 7,679 in the rest of the province. However, Dr Moreno Gómez estimates that these are certainly below the real figure, not least because, since his research was completed, there has been a flood of people emboldened in the last few years of the democratic regime to register the wartime deaths of their relatives. The Basque priest, Fr Juan José Usabiaga Irazustabarrena ('Juan de Iturralde'), was able to find the names of 1,950 people murdered by the right in Navarre, a province in which the left barely existed. Other estimates of victims in Navarre are over 7,000.

The terror in the Nationalist zone was crucial in establishing the power of the Nationalists. The dour and humourless General Franco had learned to instil loyalty through fear during his time in Africa. His military style, appropriate to a minor colonial war, also reflected his experience in Morocco. He was cold, ruthless and secretive. His taciturn *Gallego* caution tended to obscure his lack of clearly defined political views. No one, however, could doubt his sense of political purpose. This was made starkly clear by his conduct of the Nationalist war effort. He was ponderous as a decision maker, and doubts have been cast on his military abilities. Certainly his leadership was dogged, uninspired and the despair of his German allies. Throughout the war he would sacrifice lives and waste time in unnecessary campaigns to gain militarily unimportant territory. However, his tortoise-like strategy of slowness facilitated the elimination of leftists and liberals

Like the Carlist *Requetés*, the members of the Spanish fascist party, *Falange Española*, lent massive armed support to the military rebellion. In the early days of the war, few people raised their hand in the fascist salute as the columns of blue-shirted volunteers passed, for *Falange* was a minority group. The war was to change it into the basis of a Francoist mass movement.

which was to be one of his greatest sources of strength after 1939. Although his decision to liberate the Alcázar gave a breathing space to the Republicans and was indefensible in military terms, it clinched his own grasp on power within the Nationalist Junta.

After his appointment as 'Head of Government of the Spanish State' at the end of September 1936, Franco had set about limiting threats to his own long-term pre-eminence from the various rightist political groups. They were all united behind the military in the desire to crush the left for once and for all, but still nurtured ambitions of putting their own special stamp on the authoritarian regime to which they all aspired. The monarchists wanted a restoration; the Carlists, a virtual theocracy under their own pretender; the Falange, a Spanish equivalent of the Third Reich. Since the generals had expected to take power swiftly, they had postponed resolving problems of political organization until after their expected victory. However, when it became apparent that a long struggle was necessary, it was recognized that some form of political structure would have to be produced to unite the Nationalist zone. The brain behind the creation of a new political movement, and indeed the chief architect of the Francoist state, was Ramón Serrano Suñer, the general's brother-in-law.

A prominent figure in the Juventud de Acción Popular, the CEDA'S extremist youth movement, Serrano Suñer had been instrumental in bringing over much of its rank and file to the Falange in the spring of 1936. Having witnessed the murder of friends in jail in the Republican zone and only just evaded the *sacas* himself, he was an emotional and totally committed opponent of democracy. It was he who, along with Franco's brother Nicolás, devised a way to fill the political void on the Nationalist side. The most feasible vehicles for the creation of a mass political movement were the *Falange*, whose membership had risen to nearly a million by early 1937, and the Carlist Traditional Communion. Since the autumn of 1936 Nicolás Franco had been toying with the idea of uniting them. The notion took off in February 1937 with the arrival of Serrano Suñer in Salamanca after he had escaped from the Republican zone. On 19 April, after Serrano Suñer had held preliminary talks with all the elements in the Nationalist camp, the Falange was forcibly unified with the Carlists to form a single party, the Falange Española Tradicionalista y de las Juntas de Ofensiva Nacional Sindicalista, remarkable more for its name than for its ideology.

The job was made easier by the fact that the *Falange* had been weakened by the arrest of many of its national and provincial leaders before the war started. Decapitated by the execution of its founder, it was now in the throes of an increasingly bitter power struggle between his designated successor Manuel Hedilla, the provincial *Jefe* from Santander, and another group of José Antonio's close friends led by Agustín Aznar and his cousin Sancho Dávila. They regarded Hedilla as too proletarian and too pro-Nazi. Franco and Serrano Suñer were more preoccupied by the fact that Hedilla was taking too seriously José Antonio's warnings about letting the Falange become a tame adjunct of the army. Hedilla had tried to forestall the unification, and from 16 to 18 April there was some sporadic street fighting between the two opposed Falangist factions in Salamanca. When he continued to oppose the unification, Hedilla was simply placed under arrest along with several other Falangist dissidents. After a sentence of death was commuted, Hedilla spent another four years in a Francoist jail.

Franco had had the decree of unification drawn up by Serrano Suñer without discussion of the details with either Hedilla or the Carlist leadership. The bulk of the Carlists were furious but, in the interests of the war effort, they silenced their outrage. The rank and file of the Nationalist zone welcomed the unification as a way of putting a stop to the friction between the various groups. However, since the new party was now the only political formation allowed in the Nationalist zone, the independence of the Spanish fascist movement was at an end. Thereafter, the *Movimiento* (Movement), as the new single party was known, had little or no political autonomy. Forced to accept Franco as their new leader, the Falangists saw their ideological role usurped by the Church, their party turned into a machine for the distribution of patronage, and their 'revolution' indefinitely postponed.

The unification enshrined Franco's determination to eliminate any political rivals. It was not a difficult task. Calvo Sotelo was dead. His deputy, the effete Antonio Goicoechea, dutifully accepted the decree of unification and dissolved Renovación Española. Gil Robles was a broken reed as far as the Nationalists were concerned. Franco allegedly loathed him, resentful of the fact that, as Minister of War in 1935, Gil Robles had been his superior. In any case, Gil Robles had been left politically isolated by the collapse of the CEDA after the Popular Front elections. Moreover, in the fevered atmosphere of Salamanca, his legalist, 'accidentalist' tactics were derided as having delayed the inevitable war against corrupt democracy. When he visited the Nationalist zone, in August 1936 and May 1937, it was made clear that he was not welcome. It served for nothing that he too had accepted the unification, and indeed as early as February had ordered the remnants of Acción Popular to desist from political activity. A more serious rival to Franco had been José Antonio Primo de Rivera. Accordingly, little had been done to facilitate attempts to save him from execution. Once he was dead, of course, Franco had not scrupled to allow the Falangist leader's death to be mythologized into martyrdom as a means of attracting supporters. In December 1936 Manuel Fal Conde, leader of the Carlists, had been sent into exile for having dared to set up a military academy for the separate training of *Requeté* officers.

Franco's competitors within the Army were also steadily eliminated. Sanjurjo had been killed at the outset, Goded and Fanjul executed by the Republicans in August 1936. This left only Mola as an even remotely realistic rival. If only in the suspicious mind of the *Caudillo* himself, Mola would always have been an implicit challenge. As it was, relations between them worsened after Franco's rise to power. Decisive and flexible in military matters, Mola was keen to terminate the war in the North. Franco's plodding style of military leadership drove him to distraction. Moreover, perhaps out of a desire to emphasize Mola's subordination, Franco put constant obstacles in the way of the northern campaign. He interfered with Mola's air forces and often took troops away from the northern front for sterile offensives against Madrid. Some sort of clash seemed to be on the cards; then Mola was killed in an air crash.

On 3 June 1937 Mola had set out by air from Pamplona to Vitoria and thence to Valladolid to inspect the front. When his plane crashed near Burgos everyone on board was killed. There have been many theories about what happened. The most convincing is that the aircraft was mistakenly shot down by Nationalist fighters. Mola was flying in a captured Airspeed Envoy with English markings, similar to planes used to fly supplies into the Republic from France. Franco received the news coldly. Wilhelm Faupel, the German Ambassador to the Nationalist government, wrote to the Wilhelmstrasse on 9 July that 'Franco undoubtedly feels relieved by the death of General Mola. He told me recently: "Mola was a stubborn fellow, and when I gave him directives which differed from his own proposals he often asked me: 'Don't you trust my leadership any more?'"' Hitler is reported to have said that 'The real tragedy for Spain was the death of Mola; there was the real brain, the real leader.... Franco came to the top like Pontius Pilate in the Creed.'

Franco was left without any serious competition. From the first floor of the Bishop's Palace in Salamanca, he now directed the Nationalist war effort. This was little in the way of an organized bureaucracy. The improvisatory nature of things was reflected in the rise to important positions of a number of bizarre characters. The much-mutilated General José Millán Astray, lacking an arm and an eye, was appointed chief of the press and propaganda department. Famous as the frenzied founder of the Spanish Foreign Legion, he was hardly the best man to present the Nationalist cause to the outside world. On 12 October 1936 he had brought that cause into considerable international disrepute by his behaviour during the celebrations of the anniversary of Christopher Columbus's discovery of America. When a bystander had shouted out the battle-cry of the Legion, '¡Viva la muerte!' (Long live death), Millán Astray began shouting out the triple Nationalist chant of '¡España!' and back came the three ritual replies of '¡Una!', '¡Grande!' and '¡Libre!' (Spain! United! Great! Free!). When he was reproached by the Rector of the University of Salamanca, the philosopher Miguel de Unamuno, Millán Astray screamed at him '¡Mueran los intelectuales!' (Death to intellectuals). Unamuno replied with the moving words, 'You will win (vencer) but you will not convince (convencer).' He was threatened by Millán Astray's bodyguards. Unamuno was removed from his position in the University and died at the end of December 1936 under virtual house arrest.

As chief of propaganda, Millán Astray regularly encouraged his subordinates to threaten foreign journalists with execution. One of them was Luis Bolín, who had helped organize Franco's transit from the Canary Islands to Morocco. He was to achieve lasting notoriety for his efforts to prove that the bombing of Guernica had never taken place. Another was the notorious Captain Gonzalo de Aguilera, Conde de Alba y Yeltes, who was responsible for explaining the Francoist position to foreign visitors. Peter Kemp, the British Francoist volunteer, felt that the Count did more harm than good:

Loyal friend, fearless critic and stimulating companion that he was, I sometimes wonder if his qualities really fitted him for the job he was given of interpreting the Nationalist cause to important strangers. For example, he told a distinguished English visitor that on the day the Civil War broke out he lined up the labourers on his estate, selected six of them and shot them in front of the others – 'Pour encourager les autres, you understand.'

He had some original ideas on the fundamental causes of the Civil War. The principal cause, if I remember rightly, was the introduction of modern drainage.

Captain Aguilera's theory on the evils of modern drainage was also elaborated to Charles Foltz, Associated Press correspondent during the war:

Sewers caused all our troubles. The masses in this country are not like your Americans, nor even like the British. They are slave stock. They are good for nothing but slaves and only when they are used as slaves are they happy. But we, the decent people, made the mistake of giving them modern housing in the cities where we have our factories. We put sewers in these cities, sewers which extend right down to the workers' quarters. Not content with the work of God, we thus interfere with His will. The result is that the slave stock increases. Had we no sewers

Left: Having studied the organization of the French Foreign Legion in Algeria, Lieutenant Colonel José Millán Astray (seen here in Cádiz, in 1936) was appointed chief of the Spanish Legion on its creation in 1920. The loss of an eye and an arm in combat added a sinister physical appearance to his bellicose character.

Above: Franco's Moorish Guard stands to attention as the *Generalísimo* leaves the building where the new German ambassador, Faupel, has presented his diplomatic credentials. Two days earlier, Roberto Cantalupo had similarly formalized diplomatic relations between Italy and Nationalist Spain.

Left: The outward symbols of political identification acquired a heightened significance during the war and partisans of both sides were inordinately proud of their respective flags, badges or colours. The illustration (*left*) shows the badge of the Third Falangist Unit (*bandera*) of Asturias, with the red yoke-and-arrows symbol of the *Falange* and the blue cross of Asturias.

Franco gives the fascist salute (declared 'national' on 24 April 1937) as blue-shirted militants of the Party, *FET y de las JONS*, stride past.

in Madrid, Barcelona, and Bilbao, all these Red leaders would have died in their infancy instead of exciting the rabble and causing good Spanish blood to flow. When the war is over, we should destroy the sewers. The perfect birth control for Spain is the birth control God intended us to have. Sewers are a luxury to be reserved for those who deserve them, the leaders of Spain, not the slave stock.

He confided to Peter Kemp his theory that Nationalists had made a major error in failing to have shot Spain's boot-blacks. 'My dear fellow, it only stands to reason! A chap who squats down on his knees to clean your boots at a café or in the street is bound to be a Communist, so why not shoot him right away and be done with it? No need for a trial – his guilt is self-evident in his profession.'

Millán Astray, Bolín and Aguilera were at the extreme margins of Nationalist propaganda. Altogether more effective in international terms was the legitimization of the Francoist cause provided by the Catholic Church. Long hostile to rationalism, Freemasonry, liberalism, socialism and communism, the Church played a central role in the political life of the Nationalist zone. With the exception of the Basque clergy, most Spanish priests and religious sided with the Nationalists. They denounced the 'reds' from their pulpits. They blessed the flags of Nationalist regiments and some even fought in their ranks. Clerics took up the fascist salute. Catholic Action declared its enthusiasm for the *alzamiento* at its congress in Burgos in September 1936. On 28 September Enrique Pla y Deniel, Bishop of Salamanca, issued a pastoral letter entitled 'The Two Cities' based on St Augustine's notion of the cities of God and of the Devil. It declared: 'On the soil of Spain a bloody conflict is being waged between two conceptions of life, two forces preparing for universal conflict in every country of the earth.... Communists and anarchists are sons of Cain, fratricides, assassins of those who cultivate virtue.... It [the war] takes the external form of a civil war, but in reality it is a crusade.'

On the same day Cardinal Isidro Gomá, Archbishop of Toledo and Primate of all Spain, broadcasting to the defenders of the Alcázar, thundered against 'the bastard soul of the sons of Moscow ... the Jews and the Freemasons ... the dark societies controlled by the Semite International'. As a young priest, Vicente Enrique y Tarancón – who as a Cardinal forty years later was to put the Church's weight behind the democratization of Spain – was perplexed by the militancy of senior churchmen. On a visit to Burgos he attended a *Te Deum* in the Cathedral to celebrate the Nationalist capture of a provincial capital. When the Captain-General and the Archbishop of Burgos spoke to the crowd afterwards, Tarancón was astonished to hear the general speak in exclusively religious terms while the archbishop delivered an aggressive military harangue. Ecclesiastical militancy was rewarded with overflowing churches. Not to attend mass in the Nationalist zone could lose a man his job or put him under political suspicion.

For Cardinal Gomá Franco's cause was God's cause. After the destruction of Guernica, when many Catholics began to question the sanctity of the Francoist cause, he rendered the *Caudillo* an inestimable service. In response to a request for public affirmation of the hierarchy's support, he organized a collective letter 'To the Bishops of the Whole World'. The text described the 'crusade' as 'an armed plebiscite' and rejoiced that on their executions, the Nationalists' enemies had become reconciled to the Church. It was signed by two Cardinals, six Archbishops, thirty-five bishops and five vicars-general. It was not signed by Cardinal Francesc Vidal i Barraquer, Archbishop of Tarragona in Catalonia, nor by Monsignor Mateo Múgica, Bishop of Vitoria in the Basque Country. Múgica was especially distressed by the execution by Nationalist firing squad of fourteen Basque priests at the end of October 1936. This should, in canon law, have led to the excommunication of those responsible. Neither the Vatican nor the Spanish hierarchy condemned the executions. Múgica, however, was told that his safety could not be guaranteed in the Nationalist zone and he remained in exile.

Throughout the world Catholics rallied to the Francoist cause. The German bishops had issued a collective pastoral on 19 August 1936 to endorse Hitler's support for Franco. In the United States the efforts of militant Catholics, and especially those of the 'Radio Priest' Father Coughlin, were probably instrumental in blocking aid to the Republic. A campaign in Britain and elsewhere to brand the Republic as the bloody executioner of priests and nuns was given greater authority by the decision of the Pope to make those who had been murdered officially martyrs. The Vatican effectively recognized Franco on 28 August 1937 and supplied an Apostolic Delegate, Monsignor Ildebrando Antoniutti, on 7 October. *De jure* recognition came on 18 May 1938, when Archbishop Gaetano Cicognani was made Apostolic Nuncio and Franco sent an Ambassador to the Holy See. The attitude to Franco of international Catholicism was summed up in a letter sent to Franco on 28 March 1939 by the Archbishop of Westminster, Cardinal Arthur Hinsley, thanking him for a signed photograph: 'I look upon you as the great defender of the true Spain, the country of Catholic principles where Catholic social justice and charity will be applied for the common good under a firm peace-loving government.' The newly elevated Pope Pius XII greeted Franco's ultimate victory with a message beginning 'With immense joy'. The Church was rewarded for its efforts on the Nationalists' behalf by being given exclusive control over education in the post-war state.

Catholicism was only one element of the Nationalist ideological armoury. The images of the *Reconquista* of Spain from the Moors was used to exalt and reinforce the notion of their war effort as a 'crusade' which was 'liberating' Spain from the Godless hordes of Moscow. *Imperio* (empire) became an ideological watchword. The Francoists latched on to the statement by the Carlist Victor Pradera that 'the New State is no more than the Spanish State of the Catholic Kings'. However, the imperial verbiage and the references to Ferdinand and Isabella were balanced by more modern borrowings from Fascism and Nazism. The Falangist symbol of the yoke and the arrows, like the swastika and the *fascio*, married the ancient and the modern. Theorists of the regime attempted to elaborate its own Führer principle, the so-called *teoría del caudillaje*, which borrowed from the doctrines of the German National Socialist Carl Schmitt. Parliamentary democracy and the rule of law were dismissed as antiquated survivals of the liberal age. All of this was designed to ensure that real power would lie exclusively in the hands of General Franco. He was to prove to be a jealous guardian of that power.

Perhaps through a cynical desire to maintain the goodwill of his benefactors, the Caudillo was unrestrained in his praise for Nazism. He told German journalists 'What the German nation has already achieved with its struggle for liberation constitutes a model which we will always keep before us'. He exchanged fulsome telegrams with Mussolini. The first three recipients of the Grand Imperial Order of the Yoke and Arrows, the highest decoration in the 'New State', were King Vittorio Emmanuele, Benito Mussolini and Adolf Hitler. After the April 1937 unification, all Nationalist newspapers had to carry the slogan 'One Fatherland, One State, One Caudillo'. Germanic borrowings could also be discerned in the emergence of anti-semitism. *The Protocols of the Elders of*

Zion was reprinted in large cheap editions. Falangists were told 'Comrade, it is your duty to root our Judaism, along with Freemasonry, Marxism and separatism.' The Catalan magnate Francesc Cambó, who had gone into exile, was denounced as 'the wandering Jew'. Fund-raising campaigns for the Nationalist war effort used slogans like 'He is a Jew who hides his gold when the Fatherland needs it.'

The 'New State' over which Franco ruled was an ideological amalgam more or less satisfactory to all the component groups of the Nationalist side. Aristocrats and army officers shuddered when addressed by Falangists as 'comrade' using the familiar *tu* form. Acid comments about the '*FAIlange*' reflected disquiet about the way ex-leftists were flooding the ranks of the *Movimiento* to escape the repression. Drapery establishments in the Nationalist zone ran out of blue cloth as orders flooded in for the *camisa azul* (blue shirt). It came to be known as the *salvavidas* (life jacket), and decrees were passed forbidding the sale of blue cloth without written authorization from Falange headquarters. The more conservative among the Francoist forces regarded the Falange with distaste but knew that it was a necessary evil. They could console themselves with the thought that, superficial appearances aside, the New State was nearer to their vision of the political future than to that of the more radical elements in the Falange.

The 'legal' formula on which the Nationalist state was based derived from the ideas of the monarchist group Renovación Española. It justified the *Movimiento* and Franco's rule as a kind of military interregnum which would eradicate the liberal and leftist poison from Spain. When this was done, the monarchy would not be restored but 'installed', to emphasize the break in continuity with the past. The Francoist institutions, and particularly the 'Vertical' Syndicates, or state-run, non-representative and non-confrontational trade unions, were based on Italian Fascist models, and were a sop to the Falangists who found that their role was less than they had hoped. The wartime regime displayed an ultra-Catholic, Nationalist and centralist rhetoric which was pleasing to all sections of the right. Basque and Catalan names were banned from baptismal ceremonies. The use of the local languages, Catalan and Euskera, was turned into a clandestine activity. There was nothing in the Republican zone to compare with the ideological cohesion or clarity of purpose provided by the Catholic Church and the unified *Movimiento*.

The dominant values of everyday life in the Nationalist zone were Catholic, hierarchical and somewhat puritanical. To eat in a restaurant without a jacket was frowned upon. Women were encouraged to dress with protective modesty and not to smoke or use make-up. Sleeves were expected to reach the wrist; necklines to stay at the neck; skirts to be full and long. Children over the age of two were obliged to wear bathing suits at the beach. In the war-time conditions of social upheaval, uncertainty and bereavement, however, there was a degree of sexual license which horrified the authorities. Moreover, economic necessity and the demands of troops on leave led to a prostitution boom. Decrees were passed against 'carnal traffic'. In general, women were expected to contribute to the war effort by joining various social services run by the Feminine Section of the Falange.

The intellectual life was stultifying in the extreme. Ritualistic book burnings eliminated any remnants of liberal culture and a lot more besides. Books printed in the Nationalist zone usually had a *nihil obstat* and were dated 'I, II or III Triumphal Year' rather than by the calendar. The best sellers were lurid descriptions of red atrocities, eulogies of Nationalist military victories and glutinous works of Falangist theory. Art was doggedly

Although, in post-war years, apologists of the Catholic Church were anxious to minimize its participation in the Spanish Civil War, the fact remains that the Vatican gave its blessing to the 'Crusade' and its ministers were always in the vanguard of the Nationalist advance. In this photograph, a priest celebrates mass in the open air at Posada (Santander) while Nationalist troops pass through the village.

The members of the first National Council of the Francoist 'single party', photographed with the *Generalísimo* after their appointment to office in Burgos on 2 December 1937.

Far left: Not even the children escaped the propagandistic onslaught of this essentially ideological war. On the contrary, they were the militants of the future and great importance was attached to their indoctrination from an early age. *Pelayos* was the magazine published to instil into Carlist children that they were 'the hope of Religion and of the Fatherland'.

Left: This poster is typical of the sycophantic personality cult organized by the Nationalist propaganda apparatus: 'Long live the Army. The Caesars were unvanquished Generals. Franco.'

'Efficient governmental action, such as must be that of the new Spanish State . . . is incompatible with the struggle of parties and political organizations . . .' So began Decree 255, of 19 April 1937, which effectively abolished all political parties except the official *Falange Española Tradicionalista y de las JONS.* They were not to return legally until 1976. In the illustration, a series of stamps issued in Seville on the occasion of the 'Unification'.

Ramón Serrano Suñer (*left*) reached Salamanca in February 1937 and immediately devoted himself to the task of organizing the structures which would provide an ideological and political framework for what, otherwise, was a régime based solely on the force of arms.

The Falangists who appointed Manuel Hedilla Larrey, photographed here in 1937, as provisional leader of the party in the summer of 1936 believed that this was a temporary measure until the party's founder, José Antonio Primo de Rivera, could be liberated from the Republican zone. Hedilla's attempt to succeed Primo de Rivera as *Falange's* national chief was aborted by Franco in April 1937.

representational and music virtually non-existent. The political debate of the Republican zone had no equivalent. Propaganda was dreary and ubiquitous. A typical slogan to be found stencilled on walls all over the Nationalist zone was 'Honour – Franco, Faith – Franco, Authority – Franco, Justice – Franco, Efficacy – Franco, Intelligence – Franco, Will – Franco, Austerity – Franco'. Beneath a surface of religious and patriotic exaltation there was core of cheap and prurient scurrillity. Azaña was described as a monster created by Frankenstein rather than born of woman. Other Republican leaders were described as sexual perverts. Some of the more absurd assertions came from the pen of the Falangist writer Ernesto Giménez Caballero, whose early novels have led to his being regarded nowadays as the father of Spanish Surrealism. His views on the causes of the war were on a par with those of Captain Aguilera. 'If French women had not shown their thighs in the vaudevilles and swimming pools of Paris where our Republicans were educated, if there had not been so much tennis played by the American women who have filled our cinema screens for years, if Nordic women had not thrown themselves into the cult of the sun, perhaps our horrible Spanish Civil War would not have broken out.' Amongst his more deranged fancies he nurtured ambitions of creating a new fascist dynasty by mating Hitler with a Spanish woman.

Representative of the atmosphere in the Nationalist zone was the way in which the bellicose and triumphal tone of official propaganda crept into commerce. The sherry producers González Byass cashed in on the liberation of the Alcázar by naming one of their brands *Imperial Toledano* and having it endorsed by General Moscardó. Hatters pointed out that the reds went bareheaded. Newspapers were full of advertisements which both contributed to and exploited the war effort. A Malaga pharmaceutical laboratory announced that 'Now that the city has been liberated from the Marxist hordes, [its] products are available at all good pharmacies in Seville.' The Firestone company expressed its confidence in Franco with a publicity campaign which blatantly identified its product with the war effort: 'Victory smiles on the best. The glorious Nationalist army always wins on the field of battle. Firestone Tyres has had its nineteenth consecutive victory in the Indianapolis 500.' The tone of mutual support was most aptly and graphically expressed in the advertisement which ran: 'Araceli (brassières and corsets) salutes the Nationalist army. *¡Viva Franco! ¡Arriba España!*'

Daily life in the Nationalist zone was rather more agreeable than in the Republican half of the country, provided you had money and were in agreement with the prevailing political atmosphere. Food was plentiful; restaurants brightly lit and crowded. Hardly representative, but somehow indicative of the dramatic difference between patrician San Sebastian and the dourly serious and dispirited atmosphere of beseiged Madrid, is the account given by Juan Antonio Ansaldo of a typical day he spent during the campaign in the North. It will be recalled that Ansaldo was the pilot at the controls when Sanjurjo died. His arduous day of combat went as follows:

8.30. Breakfast with the family.
9.30. Take-off for the front; bombard enemy batteries; machine-gun convoys and trenches.
11.00. Rudimentary golf in the club at Lasarte, next to the airport and partially usable.
12.30. Sun-bathing on the Ondarreta beach and quick splash in the calm sea.
13.30. Shellfish, beer and a chat in a café in the Avenue.

Modelled on the Italian *Carta del Lavoro* (Labour Charter), the Spanish *Fuero del Trabajo* was the first major piece of legislation enacted by the Cabinet appointed by Franco in January 1938. It promised that the New State would, 'with a military, constructive and deeply religious spirit', carry out a revolution against 'liberal capitalism and marxist materialism'

This was soon to become a familiar sight in the Levant and Catalonia. Girls in the town of Castellón salute fascist-style as a truck full of Nationalist soldiers drives through the town in a cloud of dust.

Tourism, however, was fostered even while the war continued. This map of Asturias is taken from a series of pamphlets published by the Nationalist government in late 1937, inviting tourists to 'visit the routes of the war'. The cover of the pamphlets promised that Route 3, Madrid, would be 'open to traffic by 1 July 1938'.

14.00. Lunch at home.
15.00. Short siesta.
16.00. Second sortie, similar to this morning's.
18.30. Cinema. Old, but wonderful movie, with Katherine Hepburn.
21.00. Aperitive in the Bar Basque. Good Scotch, animated atmosphere.
22.15. Dinner at the Nicolasa Restaurant, war songs, camaraderie, enthusiasm.

It was a far cry from the daily rations of 'Dr Negrín's victory pills', the lentils on which the bulk of the Madrid population had to depend.

8

Politics Behind the Lines: Revolution and Terror in the City of the Devil

The Republicans suffered from numerous problems which were virtually unknown to the Nationalists. They were never able to achieve anything like the singleness of purpose enjoyed in Salamanca. Political rivalries in the loyalist zone were closely linked to the questions of foreign aid and Republican dependence on the Soviet Union. Another acute problem which afflicted the Republic, but not the Nationalists, was the questionable loyalty of its military personnel. Estimates vary as to how many army officers remained loyal to the Republic. In the last ten years much has been made by Francoist military historians of the fact that 'the army' as a whole did not rebel. Certainly, it has now been established that fewer senior generals rebelled than once was thought to be the case. About 70 per cent of generals and a small majority of colonels remained ostensibly loyal. However, the balance of military advantage still lay decisively with the Nationalists. Apart from total control of the best operational unit, the Army of Africa, they had a clear majority of field officers, majors, captains and lieutenants and an adequate number of the best generals to command them.

More importantly, the officers who opted for the Nationalists were committed to the cause and were immediately usable. Those who remained loyal to the Republic were not. They were mistrusted because of the simple fact that so many of their brothers-in-arms had already rebelled. Thus it was feared that they were often loyal to the Republic only through expediency, based on the geographical accident of where they happened to find themselves on 18 July. The deceptions practised by Queipo de Llano in Seville, by Aranda in Oviedo or by the officers who took Vigo and La Coruña did nothing to enhance the idea that army officers were honourable or trustworthy. Once the war was under way there were numerous examples in the Republican zone of treachery, sabotage, deliberate incompetence and desertion. Artillery officers had their batteries aimed to miss their targets or 'accidentally' to rain shells on Republican troops. Others crossed the lines with their units at the first opportunity, taking with them Republican battle plans. The suspicion with which regular army officers were regarded by the forces of the left was entirely comprehensible. In consequence, even competent and loyal officers were often not used to their fullest capabilities. A committee was set up under the fanatical Communist Major

Leader of the Catalan republican party *Esquerra Republicana* (Republican Left) and one of the most important figures in contemporary Catalan politics, D. Lluis Companys i Jover was appointed President of the autonomous government (*Generalitat*) of Cataluña in 1933. The photograph was taken in 1934 and shows Companys in the prison of Puerto de Santa María (Cádiz), where he was to serve a thirty year sentence for his participation in the 'October revolution' that year. He was amnestied after the electoral victory of the Popular Front in February 1936.

In the centre of the photograph, wearing spectacles, Andreu Nin, co-founder in 1935 of the *Partido Obrero de Unificación Marxista* (POUM), regarded by Spanish Communists and Socialists as a Trotskyist group.

A poster produced by the CNT, which graphically expresses the anarchists' belief in the power of the working classes to overcome the insurgents. A broad-shouldered militiaman forces his adversary to drop a blood-smeared dagger, as the background to a text which reads: 'Against military brutality, the invincible strength of the Proletariat'.

One of the most influential members of the
Comité Central de Milicias Anti-fascistas, created in
Barcelona soon after the rising in July 1936, was
the anarchist Juan García Oliver, responsible for
the Committee's War Department.

Above: The verbal revolutionism of the Socialist
leader Francisco Largo Caballero contributed in no
small measure during the Republic to the internal
divisions of the Socialist party and to the polarization
of politics in general. His radical positions were
greatly admired by the Socialist Youth Movement,
some of whose members Largo Caballero addresses
here, during a summer school held in 1936.

Right: To the militiamen, who felt a certain
traditional mistrust towards the professional
soldiers, the political commissar was 'a man they
trusted, a man of the people, a man with a history
of struggle, a man from the union or Popular Front
party'. Former commissar Santiago Alvarez, seen
here, on the right of the photograph, with
Communist Dolores Ibárruri, on the eve of the
battle of Brunete.

Eleuterio Díaz Tendero to classify officers as *faccioso* (rebel), indifferent or Republican. From his efforts emerged the nucleus of what was to be the Popular Army.

Just as the military rising had effectively denuded the Spanish Republic of a significant portion of its armed forces, so too it left the regime bereft of forces of law and order. In the short term the lack of military units was spontaneously, albeit inadequately, made good by untrained militia units. The problem of the Civil Guard and the armed police known as the Assault Guards was less easily resolved. In the areas where the Civil Guard and the Assault Guards remained loyal, such as Barcelona or Malaga, they held them for the Republic. However, in the main their loyalties lay with the insurgents, and even where they did not, the old forces of order were the object of understandable mistrust. The revolutionary enthusiasm that took workers to the front did not serve to make them volunteer to become policemen. As a result the first two months of the war saw a breakdown of law and order in the Republican zone. Julián Zugazagoitia, the moderate Prieto supporter who was editor of the daily *El Socialista*, and who was later to be executed by the Francoists, wrote that 'the power of state lay in the street'.

There was widespread terrorism for a brief period, mainly directed against the supporters of right-wing parties and the clergy. Courts were replaced by revolutionary tribunals. In the view of Juan García Oliver, the anarchist who was to become Minister of Justice in November 1936, such action was justified: 'Everybody created his own justice and administered it himself. Some used to call this "taking a person for a ride", but I maintain that it was justice administered directly by the people in the complete absence of the regular judicial bodies.' Much less organized even than the 'tribunals' were the uncontrolled acts of reprisal and revenge for earlier offences real and imagined. The gruesome products of midnight *paseos* (car rides) at the hands of militia patrols or private-enterprise hoodlums were corpses to be found at dawn strewn along roadsides. The government did take steps to put a stop to irregular 'justice'. Under the premiership of José Giral, it set up Popular Tribunals in order to temper the revolutionary excesses. These had only a limited effect in the early weeks of the war.

It was impossible to keep the groundswell of long repressed anti-rightist feeling entirely in check once the restraints were off. Churches and convents in the Republican zone were sacked and burned. The most reliable study of religious persecution during the Civil War, by Fr Antonio Montero, claims that 6,832 members of the clergy and religious orders were murdered or executed. Many others fled abroad. The popular hatred against the Church was a consequence both of its traditional association with the right and its open legitimation of the military rebellion. About 55,000 civilians were killed in the Republican zone in the course of the war. It is difficult to find a simple explanation. Some, like those who were killed at Paracuellos del Jarama and Torejón de Ardoz, were victims of decisions based on an assessment of their potential danger to the Republican cause. Some were executed as known fifth columnists. Others died in explosions of mass rage which occurred as news arrived of the savage purges being carried out in the Nationalist zone, and especially of atrocities committed by Franco's Moors. Others still were the victims of sordid personal feuds. However, with the determined help of all the proletarian organizations, particularly the Communist Party, order was eventually reimposed. After the autumn of 1936 terror in the Republican zone was to be directed not against rightists but against revolutionaries.

The delay in reimposing law and order and organizing the war effort was a direct consequence of the confused relationship between the institutions of the state and the power which had passed into the hands of the people. The ambiguity was most acute in Barcelona and had been overtly recognized by the President of the *Generalitat*, Lluis Companys, leader of the bourgeois Republican party, the Esquerra. On 20 July 1936, immediately after the rising had been defeated, he was visited by a delegation from the CNT consisting of Buenaventura Durruti, Ricardo Sanz and Juan García Oliver. With astonishing candour, and not a little cunning, he told them, 'Today you are masters of the city and of Catalonia.... You have conquered and everything is in your power; if you do not need or want me as President of Catalonia, tell me now. If, on the other hand, you believe that in my post, with the men of my party, my name and my prestige, I can be useful in the struggle... you can count on me and on my loyalty as a man and a politician.' Taken by surprise, the anarchist delegation asked Companys to stay on. They were then persuaded to join with the members of the Popular Front, to which the CNT did not officially belong, and create an Anti-Fascist Militia Committee to organize both the social revolution and its military defence.

Even after full consultation, the CNT leadership went along with the spontaneous decision of Durruti, Sanz and García Oliver. A combination of an apolitical anti-statist ideology and years of involvement in the day-to-day trade union activities of the CNT had left the anarcho-syndicalists ill-prepared to improvise the institutions necessary to handle the simultaneous organization of a revolution and a war. The Anti-Fascist Militia Committee was a great face-saving device for them. It seemed as if the workers were in control. However, Companys had effectively ensured a continuity of state power even if it was temporarily in the background. The presence in the Committee of the Catalan Communist Party, the Partit Socialista Unificat de Catalunya, was a guarantee of this. The PSUC was as committed as Companys to taming the revolution. Companys had manoeuvred the CNT into accepting responsibility without long-term institutionalized power. It did not occur to the anarchists that their effective authority in the streets could be short-lived.

In Madrid, the unions dominated the government through their control of transport and communications, but ultimately the state apparatus survived, despite the appearance of a revolutionary take-over. In small towns and villages, Popular Front Committees and Committees of Public Safety were set up. In a frenetic atmosphere of revolutionary enthusiasm, the question of state power seemed irrelevant. Lorryloads of trade unionists set off for the front accompanied by hastily improvised armoured cars. The luxury hotels of Madrid and Barcelona were commandeered, their dining rooms converted into militia canteens. Symbols of middle-class respectability disappeared overnight. Hats, ties, tipping in restaurants, the polite *Usted* form of address all became things of the past. In Barcelona brothels and cabarets were closed down. For two months the trade unions were in control. They euphorically believed that the seizure of the means of production *was* the revolution. The advances of Franco's Army of Africa and Mola's northern army, however, pointed unavoidably to the need for military and economic coordination. By the end of September the Militia Committee was dissolved and the CNT joined the *Generalitat*, along with the PSUC and the Esquerra.

The co-existence of the traditional institutions of the state and the spontaneous revolutionary committees of the workers was the clearest symptom of the Republic's most dramatic difficulty. This was born of the contradictory ambitions of the various component

Above: In the working class area of Cuatro Caminos in Madrid, the local group of the Communist *Milicias Antifascistas Obreras y Campesinas* (Workers' and Peasants' Antifascist Militias) formed the basis of the 5th volunteer battalion, later transformed into the celebrated 5th Regiment of the popular militias. In the picture, a group of volunteers lines up for inspection in the courtyard of the convent which served as the 5th Regiment's headquarters.

Left: Whilst both Nationalists and Republicans were aware of the value of propaganda for mass mobilization, the Republicans produced the greater quantity of posters, pamphlets, films and other propagandistic materials. Here, a group of artists are seen producing posters for the Republican war effort.

Above: The mobilization of women was significant but not as massive as has sometimes been suggested. Women on both sides played an important, but temporary, rearguard rôle in the hospitals, clothing and munitions factories, children's homes and collective kitchens necessitated by the war. In addition, some women of leftist sympathies volunteered for active service – like the girls shown here drilling with rifles – but the presence of women in fighting units was prohibited in 1937.

Above: As in all wars, there was always the danger that the enemy might obtain vital information through the negligence of his adversary. This impressive poster formed part of a Republican campaign to make people aware that careless remarks could cost lives.

Left: The creation of a well-disciplined, fully militarized army from the unruly mixture of volunteer militias and regular armed forces was an essential but by no means easy task for the Republican government. The sentiments expressed by the board above the door in the photograph were not shared by all the forces fighting on the Republican side: 'Without culture and discipline there cannot be a powerful Army'.

groups of the Popular Front. The ultimate issue was to do with the primacy of war or revolution. The view argued by the Communist Party, the right wing of the Socialist Party and the bourgeois Republican politicians was that that the war must be won first in order to give the revolution any possibility of triumphing later. With the possible exception of the Prieto wing of the PSOE, this was a not entirely disinterested argument. For the anarcho-syndicalist CNT, the more or less Trotskyist POUM and the left wing of the PSOE, proletarian revolution was itself the essential precondition for the defeat of fascism. The revolutionary viewpoint is best summed up in the aphorism that 'The people in arms won the revolution; the People's army lost the war.' However, neither the popular victories over the insurgents in Barcelona and Madrid in the first few days of the war nor the ultimate defeat of the Communist-organized Popular Army can definitively resolve the argument. After all, the Republic lost far more territory in the first ten months of the war before the Communists had finally established their hegemony than it did in the subsequent twenty-three months during which they dominated the war effort.

After 1939 Spanish Republicans engaged in bitter polemics about the responsibility for their defeat. The position put forward by the Communists and their allies was that the Spanish Civil War was fought between fascism and a popular, democratic anti-fascist Republic. In this view popular revolutionary movements were an obstacle which not only hindered the central task of creating an efficient army to win the war but also threatened to bring down on the head of the Republic an alliance of the conservative Western democracies with the Axis powers. The contrary position was best expressed in the words of the Italian anarchist Camilo Berneri, whose opinions led to his being murdered by Russian agents in Barcelona in May 1937: 'The dilemma, war *or* revolution, has no meaning. The only dilemma is this – either victory over Franco through revolutionary war *or* defeat.' In other words, only a full-scale proletarian revolution could destroy the capitalism which spawned fascism. This had been recognized by the vacillating Republican authorities who had hesitated to arm the workers on 18 July. They rightly feared that by arming the workers to defeat the military uprising they risked unleashing proletarian revolution.

The two diametrically opposed positions are each based on a partial view of the war. In denouncing the revolutionaries as wreckers and the objective enemies of the popular cause, the Communists ignore the fact that the one great and unique weapon the Republic possessed was popular enthusiasm. That weapon was destroyed when revolutionary structures were dismantled by ruthless methods. The revolutionary position tends to ignore the international situation. It is unlikely that Chamberlain's Britain or even Blum's divided France would stand idly by and watch a full-blown revolutionary society being built at the mouth of the Mediterranean. The Communist argument implies that the final outcome of the Civil War was inevitable. The revolutionary argument avoids that trap only at the expense of falling into another, the counter-factual proposition that 'If revolutionary war had been unleashed, Franco would have been defeated'.

The entire debate was revived in 1969 by Noam Chomsky, who tried to link the Spanish struggle with the popular liberation movements then active in South-East Asia. In doing so, Chomsky provided valuable insights into the power of popular revolutionary enthusiasm. On the other hand his analogies fell down on the fact that neither Largo Caballero nor even Durruti was of the stature of Ho Chi Minh and, more crucially, on the fact that there was no Ho Chi Minh Trail weaving its way across the Pyrenees to a strong ally. The attractiveness of Chomsky's views is threefold. In the first place, the Communist destruction of the popular revolution seems a tragic waste to genuine supporters of the Spanish people's struggle against the most reactionary elements in Spanish society and their foreign fascist allies. At the same time many conservative historians have delighted in being able to condemn Communist atrocities in Spain against revolutionary groups with which they would otherwise have no sympathy. Finally, since the Communist proposition of the primacy of war over revolution was tried and found wanting, it is easy to clutch at the counter-factual straw that, had it not been for the Communists, the Republic would have won the Civil War. Against all of this stands the indisputable perception of the Communists, the bourgeois Republicans and the moderate Socialists that once the uprising had developed into a civil war, the first priority had to be to win that war.

However, the reality of the revolutionary developments which took place in the first few days of the war could not simply be ignored. It had sweeping implications both in terms of the attitude of the masses to the loyalist war effort and of the international context in which the Republic had to exist. In all Spain before July 1936 there had been various class wars being fought out. In the Nationalist zone they were snuffed out by the draconian repression. Not only were working-class organizations and their members crushed, but a similar fate was also meted out to the adherents of the bourgeois Republican parties. This brutal resolution of the class problem was not emulated in the Republican zone. There were cases of factory owners and landlords being killed and the means of production passed to the urban and rural working classes. However, the contradictions between the bourgeois democratic Republicans and the moderate Socialists on one hand and the revolutionary proletarian groups on the other remained a burning issue. The defeat of the rising by the workers gave rise to the situation of dual power epitomized by Companys' meeting with the CNT leaders. The Republican government in Madrid and the *Generalitat* in Catalonia theoretically ran the country but effective authority had passed, albeit briefly, to the anarcho-syndicalist workers in Barcelona and to the UGT in Madrid.

The CNT delegation's decision to let Companys stay on meant a tacit acceptance that the libertarian revolution should take a back seat to the more immediate task of defeating the common enemy. However, impelled by their rank and file, the individual CNT unions ignored the leadership and ensured that a revolutionary take-over did indeed occur. Wholesale collectivization took place in industry and commerce, involving not just large enterprises but also small workshops and businesses. This was sufficiently dramatic to impress even Communists. One, Narciso Julián, a railway worker who had arrived in Barcelona the night before the rising, told the British oral historian Ronald Fraser, 'It was incredible, the proof in practice of what one knows in theory: the power and strength of the masses when they take to the streets. Suddenly you feel their creative power; you can't imagine how rapidly the masses are capable of organizing themselves. The forms they invent go far beyond anything you've dreamt of, read in books.'

However, Barcelona was not representative of the whole of Republican Spain. The revolutionary take-over of lands and industry occurred to differing degrees according to the area in question. The only common features were the disorder and chaos that marked the first months of the war in the Republican zone. Moreover, few other cities experienced the revolutionary fervour felt in Barcelona. In Madrid, where there was far less industry anyway, the atmosphere was more sombre and warlike than revolutionary. Valencia experienced no social cataclysm on a scale comparable to Barcelona, while in San Sebastian and Bilbao affairs carried on much as they had before 18 July. Throughout rural Spain, above all in the areas of latifundia estates and poor soil, the peasants quickly resolved the land question by collectivization. In Andalusia, there was socialized austerity of an impressive kind. The 'tyranny of property' was abolished, and with it vices such as the consumption of coffee and alcohol. In parts of Aragon the same was true, although the spontaneity and revolutionary nature of much of the collectivization that took place has been exaggerated. In parts of Republican-held Castile, poverty overcame the instinctive individualism of the small holders. The prosperous farmers of Catalonia, the Levante and Asturias, however, were anything but enthusiastic.

The collectives varied enormously in the way they were set up and run. Moreover, they were not all organized by the CNT. In the Levante, for instance, there occurred situations in which one small *pueblo* would have three collectives, one controlled by the CNT, one by the UGT and one by left Republicans. Not all the land that was expropriated was collectivized, and the amount of land seized varied according to the region. For instance, the recent study by Professor Aurora Bosch has shown that, while in Jaen 65 per cent of the useful land surface was expropriated, and 80 per cent of that land collectivized, in Valencia only 13.8 per cent of the land surface was seized, of which a mere 31.58 per cent was turned over to collectives. In general, however, in all Republican areas, collectivization was most intense where the CNT was strongest. This was particularly evident in Aragon. There the areas with the greatest UGT strength were in the west of the region and had fallen to the insurgents. The PCE, meanwhile, was very weak in Aragon, while the Republicans did not have sufficiently compact local organizations to command power. This left the field open to the CNT, even though its only real centre of strength was in the province of Zaragoza. The Aragonese anarcho-syndicalist collectivizers were bolstered by the military assistance granted by their Catalan comrades.

Indeed, the initial predominance of the CNT in the revolutionary committees of Aragon has been seen as largely the result of the influence of the Catalan militia. After the failure of the military uprising in the east of Aragon, Catalan CNT militia columns played a fundamental role in creating the 'climate' for social revolution. According to the Communists, this was done at the point of a gun. In much of the region the collectives, far from being the spontaneous creation of peasants, were imposed by force. Moreover, whether genuinely spontaneous or forcibly created, they all faced the problem of putting into practice what had up to that point been only abstract theory. In the view of Juan Zafón, a Catalan *cenetista*, who later wrote a book about his experiences as propaganda counsellor on the Revolutionary Council of Aragon, 'We were attempting to put into practice a libertarian communism about which, it's sad to say, none of us really knew anything.'

The Council of Aragon had been established in early October 1936 in an attempt to fill the political void created by the military rising and the widescale collectivization. As the fief of the CNT, the Council was from the first the target of hostile reaction from Communists, Socialists and Republicans alike. It was granted recognition by the central government of Largo Caballero in December. This entailed the creation of municipal councils, and the inclusion in the Council of representatives of the other Popular Front parties. The Council soon found itself caught in the dilemma of trying to provide a coherent structure for a highly disorganized series of local bodies without impinging upon their 'spontaneity'. In the event, it was forced to engage in economic centralization and thereby to abandon the anarchist principle of autonomous local government. Indeed, the Council of Aragon was attacked by other Popular Front organizations for its interventionism, particularly in the sugar-producing factory at Monzón, and it was even accused of 'counter-revolutionary activity' within the CNT. This did not prevent the Communists from denouncing the Council for imposing the 'tyranny of gangsters'.

Much the same story was true of Valencia, where there was little clear idea of how to run collectives in practice. Moreover, the local provincial delegates of the government's Institute of Agrarian Reform were quite unable to impose any kind of order. In consequence, the Valencian agricultural collectives were permitted to operate with complete independence and autonomy. This, together with the violence which accompanied much of the collectivization, had a disastrous effect on the Valencian agricultural economy. Production of the Valencian export crops of rice and oranges, a crucial source of foreign currency for the Republic, was disrupted. The extent of the economic chaos was so great that even the provincial revolutionary powers recognized the need to impose some central control. However, although a *Consejo de Economía de Valencia* was set up, it had little or no effect. In fact, the instances in Valencia of total collectivization and the proclamation of libertarian communism were few and short-lived. War was hardly the best context for massive economic experiments. Collectivization tended to disrupt both continuity of production and market mechanisms at precisely the time when planning and co-ordination were most urgently needed.

As a general rule rural collectivization was accepted wholeheartedly by the landless *braceros* but resented by smallholders who saw the labour market drained, the threat of competition from units large enough to enjoy economies of scale and the ultimate possibility of their own expropriation. At the risk of simplification, it could be said that the Republican countryside witnessed a potential conflict between the rural proletariat gathered in the collectives and the smallholding rural middle classes. Similarly, in industrial towns, small businessmen, who might in fact be Republican voters, warily awaited the process of collectivization. These two conflicting groups in town and country looked to different national authorities: the collectivizers to the CNT and the UGT; the small holders and businessmen to the Republican government. The overwhelming power of the proletariat might have been expected to prevail. However, the need for foreign aid and the fact that the Soviet Union provided it soon altered the relation of forces within the Republican zone. The Communist Party was pushed from its relative obscurity to be, as the channel through which Russian aid passed, the arbiter of Republican politics.

Soviet policy on Spain was constrained by Stalin's search for Western allies against Hitler. Accordingly, Russian help had to ensure that political and social developments in Spain would stop short at the maximum which French and British policy makers would tolerate. This meant guaranteeing that the Spanish Republic remained a bourgeois democratic parliamentary regime. In any case, the Spanish Communists were convinced that Spain was obliged by an iron historical destiny to pass through a bourgeois democratic stage on its road to socialism. They failed to perceive that in legal and economic terms Spain had already passed through a bourgeois revolution, albeit without a democratic political revolution, in the nineteenth century. Soviet directives and the Party's own erroneous analysis of Spanish history thus meant that, in the potential class conflicts of the loyalist zone, the newly powerful PCE would throw its weight behind the bourgeois

Republican forces. The consequent hostility between the Communists and the forces of revolution was bitter and violent. It would be intensified in 1937 by the PCE's mimetic emulation of the Moscow trials and Stalin's witch-hunt against Trotskyists.

By August 1936 the Communists were working to ensure that the war effort would have as its central objective the defence of the legitimately elected bourgeois democratic Republic. At first they gave their backing to the Giral government. This brought them into conflict with the reality of the revolution in the fields and the factories. However, the PCE had a certain advantage in its control of Soviet aid, which would be cut off unless certain adjustments were made. Thus, in late August, plans for a revolutionary junta of the PSOE-UGT, the CNT-FAI and the PCE under Largo Caballero were spiked by Marcel Rosenberg, the Russian ambassador, who pointed out plausibly that the Western powers would not tolerate a workers' government within their sphere of influence. The Communists realized that the Republic still needed a more broadly based government. Accordingly, the government formed by Largo Caballero on 4 September included Republicans as well as representatives of the workers' parties. Largo Caballero's undeserved reputation as the 'Spanish Lenin' served as a sop to the workers. However, Azaña and Prieto, who rather despised Largo Caballero, looked to the Communists as a guarantee that the bourgeois Republic was intact.

The position of the Communists posed a terrible dilemma for the anarchists. If the rebels should win the war, the anarchist experiment would definitely be brought to an end. For the Republic to win, the active co-operation of the anarchists was essential. The issue hinged on what form that co-operation should take, and what price should be paid in terms of sacrificing revolutionary gains. The Communists had no doubt that the CNT-FAI should join the central government, both in order to create a solid political front and to implicate them in the destruction of their autonomous revolutionary powers. It was the Communists who, according to Largo Caballero, 'asked that everything possible should be done in order that the CNT should be represented in the government, and I promised it'. Pressure was brought to bear upon the CNT, and on 3 November 1936 negotiations were finalized. On the following day their four representatives joined the cabinet in besieged Madrid. Inevitably the decision created tensions and frictions within the anarchist movement. Even for those in favour of participation it was a painful decision. Joining the cabinet reflected a recognition that if the CNT remained outside, it would be that much easier for the Communists to control the key decision-making apparatus.

The anarchist ministers quickly found themselves confronted with the PCE assertion of the need to postpone revolutionary action until the bourgeois Republic had been consolidated against fascist attack. They were slow to perceive the strength of the tacit, but unholy, alliance created between the PCE on the one hand and Azaña and Prieto on the other. They both hoped to use the Communists to control the revolutionary masses of the UGT and the CNT. The central government began a policy of bureaucratic harassment of collectivized industry and agriculture. This could be justified by the fact that production had to be integrated into a centralized war effort. However, deliberately manipulated credit shortages created major difficulties for many collectives. At the same time as the achievements of the popular revolution were being whittled away, the Communists aligned themselves with the petty bourgeois forces within Republican society. For a large sector of the rural and urban middle classes, the Communist position came as an immense relief.

During the Civil War, the Spanish Communist Party experienced an unprecedented increase in its numerical and political strength, as thousands of people in Republican-held territory responded to the call of such propaganda as this pamphlet. Addressed to 'all the peoples of Spain and all who love peace, progress and freedom', it advocated unity and discipline as the only possible 'road to victory' proclaimed by the title.

Profoundly disheartened by the trend to collectivization, they had been driven to despair by the seeming inability of their own Republican leaders to control events. The Communists consciously set out to win the support of the threatened small property owners. They began to pick up members among army officers, state bureaucrats, middle-class professionals, smallholders and small businessmen.

PCE party offices carried signs which read 'Respect the property of the small peasant' and 'Respect the property of the small industrialist'. Vicente Uribe, the Communist Minister of Agriculture in the government of Largo Caballero, legalized the expropriation of lands belonging to Francoists – but not of other collectivized land, much of which was now returned to its owners. He stated that 'The property of the small farmer is sacred and that those who attack or attempt to attack that property must be regarded as enemies of the regime.' It was all part of a policy of dismantling the revolution. Stalin wrote to Largo Caballero on 21 December 1936:

> The urban petty and middle bourgeoisie must be attracted to the government side.... The leaders of the Republican party should not be repulsed; on the contrary they should be drawn in, persuaded to get down to the job in harness with the government.... This is necessary in order to prevent the enemies of Spain from presenting it as a Communist Republic, and thus to avert their open intervention, which represents the greatest danger to Republican Spain.

The policies advocated by Stalin and pursued by the Largo Caballero government were based on a realistic assessment of the attitudes of the great powers. Unfortunately, since the five years of the Republic had stripped the Spanish working class of any illusions about the capacity for reform of bourgeois democracy, those policies dramatically damaged working-class morale in the Republican zone.

In a similar way, the dissolution of the spontaneous revolutionary militia and their replacement by regular army units diminished the revolutionary *élan* of the masses. However, after the uninterrupted defeats at the hands of the Army of Africa in the early months of the war, it seemed an elementary military requirement. It is a romantic view which sees the creation of the Popular Army as a backward step. Indeed, it is difficult to deny the military achievements of the Communists. The Spanish Communists, advised by the delegates of the Comintern and Soviet military advisers, were the first to appreciate that, if the Republic was to avoid being swept aside by the Nationalists, it must have properly trained regular troops carrying out the orders of a unified and coherent command. The Communists, by dint of their organizational structure, their fetish of rigid discipline and their access to Soviet aid, were in a position to begin immediately to organize the Popular Army. Largo Caballero was persuaded of the logic of the Communist position through the combined efforts of Mikhail Koltzov, the Soviet journalist, and Julio Alvarez del Vayo, the Socialist Foreign Minister who had developed very close ties with the Communists. In any case, the defects of the militia system were glaringly obvious. Their attempt to maintain full democracy in the field had led to costly inefficiency. Vital hours would often be lost in discussions and deliberations among committee members. Discipline was almost impossible to enforce. There had been cases of militiamen going home for the weekend while on active service.

The Communists, in contrast, demanded 'Discipline, Hierarchy, and Organization'. These three virtues reached their apogee in the Communists' own Fifth Regiment, which was to form the core of the Popular Army. Modelled on the Red Army of the Russian

Civil War, the Fifth Regiment was led by a series of outstanding Communist officers: Enrique Castro Delgado, Enrique Lister and Juan Modesto. The efficiency of the Fifth Regiment attracted thousands to its ranks. According to José Martín Blázquez, Republican army officer, 'The Communist Party must be granted the credit of having set the example in accepting discipline. By doing so it enormously increased not only its prestige, but its numbers. Innumerable men who wished to enlist and fight for their country joined the Communist Party.' The Fifth Regiment also enjoyed the advantage of being favoured in the distribution of Soviet arms.

It was precisely over the Republican army that the Communists ultimately clashed with Largo Caballero. The event was to lead to his downfall as Prime Minister. The Communists were anxious for the removal of General José Asensio, Largo's appointee as Under-Secretary for War, whom they saw as an obstacle to their plans to gain hegemony over the Republican war effort. The crude and blatant way in which they attempted to impose their viewpoint led to a famous incident in which Largo rounded on Marcel Rosenberg, the Soviet Ambassador, and on Alvarez del Vayo who had demanded Asensio's dismissal. Apparently the Soviet Ambassador spent several hours every day in the office of Largo Caballero. Rosenberg was usually accompanied by the most elevated interpreter imaginable, the Minister of Foreign Affairs, Julio Alvarez del Vayo. On the morning of the confrontation, a two-hour meeting ended when Largo Caballero was heard shouting. According to the Socialist deputy Ginés Ganga:

> Caballero's shouting increased in intensity. Then, all of a sudden, the door opened, and the aged premier of Spain, standing in front of his table, his arms outstretched and his shaking finger pointing at the door, was heard saying in a voice tremulous with emotion: 'Get out! Get out! You will have to learn, Señor Ambassador, that although we Spaniards are very poor and need help from abroad very much, we are too proud to let a foreign ambassador attempt to impose his will on the head of the government of Spain! And as for you, Vayo, it would be better to remember that you are a Spaniard and Minister of Foreign Affairs of the Republic and that you should not combine with a foreign diplomat in putting pressure on your Prime Minister.'

Relations between Largo and the Communists rapidly deteriorated. He had belatedly realized that the massive Communist contribution to Republican resistance was unfortunately linked to a sectarian view of society and a set of dictatorial methods which could only lead to conflict with other groups, who were also making a great sacrifice in the fight against Franco. After the *débâcle* at Malaga, in which all the shortcomings of the militia system were starkly revealed, Asensio was dismissed. Largo now began to try to reduce the dominance of the Communists in the army, realizing belatedly the nature of their mission. By the time he tried to take them on, however, it was too late. Soviet arms supplies, and the ordered efficiency of the Communists, left the Spanish Prime Minister with little hope of success.

Events came to a head in May 1937 in Barcelona. By this stage the 'proletarian content' of the initial revolutionary stages of the struggle had been severely emasculated. Increasingly the PCE, the Republicans and the reformist Socialists were taking command of the political and military structures of the Republic. The groups most affected by this were the left Socialist followers of Largo Caballero; the anarchists; and the POUM, made up of dissident anti-Stalinist Marxists and led by Joaquín Maurín and Andreu Nin, who had once been Trotsky's private secretary in Moscow. Until ousted by Communists in

Above: Amid the ruins of the University campus, the Republican Colonel Adolfo Prada (left, facing the camera) surrenders the troops responsible for the defence of Madrid, to the chief of the Nationalist Army of the Centre, Colonel Losas (right, wearing a Moroccan *chilaba*).

Opposite (above): Even at the eleventh hour, the Republic continued to be blighted by the internal wranglings which had characterized it since its establishment eight years earlier. Seen here are Juan Modesto (centre) and Enrique Lister (right), two of the Communist army officers whose promotion was the catalyst for Colonel Casado's *coup*.

Opposite (below): In May 1937, President Azaña had designated the Socialist Julián Besteiro to represent the Spanish Republic at the coronation of King George VI in London. Two years later, Besteiro was responsible for Foreign Affairs on the National Defence Council which took the place of the legitimate government on 5 March 1939. In the photograph, Julián Besteiro reads the Council's initial manifesto over the radio.

December 1936, Nin had been Minister of Justice in the *Generalitat*. The CNT and the POUM had come to feel that the sacrifices demanded by the Communists in favour of a bourgeois Republic were simply not influencing the Western powers, who were in the last analysis fully aware that Franco was a better bet for Western capitalism than the Republic could ever be. For the POUM, which had its main strength in Lérida and Barcelona, the war and revolution were inseparable.

The POUM was singled out for the enmity of the Communists precisely because of its Trotskyist views. Its 'bolshevist' analysis of the PCE's betrayal of the revolution in Spain was especially wounding to the Communists. The PCE began to call for the extermination of the POUM and to denounce as 'enemies of the USSR', 'fascist spies' and 'Trotskyist agents' those who criticized the Moscow trials. Blindly following the Soviet leadership, the Spanish Communists were convinced that the trials were genuinely directed against 'enemies of the people'. POUM militia units were starved of arms. Orwell and others complained that POUM units at the front had to make do with tattered uniforms, bad equipment and inadequate supplies of food and ammunition. In contrast, the Communist units in Barcelona who spent their time harassing the POUM were well equipped. As Orwell put it, 'A government which sends boys of fifteen to the front with rifles forty years old and keeps the biggest men and the newest weapons in the rear is manifestly more afraid of the revolution than of the fascists.' The collectives were deprived of funds. Communist secret police units began to pick up POUM militants. By April 1937 tension in Barcelona was reaching extreme levels. On 25 April *carabineros*, the frontier guards who were under the jurisdiction of the Minister of Finance, Dr Negrín, attacked the CNT frontier post at Puigcerdá. Several anarchists were killed. On the same day a prominent Communist, Roldán Cortada, was murdered in Barcelona. In early May the crisis exploded.

The immediate catalyst of the May events was the raid on the CNT-controlled central telephone exchange ordered on 3 May by Eusebio Rodríguez Salas, PSUC police commissioner for Catalonia. This led to the outbreak of street fighting. The CNT, the POUM, and the extreme anarchist group, the Friends of Durruti, fought the Communists for several days. The Communists and Prieto were delighted to have a chance to break the power of the CNT and limit that of the *Generalitat*. The fighting exposed the central dilemma of the CNT. The anarchists could win in Barcelona only at the cost of bloodshed which would effectively lose the war for the Republic. The CNT leadership instructed its militants to lay down their arms. The *Generalitat* lost autonomous control of the Army of Catalonia, and responsibility for public order was assumed by the government in Valencia. In victory, the Communists were anything but magnanimous. They would settle for nothing less than the complete destruction of the POUM. Orwell noted that 'There was a peculiar evil feeling in the air – an atmosphere of suspicion, fear, uncertainty and veiled hatred.'

Immediately the fighting in Barcelona was over, the Communists demanded that the Largo Caballero government dissolve the POUM and arrest its leadership. Largo refused. For the Communists, this confirmed their belief that Largo must go. In fact the decision had already been taken in March at a fiery meeting of the Spanish Politburo, a meeting at which there were more foreigners than Spaniards. The Comintern advisers, particularly André Marty and Boris Stefanov, had insisted on the removal of Largo and clashed violently with the PCE leaders José Díaz and Jesús Hernández. When the Prime Minister's fate was put to the vote, theirs had been the only two votes in his favour. By blocking Largo Caballero's plans for an offensive in Extremadura the Communists provoked a Cabinet crisis. Largo was left without support. Indalecio Prieto, the moderate Socialist, nurtured some resentment against the dour Prime Minister, and his supporters in the PSOE were glad of the chance to oust the Caballerists. Azaña, meanwhile, would not forgive Largo for the delay in getting him out of Barcelona during the 'May Events'. Thus Largo Caballero was forced to resign, and the government was offered to Dr Juan Negrín. In a sense, this marked an end to the power struggle between the revolutionists and the Communists. From this point on, the revolutionary achievements of the initial stages of the struggle would be steadily dismantled, leaving the war to follow the direction dictated by the Republicans and moderate Socialists who had taken over the key ministries in the government.

Dr Juan Negrín, the new Premier, was convinced that the only chance for the Republic lay in close co-operation with the Soviets. Dr Negrín remains an enigma. In personal terms he was a complete opposite to the puritanical Largo: charming, engaging, a gourmet and apparently a considerable sexual athlete, despite his portly figure. A brilliant physiologist, he had entered politics in the late 1920s as a moderate Socialist; he was considered to be an ally of Indalecio Prieto. By the time he assumed the premiership the relations between the two were deteriorating as a result of their differing attitudes to the Communists. In the view of Burnett Bolloten, 'He more than any other Spaniard was responsible for the success of Communist policy during the last year of the Civil War.' Certainly, Negrín's policy rested on the firm conviction that victory depended upon discipline in the armed forces, and on the continued supply of arms from the Soviet Union. As in the case of the transfer of Spanish gold reserves to Moscow, it is difficult to see what options were open to Negrín other than currying Communist favour. His government was more united than any of its predecessors. However, its unity had been bought at the price of liquidating the revolution. It was the logical conclusion and the most concrete realization of the Popular Front option, a government which enshrined the Communist alliance with bourgeois democratic forces in the interests of Russian relations with the bourgeois democracies.

Negrín was not alone in believing that the democratic powers in Europe must come to the Republic's aid if they could be persuaded of the non-revolutionary nature of the Republican struggle. His close collaboration with the Communists is therefore entirely understandable. For the Communists, once Negrín had been installed as Premier, their main objectives were to ensure the destruction of the POUM and to bring about the downfall of Indalecio Prieto, the new Minister of Defence. The POUM was purged relentlessly. In one of the most horrific incidents of the Civil War Andreu Nin, the POUM leader, was arrested, brutally tortured and then executed by being flayed alive. Clumsy Communist propaganda efforts to pretend that Nin had been spirited away by a Nazi rescue squad could not hide the fact that Nin's murder was the work of the NKVD, the Soviet secret police. The rest of the POUM leadership was brought to trial in late 1938. So outraged were Largo Caballero and the anarchists who had been in his cabinet that they went to see Azaña, and denounced Negrín as a traitor. The President of the Republic ignored their request that he should dismiss the Prime Minister.

The Communists demanded that centralization be rigidly imposed. The Council of Aragon was dissolved. However, in enacting the Decree of Dissolution of 11 August 1937,

Enrique Lister, the Communist commander, went well beyond the decree's provisions. In an unnecessarily brutal repression, when the Council was dismantled many CNT members were arrested. The effects on both morale and agricultural efficiency were devastating. After Aragon, the Communists moved against the collectives of Catalonia, and by 1938 there remained little of the autonomy granted by the Popular Front. Other centralizing measures included the use of the secret police known as the *Servicio de Investigación Militar* (SIM) which had been increasingly infiltrated by Communists, to purge opponents. Gustav Regler referred to the Comintern's obsession with spies and traitors as 'the Russian syphilis'. The crushing of the collectives and the use of secret police ensured that the last two years of the Civil War in the Republican zone were very different from the first. Without the sense of a new world to fight for, the sacrifices and the hunger were that much harder to bear.

The PCE was in an ironic sense also a loser. The Communists had backed the bourgeois Republicans and the moderate Socialists, and in the latter stages of the war those groups were suffused with defeatism. Even within the PCE, doubts were expressed about the choices that had been made, especially after Munich seemed to suggest a rapprochement between the Western powers and the Axis. The major obstacle remaining for the PCE was the continued presence in the cabinet of the increasingly anti-Communist Indalecio Prieto as Minister of Defence. Although Prieto and the PCE had been united by their opposition to the revolutionism of Largo Caballero and the anarchists, each saw in the other the means to further their own particular interests. Prieto had always been suspicious of the Communists. Once Largo had been removed, the marriage of convenience was bound to break down. Prieto, whose natural tendency to defeatism and discouragement found an echo in Azaña's traumatized state of despair, sought to reduce the prominence of the Communists. This put the PCE into an awkward position. Having laid such stress on the need to defend a moderate bourgeois Republic, they could hardly move openly against its foremost representatives, Azaña and Prieto.

Ironically, then, Communist efforts against the revolutionists had in some senses let their own control of the war effort slip. Unfortunately, the methods that it used to impose its views were to lead, in early 1939, to full-scale internecine war. It has been plausibly argued by the Spanish Marxist Fernando Claudín and by Ronald Fraser that, if the Communists had been able to find some way to harness the revolutionary enthusiasm of the first months instead of simply crushing it, the war might have been won. This would have involved a revolutionary guerrilla war in the zones occupied by the Nationalists. It would have required a genuine revolutionary policy in the loyalist zone. Given the sectarian tendencies of the Communists, that would have been unlikely to have produced a policy acceptable to the CNT and the POUM. Moreover, in the light of the international situation between 1936 and 1937, and Stalin's view of it, Communist sponsorship of revolution was virtually inconceivable. As it was, the Communist Party, for all its crimes and its errors, played a major role in keeping Republican resistance alive as long as it did.

9

Defeat by Instalments

It was hardly surprising, given the divisions which racked the Republicans, that even after the defeat of Guadalajara, in which the large contingent of Italian troops had been routed, the Nationalists continued to hold the initiative. This was starkly demonstrated by the ease with which they swept through the north in the spring and summer of 1937. In March Mola had gathered nearly 40,000 troops for an assault on the Basque Country, and he opened his campaign at the end of the month with a widely publicized threat: 'If submission is not immediate, I will raze all Vizcaya to the ground, beginning with the industries of war. I have the means to do so.' However, despite Mola's evident desire for a quick victory, the campaign was slower than either the rebels or their German allies cared for. Steep, wooded hills and poor roads held up the advance, and the dogged Basque retreat also exacted a high price from the attacking forces. Skilful use of tank traps and barbed-wire entanglements seemed merely a prelude to what would happen at the much vaunted 'iron ring' of defences of Bilbao, which had been known as the great 'city of sieges' during the Carlist wars of the nineteenth century.

Mola enjoyed the air support of the German Condor Legion, whose Chief of Staff and later leader was Lieutenant-Colonel Wolfram von Richthofen, cousin of the 'Red Baron'. Von Richthofen, who was later to mastermind the Nazi invasion of Poland, used the Condor Legion to practice the techniques of dive-bombing and saturation bombing, which were later to be incorporated into the Blitzkrieg of the Second World War. An exigent and cold-bloodedly professional commander, von Richthofen was firmly committed to the use of terror. He advised Mola that 'Nothing is unreasonable that can further destroy enemy morale and quickly.' On the same night, 25 April, Mola had the rebel radio at Salamanca broadcast the following warning to the Basque people: 'Franco is about to deliver a mighty blow against which all resistance is useless. Basques! Surrender now and your lives will be spared.'

On the following afternoon, 26 April, which was a Monday and market day in the small town of Guernica, the Condor Legion struck. Guernica, which was of deep symbolic importance to the Basque people, was destroyed in one awful afternoon of sustained bomb attacks. The scale of the atrocity was compounded by subsequent efforts on the part of the Nationalists to deny any responsibility. George Steer, correspondent of *The Times*, was one of the first journalists to arrive at the scene. With some misgiving, the editor of *The Times*, Geoffrey Dawson, published the following report by Steer on 28 April:

> Guernica, the most ancient town of the Basques and the centre of their cultural tradition, was completely destroyed by insurgent air raiders. The bombardment of this open town far behind the lines occupied precisely three hours and a quarter, during which a powerful fleet of aeroplanes consisting of three German types, Junkers and Heinkel bombers and Heinkel fighters, did not cease unloading on the town bombs weighing from 1,000 lb downwards and, it is calculated, more than 3,000 two-pounder aluminium incendiary projectiles. The fighters, meanwhile, plunged low from above the centre of the town to machine-gun those of the civilian population who had taken refuge.

Dawson who was a strong advocate of appeasement, later wrote 'I did my best, night after night, to keep out of the paper anything that might hurt [German] susceptibilities.' Steer was a first-class war correspondent. The Francoists, in an effort to discredit his report, went to great lengths to denigrate his personal and professional integrity.

Franco's foreign press service, under the direction of Luis Bolín, immediately set to work denying that the bombing had taken place. For Bolín, the London correspondent of the monarchist daily *ABC*, the cover-up was inspired in large measure by his worries about the possible reaction of the English Catholic Church. When it quickly became obvious that outright denial of the atrocity was no longer tenable, the Nationalists claimed that Guernica had been dynamited by the Basques themselves in order to fabricate an atrocity for propaganda purposes. This story was maintained by some even up to the 1970s. Unfortunately for Bolín, though, there were too many reliable witnesses. Father Alberto Onaindía, unofficial diplomatic agent of the Basque Country in Paris, reached the town on the day of the German attack:

> I arrived at Guernica on April 26, at 4.40 pm. I had hardly left the car when the bombardments began. The people were terrified. They fled, abandoning their livestock in the market place. The bombardment lasted until 7.45. During that time, five minutes did not elapse without the sky's being black with German planes. The planes descended very low, the machine-gun fire tearing up the woods and roads, in whose gutters, huddled together, lay old men, women and children. Before long it was impossible to see as far as five hundred yards, owing to the heavy smoke. Fire enveloped the whole city. Screams of lamentation were heard everywhere, and the people, filled with terror, knelt, lifting their hands to heaven as if to implore divine protection. . . . As a Catholic priest, I state that no worse outrage could be inflicted on religion than the Te Deum to be sung to the glory of Franco in the church at Guernica which was miraculously saved by the heroism of firemen from Bilbao.

Not all Nationalists attempted to deny the bombing of Guernica. Virginia Cowles, an American reporter, travelled extensively through rebel Spain in the company of Captain Gonzalo de Aguilera, the eccentric aristocrat who blamed the outbreak of the war on sewers. On meeting German soldiers in the north, he remarked to her, 'Nice chaps, the Germans, but a bit too serious; they never seem to have any women around, but I suppose they didn't come for that. If they kill enough reds, we can forgive them anything.' She visited the remains of Guernica in the company of another Nationalist press officer, Ignacio Rosalles.

> We arrived in Guernica to find it a lonely chaos of timber and brick, like an ancient civilization in process of being excavated. There were only three or four people in the streets. An old man

In their advance towards Bilbao, the 'Navarra Brigades' led by General Solchaga had a number of obstacles to contend with, amongst which was the destruction of bridges by retreating Basque forces. In this photograph, Nationalist troops replace a dynamited stone bridge with a temporary structure of wooden piles and planks.

A lone dog surveys the smoke and ruins in the streets of Guernica, after the air raid of 26 April 1937.

70 per cent of the buildings in Guernica were destroyed by the 22,000 kg of bombs dropped by three squadrons of the German 'Condor Legion'. Fires caused by incendiary bombs spread rapidly and did perhaps more damage than the explosive bombs dropped.

was clearing away debris. Accompanied by Rosalles, my official escort, I went up to him and asked if he had been in the town during the destruction. He nodded his head and, when I asked what had happened, waved his arms in the air and declared that the sky had been black with planes – 'Aviones,' he said: 'Italianos y alemanes.' Rosalles was astonished. 'Guernica was burned,' he contradicted heatedly. The old man, however, stuck to his point, insisting that after a four-hour bombardment there was little left to burn. Rosalles moved me away. 'He's a red', he explained indignantly. A couple of days later, we were talking to some staff officers. Rosalles described our drive along the coast and told them of the incident at Guernica. 'The town was full of reds,' he said. 'They tried to tell us it was bombed, not burnt.' The tall staff officer replied: 'But of course it was bombed. We bombed it and bombed it and bombed it, and bueno, why not?' Rosalles looked astonished, and when we were back in the car again he said, 'I don't think I would write about that if I were you.'

Such attempts at intimidation, if not particularly effective, were nevertheless not uncommon. Luis Bolín, in particular, having already threatened a French journalist with execution for filming the Badajoz massacre, was used to the press submitting to his wishes. In the last resort, though, the myth of the Basque dynamiters was counterproductive. Had the Nationalist authorities taken the same line as the nonchalant staff officer, the bombing could have been dismissed as a regrettable consequence of war. As it was, the controversy made it a central symbol of the war, immortalized in the painting by Pablo Picasso. That Guernica was destroyed by the German Condor Legion is no longer open to any doubt. Moreover, it is this fact which gives the event its military significance, for the town was the first in the world's history to have been entirely destroyed by aerial bombing. The only controversy that remains in relation to the atrocity is whether it was carried out at the behest of the Nationalist high command, or on the initiative of the Nazis. Dr Herbert Southworth, the world authority on the destruction of Guernica, reached the unequivocal conclusion that Guernica was destroyed by explosive and incendiary bombs dropped from aircraft of the Condor Legion piloted by Germans. The bombing was undertaken at the request of the Nationalist high command in order to destroy Basque morale and preclude the defence of Bilbao.

The devastation of Guernica certainly shattered Basque morale. The meetings between General Mola and Lieutenant-Colonel von Richthofen on the evening of 25 April and the morning of 26 April suggest that this was precisely why it had been bombed. If that was not the case, the most plausible tactical objective would have been to knock out the Rentería bridge across the River Mundaca across which Basque troops could retreat. However, light incendiary bombs were an odd choice of projectile for use against a stone bridge. Besides, von Richthofen, an austerely efficient man, had access to the new Stuka dive-bomber, by far the most suitable aircraft in existence for small-scale precision bombing. Yet he chose not to use it. Even so, eyewitnesses have testified to the fact that the conventional bombers he did use were low enough to have been able to drop bombs with some accuracy. However, they flew too wide apart for them to have been concentrating on a given target. In fact, it seems that under the Rentería bridge was by far the safest place to be in Guernica during the bombing.

The key to the defence of Bilbao, the 'iron ring' of fortifications, had been betrayed by a Basque officer, Major Alejandro Goicoechea, who had deserted with its blueprints in March. By late May Mola's troops had Bilbao surrounded. The orders of Prieto, Minister for Defence, to destroy all industrial installations were ignored by the Basque President,

José Antonio Aguirre. Constant air attacks by the Nationalists enabled them to break through the defensive lines on 12 June. A week later Bilbao fell. The newly imposed rebel mayor, the Basque Falangist, José María de Areilza, in an effort to minimize the advantage enjoyed by the Nationalists on account of the leaked information, exalted the victory in the following terms:

> Bilbao was conquered by arms. No deals and posthumous back-scratching. The rules of war – harsh, virile and inexorable. The revolting, sinister, heinous nightmare known as Euskadi has fallen for ever. You have fallen forever, self-seeking, bickering, worthless, Basque Nationalist toady, President Aguirre. You, who cut an elegant figure during eleven months of crime and robbery while the poor Basque soldiers were being hunted down in the villages with lassoes like quadrupeds, leaving their pelts scattered over the length and breadth of the Biscayan mountains. As for Basque nationalism, there exists as from now an argument which supersedes all historical sophistry and legalistic manouevres. This argument, written in the blood spilt in Vizcaya, is that it has become once again a part of Spain purely and simply by conquest of arms. Spain has recovered the full independence of her sovereignty. And she is using it to proclaim her friendship for the great European nations who have befriended her in these tragic times of national crusade. I refer to the Germany of Hitler, the Italy of Mussolini, and the Portugal of Oliveira Salazar.

Thirty years later, after a distinguished career in Franco's service, Areilza was to repent of his past, and he joined the moderate opposition to the dictatorship.

After the fall of Bilbao the Nationalists' northern campaign met few obstacles. An army of sixty thousand troops, amply supplied with Italian troops and equipment, easily dealt with disorganized Republican militia and entered the elegant coastal resort of Santander on 26 August. The Italians claimed this as a great triumph, and their troops paraded through Santander holding aloft giant portraits of Mussolini. In Italy the press gloried in this revenge for Guadalajara, even though in reality the Italian troops had faced virtually no resistance. By this stage the Basques defending Castilian Santander were thoroughly dispirited after the capture of their homeland. Fearful of the vengeful attitude of the Nationalists, they had tried to sue for peace with the Italian General, Ettore Bastico. The Nationalists, however, got wind of the plan and sent troops to curtail negotiations. Thereafter the remainder of the north was quickly mopped up during September and October. Gijon and Avilés in Asturias fell on 21 October, and by the end of the month northern industry was at the service of the rebels. This gave them a decisive advantage. Already better off in terms of tanks and aeroplanes, the Nationalists were now able to consolidate their military superiority through control of the production of iron ore. Moreover, conscription had been introduced in the rebel zone, giving the Nationalists an advantage of approximately 200,000 troops over the Republicans.

During the summer the Republicans had tried to halt the seemingly inexorable process by which their territory was being whittled away. A well-planned offensive at Brunete, fifteen miles west of Madrid, achieved initial surprise on 6 July. The attack was conceived by General Vicente Rojo, the shrewd Republican Chief of Staff. His idea was to break through the Nationalist lines at their weakest point. Nearly 50,000 troops smashed through enemy lines, but in conditions of extreme heat and great confusion Republican discipline broke down. Political rivalries hampered the effective prosecution of the campaign, and within two days General Varela was able to call up enough reinforcements to plug the gap. For ten days, in one of the bloodiest encounters of the war, the Republicans defended

Opposite top left: Nationalist troops and vehicles fill the Plaza Elíptica in the centre of Bilbao, after the occupation of the Basque capital on 19 June 1937.

Opposite top right: A column of Nationalist troops winds its way through the impressive mountain scenery of the province of Santander in the summer of 1937.

Opposite below: After the disaster of Guadalajara, Mussolini's 'volunteers' were incorporated into a series of mixed, Hispano-Italian units, the Black, the Red and the Green Arrows. The troops seen here entering Santander in one of the fast-moving Fiat 'mini tanks' belong to the first of these units.

Left: A group of Republican soldiers stands around part of their arsenal at the entrance to the village of Brunete on the eve of the battle there. Brunete was to be the first serious test of the newly-organized Popular Army as an offensive force.

Below: After the war, the ruins of Belchite were left as they are seen here as a monument to the Nationalist dead. A new village was built nearby to house Belchite's surviving inhabitants.

the salient they had gained against overwhelming air and artillery attacks. The Nationalists were hugely aided by the introduction at the Battle of Brunete of the new German fighter, the Messerschmitt 109, which was to play such an important role in the Second World War. In conditions of total chaos, with both sides mistakenly dropping shells on their own troops, the Nationalists gradually forced the attackers back to their starting point. At the cost of many of its best troops and much valuable equipment, the Republic had done little except slightly delay the eventual collapse of the north.

Nevertheless, the Republicans maintained their efforts to take the initiative. In August 1937 an offensive was made on the Aragon front – chosen in part because of the government's desire to end the anarchists' control of the lines there. Again the brainchild of General Rojo, the objective was to approach Zaragoza through a bold pincer movement. However, difficulty was experienced in capturing small towns along the way, such as Belchite, and the offensive ground to a halt by mid-September. The story at Belchite was similar to that at Brunete. The Republicans gained an initial advantage, but then got bogged down owing to a combination of the intense midsummer heat and poor communications. In particular, the strategy of the Russian tank commander came to grief largely as a result of his insistence on giving orders in Russian. Once more, fierce resistance led to very heavy casualties. The Republican offensive was again hampered by political conflicts. The Communists' determination to dominate the war effort meant that the CNT militia were denied adequate weaponry. The Republican attacking force as a whole suffered from its internal political divisions, despite the Popular Army's discipline. At its side fought both units of the International Brigades and the remains of the former anarchist militia columns, which were still smarting under their forced militarization.

The disappointments of the Brunete and Aragon campaigns intensified divisive recriminations within the Republican camp. Largo Caballero had long been in favour of an offensive in Extremadura aimed at cutting Andalusia off from the rest of the rebel zone, but the opposition of the Communists, and particularly of Miaja, scuppered his plan. Now Indalecio Prieto, the Minister of Defence, attacked the Communists' handling of the Aragon offensive. This confirmed the increasingly pessimistic Socialist leader as the main enemy of the Communists in the government. Prieto also came under attack from the anarchists for his role in sanctioning the dissolution of the Council of Aragon in August 1937. Although he always denied having also authorized the brutal destruction of the anarchist collectives by the heavy-handed Stalinist General Enrique Lister, it was clear that morale in the Republican zone was increasingly being undermined by political disputes.

In the Nationalist zone there were no such divisions. General Mola's death on 3 June allowed Franco to run the war effort without interference. Franco was able to direct the Nationalist forces unhindered by problems of insubordination and indiscipline. None the less, the rebel leader was profligate with the lives of his troops in a series of decisions of questionable strategic wisdom. Having squandered his opportunity to take Madrid by his insistence on relieving El Alcázar, he now committed his men to costly counter-offensives, particularly at Brunete. Franco's battle tactics reflected his character: cruel, unforgiving, and vengeful. These attributes, however, were of inestimable value in allowing him to impose his will on the rebel zone. With his major potential rivals all dead, Franco was free to control not just the military, but also the political direction of the Nationalists.

The *Caudillo*'s political dominance was confirmed at the start of 1938. On 30 January

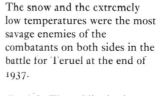

The snow and the extremely low temperatures were the most savage enemies of the combatants on both sides in the battle for Teruel at the end of 1937.

Top left: The soldier in the photograph endured temperatures below $-20°$C in his snow-covered trench.

Top right: In the streets of Teruel, Republican troops lay siege to the buildings occupied by Lieutenant Colonel Rey d'Harcourt and the garrison of Teruel.

Centre: When the Nationalists could hold out no longer, the civilians were evacuated and the military personnel were taken prisoner, along with the Bishop of Teruel, on 7 January 1938. However, the Republican occupation of Teruel was short-lived. (*Bottom*) On 22 February, General Aranda's troops carried the Nationalist flag into the battle-scarred city.

he formed his first regular ministry. Thus the rule of the Burgos junta of generals was brought to an end. Ramón Serrano Suñer, the *cuñadísimo* (most brother-in-law of brother-in-laws), was made Minister of the Interior, and other posts went to a carefully balanced selection of soldiers, monarchists, Carlists and Falangists. The dominant tone, however, was military. The Ministries of Defence, Public Order and Foreign Affairs all went to generals. The 'New State' was formalized through the *Ley de Administración Central del Estado*. According to this, 'The organization which has been created will be subject to the constant influence of the National Movement. The administration of the new State must be imbued with the spirit of its origin: noble and impartial, strong and austere, deeply Spanish down to the marrow.' The Falange was awarded control of the labour movement, and with it a hugely lucrative fount of patronage. The Church too was rewarded for its services by the concession of sole authority over education. This was in part reward for the Vatican's formal recognition of Franco in August 1937. The ideology of the New State was wholly backward-looking, concerned above all with the destruction of such symbols of progress as parliamentary democracy and trade unionism. Its political purpose was to rebuild Spain in the image of an imperial past. The only novelty was to be found the rallies and other trimmings adopted to facilitate its incorporation into the fascist world order envisaged by Hitler and Mussolini.

That Franco was able to give time to his political future was a sign of the way the military balance was pointing to his ultimate victory. After the Republicans' Aragon offensive there had been a lull in fighting. Towards the end of 1937, though, Franco decided to launch another attack on what had now become virtually his obsession, Madrid. His plan was to break through the Guadalajara front and move in for the kill on the Spanish capital. However, the Republicans were able to mount a successful spying mission to discover Franco's battle tactics. According to the Francoist historian, Ricardo de la Cierva, this was done by the anarchist commander of the Republic's Fourth Corps, Cipriano Mera, crossing the lines disguised as a shepherd. In his own memoirs, however, Mera makes it clear that he knew little of what was going on. Whoever deserved the credit, the information gathered led the Republicans to decide in December to launch their own pre-emptive attack in the hope of turning Franco away from Madrid. It was to be directed against Teruel, capital of the bleakest of the Aragonese provinces. The Nationalist lines there were weakly held and the city was already virtually surrounded by Republican forces.

Once more the strategy had been skilfully elaborated by General Vicente Rojo, and again complete surprise was achieved. The campaign took place in the midst of one of the cruellest winters Spain had ever suffered, the bitter cold intensified in the rocky terrain around Teruel. The Nationalists, caught unawares, discovered that their German and Italian aeroplanes were grounded by the weather. Their truckloads of reinforcements were delayed by snow and icebound roads. This allowed the Republican forces, principally composed of units of the Popular Army, to press home their initial advantage. The rebels thus had to postpone their planned advance on Madrid and switch their forces to the East. However, the Nationalist counter-attack, headed by Generals Varela and Aranda, was slowed by the appalling weather conditions. Although the snow stopped on 29 December, two days later the lowest temperature of the century was recorded. In such conditions the only feasible strategy for either side was one of attrition, in which the Nationalists enjoyed a distinct advantage. With more weapons and more men at their command, and driven by Franco's ruthless determination to recapture all lost territory, the rebels were always likely to be able to outlast the loyalist troops.

After bloody house-to-house fighting the Republicans managed to capture the Nationalist garrison on 8 January. They were then subjected to a heavy battering by artillery and bombers. In the freezing conditions, morale was sapped. Deaths from the cold were high on both sides, many troops dying in their sleep partly as the result of the alcohol they had taken to stay warm. Inevitably, political conflicts broke out once more. Indalecio Prieto visited the front and made scathing remarks about the inefficiency of the operation. Costly rivalries flared up between the commanders. Valentín González, 'El Campesino', the illiterate and fiery Communist commander, claimed later that during the Nationalist offensive against Teruel 'The advanced positions were lost, and I quickly found my force of 16,000 men surrounded. Outside the town, Lister and Modesto commanded six brigades and two battalions. They could have helped me. They did nothing of the kind. Even worse, when Captain Valdepeñas wanted to come to my rescue, they prevented him from doing so.' According to El Campesino, his division escaped only by dint of a desperate break-out. Some brigades refused to obey orders. Lister and El Campesino got away with it. Forty-six CNT mutineers, however, were executed. El Campesino was later to claim that the Communists deliberately sabotaged the capture of Teruel in order to prevent Prieto's position from being unduly strengthened. However, his accusations were made when he had become a virulent anti-Communist after being imprisoned in Siberia.

Nevertheless, after another costly defence of a small advance, the Republicans had to retreat on 21 February 1938, when Teruel was on the point of being encircled. The casualties on both sides had been enormous, the Nationalists losing over 50,000 men and the Republicans more than 60,000. What the successive breakdown of the three Republican offensives at Brunete, Belchite and Teruel demonstrated was that the sheer material superiority of the rebel forces could always prevail over the courage of the loyalist troops. Each time the Republicans had been unable to follow up their initial advantage. In part, this reflected political conflicts within the Republican zone. However, it was also a consequence the fact that by early 1938 Franco had an overwhelming advantage in terms of men and equipment. His exploitation of that superiority in regaining Teruel made it the military turning point of the Civil War.

The Nationalists now prepared to consolidate their victory with a massive offensive through Aragon and Castellón towards the sea. 100,000 troops, well covered by 200 tanks and nearly 1,000 German and Italian aircraft, began their advance on 7 March 1938. Colonel Wilhelm von Thoma, in command of the Condor Legion's fast tank units, wanted to use swift Blitzkrieg tactics but came into conflict with Franco's conservative instincts. In the style of First World War generals, Franco planned to use them as infantry support. Von Thoma made his point but it hardly mattered. After an opening artillery and aerial bombardment, the Nationalists found their Republican opponents exhausted, short of guns and ammunition and generally unprepared. Demoralization after the defeat of Teruel was compounded by organizational confusion. By the last week of March the River Ebro had been crossed. The population fled in terror before the advancing Nationalists. With their furniture piled on carts and their animals tied behind, they were strafed from the air. By early April the rebels had reached Lérida, which fell after a brave defence by El Campesino's division. They then moved down the Ebro valley, cutting off Catalonia from the rest of the Republic. By 15 April they had reached the sea at the fishing village of

Not only those in the armed services suffered the effects of gunfire and bombardment. As the front line came closer, the civilian population hurriedly evacuated their towns and villages. Some were able to load their possessions onto carts or animals. Others took what they could carry in their arms or on their heads.

Right: When the Republican government left Madrid for Valencia in November 1936, General Miaja, as military leader of the defence of the capital, appointed Major Vicente Rojo Lluch (right) chief of his General Staff. Promoted to the rank of Colonel in March 1937 and to that of General in October of the same year, Rojo was undoubtedly one of the most brilliant officers of the Republican army. In spite of his professional capacity and unstinting efforts, his work on the organization of the Popular Army did not bear the hoped-for fruits of victory.

Below: General Juan Yagüe, known for his Falangist sympathies and his part in the Badajoz massacre, poses for the photographer in Lérida, in April 1938. With him are two unidentified citizens of Lérida, presumably Nationalist sympathizers proud to be photographed with the man known by the Left as the 'hyena of Asturias' because of his repressive rôle there in October 1934.

Vinaroz. On the beach at Benicasim joyful Carlist soldiers cavorted in the waves. Serrano Suñer declared that the war was approaching its close.

Divided in two and suffering gravely from lack of food, the Republic was in dire straits. The Soviet Union had begun to ease off deliveries of armaments. Indeed, so bleak did the prospects seem that the unhappy Indalecio Prieto had come to share Azaña's long-held conviction that all was lost and that a negotiated peace was necessary to avoid the senseless loss of more lives. This gave the Communists the opportunity they were looking for to oust the Minister of Defence. After a lengthy exchange of views with Negrín, with Julián Zugazagoitia as intermediary, it was suggested that Prieto become Minister in charge of public works and railways. Prieto was thus provoked into resignation from the cabinet on 5 April, despite appeals to remain from the PSOE executive and a delegation of CNT leaders. Negrín told Prieto that he could not afford to have a pessimist in the Ministry of Defence.

Franco was equally convinced that the end was nigh. He cautiously suggested that the Germans might recall their troops as a sop to British and French sensibilities. Hitler, in turn, had decided by this stage that there was nothing more for the German technicians to learn from the Spanish conflict. However, the two fascist leaders had not reckoned with the tenacity of Republican resistance. The Nationalists found that they could not yet afford to dispense with the Condor Legion. The opening of the French frontier in March brought supplies and renewed hope to the defenders of the Spanish Second Republic.

The arms that the Republic was able to secure as a result of the reopening of the border with France led to the halting of the Nationalist advance, or at least to its slowing to a painful crawl. Indeed, Franco's Italian backers began to experience doubts. Mussolini became pessimistic about Spain and told Ciano, 'Put on record in your diary that today, 29 August, I prophesy the defeat of Franco.... The reds are fighters, Franco is not.' In fact, weighed down by the atmosphere of stalemate and war weariness, Negrín was looking for a compromise peace; but Franco was set on exacting nothing less than unconditional surrender. Had he mounted an offensive against Catalonia, where the Republic's remaining war industry lay, he could probably have brought the war to a speedier conclusion. Instead, in July he launched a major attack on Valencia.

Franco's decision was in part motivated by the fear that, following the German *Anschluss* in Austria in March, the French would intervene on the side of the Republic in Catalonia. Moreover, Hitler was now worried about possible repercussions should the Nationalists achieve an outright victory so soon after the annexation of Austria. In Hitler's opinion, expressed in November 1937, 'a 100 per cent victory for Franco' was undesirable 'from the German point of view' given that Germany's 'interest lay rather in a continuance of the war and the keeping up of the tension in the Mediterranean.' In fact, the Führer's worries were misplaced. Blum's second administration, which in any case had been hamstrung by the lack of a clear-cut majority, lasted just over a month before Daladier took over in April. He closed the border with Spain again on 13 June. Britain, meanwhile, was going ever farther down Chamberlain's road of appeasement at any price. A treaty had been signed with Italy in April, thereby tacitly condoning Italian intervention in Spain. Worse was to follow with the British reaction to the Czechoslovakian crisis during the summer. Rather than risk war with Hitler, Czechoslovakia was effectively surrendered to the Nazis at the Munich Agreement of 29 September. The Republicans awaited the

When the Nationalist troops reached the Mediterranean coast at Vinaroz on 15 April 1938, their regimental banners were dipped in the sea, then blessed by a priest. Here, some of the soldiers stand on the beach, saluting and perhaps singing the Falangist anthem, 'Cara al sol' ('Face to the sun').

The moderate Socialist Indalecio Prieto, Defence Minister between 17 May 1937 and 5 April 1938, addresses a large crowd outside Madrid's East Cemetery, at a gathering to pay tribute to the memory of the founder of the Spanish Socialist Party, Pablo Iglesias.

Like so many towns all over Spain, Tortosa was a mass of half-fallen buildings and rubble by the time it was occupied by the Nationalists in April 1938.

outcome of the Munich meeting in painful suspense. Negrín's naïve hopes of a European war in which a Republican Spain would be a vital ally of the Western democracies were dashed by the cynicism of the democracies. As Prieto stated, Europe had betrayed Spain.

Negrín's immediate response to the Anglo-Italian treaty had been to launch a diplomatic offensive of his own. In a bid to find a formula for peace negotiations, he had issued his 'Thirteen Points', inspired by Ivor Montagu, the British Communist film producer, in which he promised a Spain free of foreign interference, with free elections and full civil rights. The Western democracies were unmoved by his moderate package. In the United States hopes that the arms sale embargo would be lifted crashed against the power of the Catholic lobby. A telegram from the reactionary Ambassador in London, Joseph Kennedy, claimed that to drop the arms embargo would be to risk the spread of the war beyond Spain's borders. Father Coughlin broadcast an appeal for Catholics to flood the White House with telegrams. They raised a spectre which frightened President Roosevelt. He told his Secretary of the Interior, Harold Ickes, that he feared 'the loss of every Catholic vote next fall'. The President ordered that the embargo be maintained. His wife Eleanor, who sympathized with the Republic, considered this to be 'a tragic error' and regreted that she had not 'pushed him harder'. On 11 May Portugal granted diplomatic recognition to the Franco regime. Two days later Alvarez del Vayo's pleas to the League of Nations to end the policy of non-intervention fell on deaf ears. The Republic appeared to be doomed.

However, Franco's offensive against Valencia did not go as planned. Once more the Republicans demonstrated their heroic determination in defence, and the Nationalist Generals Varela, Aranda and García Valiño found progress towards the coast slow and exhausting. Indeed, the Republicans' achievement in holding up Franco's troops has been much underplayed. Through the use of well-planned trenches and properly protected communications lines, the Republicans were able to inflict heavy casualties on the Nationalists while suffering relatively few themselves. None the less, the progress of the rebels was inexorable, if painfully slow. By 23 July 1938 Valencia was under direct threat, with the Nationalists less than twenty-five miles away. In response, Negrín decided to mount a spectacular diversion in the form of a counter-offensive to stem the continual erosion of Republican territory.

In an attempt to restore contact with Catalonia, an assault across the River Ebro was conceived and planned by the ever-thoughtful General Vicente Rojo. It turned out to be the most hard-fought battle of the entire war. A special Army of the Ebro was formed for the offensive and was placed under the command of General Juan Modesto, the domineering Communist. All the division commanders were also Communists, even though some of them, such as Lister, had fallen out with Modesto. The Fifteenth Corps was under Manuel Tagüeña, at twenty-six already an outstanding leader. As in previous offensives, the best of the arms went to the Communists. The Nationalists placed the onus of defence on the blunt and outspoken General Juan de Yagüe. However, through a combination of over-confidence and poor intelligence, the scope and scale of the Republican attack was again misjudged.

A huge concentration of men, numbering some 80,000, was secretly transported to the river banks. Using boats, the first units of Modesto's army crossed the river on the night of 24–5 July. The remainder crossed on pontoon bridges on the following day. They surprised the thinly held Nationalist lines. The Popular Army was able to inflict serious

In the summer of 1938, Dr Negrín believed that war in Europe was imminent and that the Spanish Republic should and could resist until its outbreak. The Ebro offensive, begun on 24 July 1938, was part of that resistance plan. The boats used to cross the Ebro were carried overland to the river on trolleys, as can be seen in this photograph.

The Nationalist troops transferred to the Ebro from the Valencia front, under the leadership of General García Valiño, line up for review at Gandesa where, during the summer and autumn of 1938, the fiercest fighting of the battle of the Ebro took place.

casualties on Yagüe's troops, although the Fourteenth International Brigade sustained heavy losses and was forced to withdraw. Further upstream, however, the Republican forces succeeded in establishing a massive bridgehead within a broad bend in the river. By 1 August they had reached Gandesa, twenty-five miles from their starting point, but there they were bogged down. As usual, reinforcements, including the Condor Legion, were rushed in to contain the advance and a desperate and ultimately meaningless battle began for the territory that had been taken. It was to last for over three months. Despite its strategic irrelevance. Franco was determined to recover the lost ground irrespective of the cost. With nearly one million men now under arms, he could afford to be careless of their lives. His background in the African wars did not incline him to behave otherwise.

Opening the dams on the Pyrenean tributaries of the Ebro, the Nationalists managed to cut off the Republican forces, which were trapped in hilly country with little cover and short of supplies. Under orders not to retreat, the Republicans doggedly clung on despite fierce artillery bombardment. Five hundred cannon fired an average of over 13,500 rounds at them every day for nearly four months. In sweltering heat, with little or no water, shelled from dawn to dusk, they held on. Determined to smash the Republican army, Franco gathered over 30,000 fresh troops with new German equipment. The Nationalists relied on the tactic of concentrating air and artillery attacks on selected small areas, and then following these up with regular battalion attacks. It was, incidentally, at the Battle of the Ebro that Lieutenant Wernher Molders, the German air ace, conceived aerial fighter tactics which were to become standard practice thereafter. By mid-November, at appalling cost in casualties, the Francoists had pushed the Republicans out of the territory captured in July. The retreating Republicans left behind them many dead and much precious equipment. Both sides had suffered heavily during the battle of the Ebro, although there remains controversy as to the number of casualties. The Nationalists lost more, 6,500 troops dead and, if the new German Ambassador, Baron Eberhard von Stohrer, is to be believed, nearly 30,000 wounded. They were the heaviest casualties of the war, but the Republic had lost its army. Its last despairing effort had seen the Nationalists gain a decisive victory.

Effectively the Republic was defeated, yet it simply refused to accept the fact. Madrid and Barcelona were swelled with refugees and their populations on the verge of starvation. Negrín again began to search for a possible formula to allow a compromise peace. As a gesture of sincerity, the Republic proposed the withdrawal of foreign volunteers. Fernando de los Ríos, the Republican Ambassador to the United States, outlined the government's view: 'Spain, from the beginning, has been in favour of the withdrawal of all foreign elements, for two reasons. First, because it is wrong to have foreign elements interfere in a purely domestic struggle. And second, because we are sure that the moment these foreign elements are withdrawn, the end of the civil war will be very near.' Republican propaganda increasingly presented the war as a patriotic struggle to rid Spain of foreign invaders. Along with the liquidation of the last remnants of revolution and the reopening of churches, it was part of a vain effort to pave the way for a possible negotiated peace.

A farewell parade was held in Barcelona for the International Brigades on 29 October 1938. In the presence of many thousands of tearful, but cheering, Spaniards, the Communist leader Dolores Ibárruri, 'La Pasionaria,' gave an emotional and moving speech:

By September 1938, the International Brigades were no longer the crucial military and moral support they had been in 1936. In fact, since they had suffered heavy losses and recruiting had by then stopped, most of their units contained a majority of Spaniards. On 1 October 1938, the League of Nations agreed to supervise the repatriation of the Brigadiers. They were seen off from Barcelona with a massive parade, attended by enthusiastic crowds and the leading Republican politicians.

Opposite (above): Mozos de Escuadra stand guard over the remains of a tailor's shop in Barcelona, after one of the many air raids suffered by the city in the latter half of 1938.

Opposite (below): Typical of his insensitive character and the priority always given to military matters was Franco's disregard of the Church's request for a Christmas cease-fire in 1938. Franco is seen here on the Catalan front in December 1938, closely observing the progress of his troops with the aid of map and binoculars.

Right: The Nationalist occupation of Catalonia was the penultimate phase of 32 months of war. The column seen here crossing a bridge on the Catalan front would soon be in the region's capital, Barcelona.

Below: General Juan Yagüe, accompanied by a huge crowd of soldiers and civilians, walks through the streets of Barcelona, occupied by Nationalist troops on 26 January 1939.

Comrades of the International Brigades! Political reasons, reasons of state, the good of that same cause for which you offered your blood with limitless generosity, send some of you back to your countries and some to forced exile. You can go with pride. You are history. You are legend. You are the heroic example of the solidarity and the universality of democracy.... We will not forget you; and, when the olive tree of peace puts forth its leaves, entwined with the laurels of the Spanish Republic's victory, come back! Come back to us and here you will find a homeland.

Under the mournful gaze of President Azaña, the brigaders then marched past as the onlookers threw flowers. In total, 59,380 of them had come to fight against fascism in Spain. 9,934 (16.7 per cent) of them had died and 7,686 (12.9 per cent) had been badly wounded. In October 1938, 12,673 were still in Spain. They began the slow trek home or back into exile, often to fates more appalling than anything they had yet suffered. Those who survived were not to return to Spain until after the death of Franco thirty-seven years later.

The departure of the International Brigades left the Republican population with no doubt that defeat was imminent. The war effort was kept alive only by the fear born of Franco's much-publicized determination to annihilate liberalism, socialism and communism in Spain. Baron von Stohrer wrote to the Wilhelmstrasse on 19 November 1938, 'The main factors which still separate the belligerent parties are mistrust, fear and hatred. The first of these exists especially among the whites, the second among the reds, while hatred and a desire for revenge are present on both sides in almost the same degree.' Francoist propaganda had declared that it had a list of two million reds who were to be punished for their 'crimes'. The political files and documentation captured as each town had fallen to the Nationalists were gathered in Salamanca. Carefully sifted, they provided the basis for a massive card index of members of political parties, trade unions and masonic lodges. It was hardly surprising that the Republican zone was kept on a war footing by fear of Nationalist reprisals.

On 23 December 1938 Franco launched his final offensive. He had new German equipment and sufficient troops to be able to relieve them every two days. The shattered Republicans could put up only token resistance. The Republican government, which had moved from Valencia to Barcelona in October 1938, fled northwards to Gerona on 25 January 1939. The following day the rebels entered the starving Catalan capital. The streets were deserted. The ever-obnoxious Luis Bolín commented that 'The stench was awful. Unswept for years, the streets were full of autumn leaves and garbage, part of the accumulated filth which the Reds bequeathed to every town that they occupied.... The dust at the Ritz, the best hotel in the town, was inches thick.' While Bolín was rustling up charladies, nearly half a million refugees began to trudge north.

The rump of the Republican Cortes held its last meeting at Figueras near the French border. On Sunday 6 February, after Negrín had tried to persuade him to return to Madrid, the President of the Republic, Manuel Azaña, chose exile. The manner of his departure, described some months later in a letter to his friend Angel Ossorio, symbolized the plight of the Republic. He was to leave at dawn, with the President of the Cortes, Diego Martínez Barrio, in a small convoy of police cars. Martínez Barrio's car broke down and Negrín, who was present, tried to push it out of the way. The President had to cross the frontier on foot. He was followed three days later by Prime Minister Negrín and General Rojo. Miaja was left in authority over the remaining Republican forces. At the end of February Azaña resigned, and his constitutionally designated successor,

The arrival of Franco's troops meant the suppression of Catalonia's own culture and language. Franco intended to stamp out all vestiges of pre-war regionalism. In its place came the militaristic uniformity of his personal rule. Here enthusiastic supporters parade with the Spanish flag and pictures of Franco.

While the remnants of the Republican Parliament met in Figueras, Nationalist troops approached the town of Gerona, 37 km. away. In the photograph, General Camilo Alonso Vega and an unidentified companion stroll through the streets of Gerona after its occupation on 4 February 1939.

A column of Republican prisoners is
escorted through Madrid after the end of
the war.

Colonel Segismundo Casado López became
the leader of the anti-resistance lobby
within the Republican camp when, on 5
March 1939, he and a number of
Socialists, anarchists and Left Republicans
effected a *coup* against the Prime Minister,
Juan Negrín.

Above: Jubilant Nationalists salute French frontier police at Bourg-Madame, at the western end of the Catalan Pyrenees.

Left: Exhausted and bewildered, this unfortunate woman sits with her family round her while a gendarme, whose language she almost certainly does not understand, offers her something from a piece of newspaper or, perhaps, searches one of her various packages.

Martínez Barrio, refused to return to Spain. With Britain and France having announced their recognition of Franco government, the Republic was left in a constitutional shambles: the legal validity of Negrín's government was unclear.

Nevertheless, a huge area of about 30 per cent of Spanish territory still remained to the Republic. The overall command of this central zone lay with General Miaja, although he spent most of his time in Valencia. Negrín and Alvarez del Vayo flew from France to Alicante on 9 February. Negrín still nurtured the vain hope of hanging on until a European war started and the democracies realized that the Republic had all along been fighting their fight. Even if further military resistance was impossible, the Communists were determined to hold on to the bitter end in order to be able to derive political capital out of the 'desertion' of their rivals. Non-communist elements, however, wanted to make peace on the best possible terms. Such hopes seemed vain in the light of Franco's *Law of Responsibilities*, published on 13 February, by which supporters of the Republic were deemed guilty of a crime. Whether or not Negrín was still convinced that the Republic would be saved if a European war were to break out, there seemed little option but to fight on. He returned to Spain and called on his commanders to continue resisting the rebels. Only the Communists supported him.

On 4 March the ascetic Colonel Segismundo Casado, commander of the Republican Army of the Centre and Miaja's effective substitute, decided to put a stop to what was increasingly senseless slaughter. Together with disillusioned anarchist leaders and the distinguished Socialist law professor, Julián Besteiro, Casado formed an anti-Negrín National Defence Junta, in the hope that his contacts in Burgos would facilitate negotiation with Franco. He may also have hoped that by inspiring a military uprising 'to save Spain from Communism', he would somehow endear himself to Franco. It has been suggested that Casado was a British agent. This is unlikely, but he was in touch with British representatives in Madrid who probably encouraged him in his efforts to end the war. Personally unambitious and a capable soldier, Casado was motivated by disgust that Negrín and the Communists talked of resistance to the bitter end while simultaneously arranging to get funds out of Spain and organizing aircraft for their flight into exile. The Casado revolt against the Republican government sparked off what was effectively the second civil war within the Civil War in the Republican zone.

What was happening in Madrid had echoes elsewhere. In Valencia the military governor, General José Aranguren, refused to hand over to the loutish Enrique Lister. At the Cartagena naval base a bizarre set of events was sparked off when Negrín sent the Communist Major Francisco Galán to take over command. A number of artillery officers, with views similar to those of Casado, rose against Galán. They were embarrassed to find their action seconded by secret Nationalist sympathizers, retired rightists and local Falangists. The Falangists seized the local radio station. Sporadic fighting broke out between Galán, the anti-Communist Republican artillery officers and the Nationalists. After coastal batteries had fired on the fleet, the pro-Negrín forces re-established their control.

Meanwhile in Madrid, arrests of Communists had begun on 6 March. General Miaja reluctantly agreed to join the Junta and took over its presidency. Most of the PCE leadership had already left Spain. From France, they denounced the Casado Junta in the most virulent terms. On 7 March Luis Barceló, commander of the First Corps of the Army of the Centre, decided to take more direct action. His troops surrounded Madrid, and for several days there was fierce fighting in the Spanish capital. The Fourth Corps,

The camps set up for Republican refugees in France were little more than lines of huts in barbed wire compounds. To feed the refugees, plates and chunks of bread were laid out on the ground. Each person took a plate and ate sitting on the ground.

Dr Juan Negrín (left, with General Vicente Rojo), eminent physiologist, *bon vivant*, Socialist politician and statesman, was – and remains – one of the most enigmatic and controversial figures of the Second Spanish Republic. Considered by some Socialists and anarchists to be the instrument of the Communist party, Negrín's will to resist, based on his view of the international situation, was not shared by the majority of his political and military colleagues.

commanded by the anarchist Cipriano Mera, managed to gain the upper hand, and a ceasefire was arranged on 10 March. Barceló, together with some other Communist officers, was arrested and executed. This marked the end of the dominance of the Communist Party in the central zone. In the meantime, Casado was attempting to negotiate terms with Franco. Not surprisingly, the *Caudillo* remained interested only in unconditional surrender. His determination not to compromise was reflected after the war in the labour camps, the two million prisoners, and the 200,000 executions on which his dictatorship was built.

With the bankruptcy of Casado's plans brutally exposed, troops all along the line were surrendering or just going home, although some took to the hills from where they kept up a guerrilla resistance until 1951. On 26 March a gigantic and virtually unopposed advance was launched along a wide front. The Nationalists entered an eerily silent Madrid on 27 March. Luis Bolín was as scathing as he had been in Barcelona about the bewildered and shabbily dressed bystanders and the fact that the city was 'evil-smelling and dirty'. By 31 March 1939 all of Spain was in Nationalist hands. A final bulletin was issued by Franco's headquarters on 1 April 1939 which ran: 'Today, with the Red Army captive and disarmed, our victorious troops have achieved their objectives.' Franco had the gratification of a telegram from the Pope thanking him for the immense joy which Spain's 'Catholic victory' had brought him. It was a victory which had cost well over half a million lives, and which was yet to cost many more. Those Republicans who could get transport had made a desperate bid to get to the Mediterranean ports. After waiting vainly in Alicante harbour for evacuation, some committed suicide rather than allow themselves to fall into the hands of the *Falange*. Those who had reached the French frontier were subjected to careless humiliation before being herded into concentration camps.

Gustav Regler, a German Communist commissar with the International Brigades, had been at the frontier looking for some of his men. He wrote later of the harrowing sights that he had witnessed:

That afternoon the Republican troops came. They were received as though they were tramps. . . . The Spaniards were asked what was in the haversacks and ditty-bags they carried, and they answered that in surrendering their rifles they had given up all the arms they possessed. But the French tapped disdainfully on the haversacks and demanded that they should be opened. The Spaniards did not understand. Until the last moment they persisted in the tragic error of believing in international solidarity. . . . The dirty road on which the disarmed men stood was not merely the frontier between two countries, it was an abyss between two worlds. Under the eyes of the Prefect and the generals, the men of the *Garde Mobile* took away the bags and bundles containing the Spaniards' personal belongings and emptied their contents into a ditch filled with chloride of lime. I have never seen eyes of such anger and helplessness as those of the Spaniards. They stood as though turned to stone, and they did not understand.

Epilogue

Although those who escaped across the French border faced internment in disease-infested concentration camps, they were among the lucky ones. After Catalonia was occupied the Mediterranean coast remained the last escape route. On 27 March 1939, with the Republic crumbling before the unopposed Nationalist advance, Colonel Casado together with some of his Defence Junta colleagues and their staff were taken on board a British ship at Gandía near Valencia. The veteran Socialist leader Julián Besteiro decided that it was his duty to remain with the people of Madrid in the vain hope that he might somehow limit the vengeance of the Nationalists. He was imprisoned and died in the squalid prison of Carmona. Communists left in jail in Madrid by the Casado Defence Junta were shot when Franco entered Madrid. Efforts to organize mass evacuation were inept. Refugees gathered at the Mediterranean ports, where only a small proportion of them managed to avoid being herded into prison camps by the arriving Nationalists. Even those who reached exile were far from safe. Julián Zugazagoitia, Lluis Companys and Juan Peiró were captured by the Gestapo in occupied France, handed over to Franco and shot. Largo Caballero spent four years in the Nazi concentration camp at Mauthausen and died shortly after his release. Negrín, Prieto and some other Republican leaders escaped to Mexico, where they spent the rest of their lives locked in sterile polemic about responsibility for their defeat. Manuel Azaña died in Montauban on 3 November 1940.

From 1939 until Franco's death Spain was governed as if it were a country occupied by a victorious foreign army. The training, deployment and structure of the Spanish army was such as to prepare it for action against the native population rather than an external enemy. That was entirely in keeping with the *Caudillo's* view, expressed in 1937, that he had been fighting a 'frontier war'. When Ciano visited Spain in the summer of 1939, he reported that 200 to 250 executions were being carried out daily in Madrid, 150 in Barcelona and 80 in Seville. In May 1939 the *Manchester Guardian* alleged that 300 people per week were being shot in Barcelona. The British consul in Madrid reported that by June there were 30,000 political prisoners in the city and that twelve tribunals were dealing with them at breathtaking speed. In proceedings lasting only minutes the death penalty was invariably demanded and often granted. British consular sources estimated conservatively that 10,000 people were shot in the first five months after the war.

Above: Shortages of food and fuel were noticeable in large cities like Madrid as early as October 1936. By the end of the war, the entire country was suffering similar hardships. Between 1936 and 1939, almost 2,500 people died from malnutrition. In the immediate post-war years black bread, lentils and carob beans were the staple diet of millions of people – provisions for which they often had to spend long hours queuing.

Right: Hundreds of Republican refugees crowd into Colliure, on the French Mediterranean coast, some 30 km. from the Hispano-French border. They had managed to get out of Spain, but their ordeal was far from over.

Right: Of the thousands of people who flocked to the ports of Valencia, Alicante and Almeria, only a few were able to embark on foreign ships before the arrival of the Nationalists curtailed the exodus.

Below: For some, life would never return to normal, no matter on whose side they had fought.

The killings went on well into the 1940s. In November 1940 a torchlit procession escorted the mortal remains of José Antonio Primo de Rivera from Alicante to the Escorial. Prisons were attacked along the way and Republican prisoners lynched. The military authorities complained that with 70 per cent of barracks turned into jails, army units were having to be accommodated in tents. The hundreds of thousands of prisoners were formed into 'penal detachments' and 'labour battalions' to be used as forced labour in the construction of dams, bridges and irrigation canals. Many were hired out to private firms for work in construction and mining. Twenty thousand were employed in the construction of the Valle de los Caídos, a gigantic mausoleum for Franco and a monument to those who fell in his cause. It took nearly twenty years to construct the basilica and monastery, carved into the hillside of the Sierra de Guadarrama to the north-east of Madrid, and the immense cross which towers above it.

The Civil War had been won by a rightist coalition which had arisen in response to the reformist challenge of the Second Republic. Franco rarely missed an opportunity to boast that he had eliminated the legacy of the Enlightenment, the French Revolution and other symbols of modernity. Indeed, the strength of Francoist links with the old order made the Second Republic appear to be a mere interlude in the history of Spain. During that parenthesis, an attack had been mounted against the existing balance of social and economic power. The defensive response of the right had been twofold: the violent or 'catastrophist' and the legalist or 'accidentalist'. Catastrophist violence had little possibility of success in the first years of the Republic. Indeed, its most spectacular failure, the abortive military coup of General Sanjurjo, merely confirmed the wisdom of entrusting oligarchical interests to the legalist means of the CEDA. However, the success of Gil Robles in building up a mass party, using parliament to block reform and winning the 1933 elections, drove the Socialists to despair. Their optimistic reformism hardened into an aggressive revolutionism.

The consequent rising of October 1934 suggested a leftist determination to resist the legal establishment of an authoritarian corporative state. The repression that followed united the left and paved the way to the Popular Front electoral victory of 1936. The right was not slow to perceive the impossibility of defending traditional structures by legal means. Given the unmistakable determination of working-class forces to introduce major reforms and the equal readiness of the oligarchy to resist them, the failure of the legalist tactics of Gil Robles could only lead to a resurgence of 'catastrophism' and an attempt to impose a corporative state by force of arms. That attempt, in the form of the Nationalist war effort, was crowned with success. The first objectives of the new regime were the maintenance of the existing structure of landed property and the strict control of the recently defeated working class. These tasks were carried out by an enormous political and military bureaucracy beholden to the Franco regime.

Wages were slashed, strikes were treated as sabotage and made punishable by long prison sentences. The CNT and the UGT were destroyed, their funds, their printing presses and other property seized by the state and the *Falange*. Travel and the search for jobs were controlled by a system of safe conducts and certificates of political and religious reliability. This effectively made second-class citizens of those defeated Republicans who escaped imprisonment. The Franco regime was especially committed to the maintenance of the rural social structure which had been threatened by the Republic. Among the smallholders of the north this was relatively easy owing to their social and religious conservatism. In the south, however, the regime faced the problem of maintaining a social system which had provoked the rage and militancy of the landless *braceros*. This was done by the creation of a series of institutions which compelled rural labourers to work the soil under conditions even more inhuman than those they had known before 1931. With no social welfare safety net, not to work was to starve. In 1951 wages were still only 60 per cent of 1936 levels. The Civil Guard and armed retainers, *guardas jurados*, employed by the *latifundistas*, maintained a hostile vigilance of the estates against the pilfering of hungry peasants. The Falangist corporative *Hermandades de Labradores y Ganaderos* (fraternities of farmers and cattlemen) were based on the myth that labourers and landowners shared 'fraternal' interests. A similar fraud was at the heart of the repressive system of industrial labour relations.

In fact, behind the rhetoric of national and social unity, until the death of Franco every effort was made to maintain the division between the victors and the vanquished. The *Falange*, as a fascist organization, might have been expected to attempt to integrate the working class into the regime. However, after a victorious war, the ruling classes had little need for such an operation. Falangist bureaucrats still mouthed anti-capitalist rhetoric but it rang ever more hollow. They dutifully served their masters by disciplining the urban working class within the corporative syndicates and drumming the peasantry into the rural *Hermandades*. The anti-oligarchical aspects of the Nazi and Fascist regimes had no place in Franco's Spain. The post-war state remained the instrument of the traditional oligarchy. The Falangist bureaucrats themselves openly acknowledged the class nature of the regime. José María Areilza declared that the state protected capital from internal as well as external aggressors. José Solís admitted that 'When we speak of transformation or reform in the countryside, no one should think that we intend to harm the present owners'. The emptiness of the Falangist rhetoric of revolution was so apparent that it shamed some of José Antonio Primo de Rivera's followers into timidly opposing the regime. They created a tame dissident *Falange* dedicated to the fulfilment of his heritage.

Francoism was merely the latest in a series of military efforts to block social progress in Spain. However, unlike its predecessors, it served not only the Spanish oligarchy but also international capitalism. The abandonment of the Republic by the Western democracies during the Civil War was matched by the feebleness of international action against Franco after 1945. This reflected a recognition that a military dictatorship could defend the economic interests of foreign investors far better than a democratic Republic ever could. Ironically, however, the twin defence of the interests of Spanish and foreign capitalists was to lay the foundations for the ultimate democratization of Spain. The efforts made by Francoism to put back the clock inadvertently created the social and economic conditions for the regime's ultimate transition to democracy.

The repressive labour relations of the 1940s and 1950s contributed to higher profits and the accumulation of native capital. They also contributed, along with Franco's much-vaunted anti-communism, to the process of making Spain attractive to foreign investors. Foreign capital flooded in. The boom years of European capitalism saw tourists pouring south as Spanish migrant labourers headed north, from where they would send back their foreign currency earnings. Gradually, within the antiquated political straitjacket of Francoist Spain, there began to grow a new, dynamic, modern society. The pattern of Spanish history was being repeated, with the political framework out of phase with the social and economic reality. By the time of the energy crisis of the 1970s many of Franco's

Typical of the scenes of relief and delight felt by Nationalist sympathisers at the arrival of 'their' forces are these two images taken in Madrid at the end of March 1939.

Top: Two nuns pose with a group of soldiers near the parliament building. Between them Church and State had made a significant contribution to the collapse of parliamentary democracy in Spain.

Above: Madrid women express their enthusiasm for Franco.

supporters were beginning to wonder whether their own survival might lie in some sort of accommodation with the forces of the democratic opposition. By 1977, only two years after his death, Franco's worst nightmares had begun to be realized. King Juan Carlos, backed by an overwhelming consensus of right and left, had created a democracy for all Spaniards. The cherished Francoist divisions between victors and vanquished were meaningless. Five years later the Socialists were in power in Madrid.

The day after the Madrid Victory Parade, 20 May 1939, was Palm
Sunday. Franco, accompanied by the members of the Nationalist
government, his wife and daughter and a large entourage of military
officers, Party officials and municipal authorities, attended a special
mass during which he dedicated the Nationalist victory to God. Franco
is seen here as he enters the church of St Barbara in Madrid, where the
mass was said by Cardinal Gomá, Primate of Spain.

Principal Characters

Alcalá Zamora, Niceto: conservative Republican, first Prime Minister and then first President of the Republic until deposed in May 1936

Alvarez del Vayo, Julio: left Socialist follower of Largo Caballero, became a close ally of the Communists

Azaña, Manuel: left Republican writer and intellectual, Prime Minister from 1931 to 1933 and again in 1936, President from 1936 to 1939

Besteiro, Julián: moderate right-of-centre Socialist, opposed leftward trend of PSOE, joined Casado's Defence Junta in 1939

Bolín, Luis: right-wing journalist, helped arrange Franco's trip to Morocco in 1936, enthusiastic defender of the Nationalist cause to international press

Calvo Sotelo, José: authoritarian monarchist, leader of Renovación Española, murdered on 13 July 1936

Casado, Segismundo: colonel in command of Republican Army of the Centre, organized coup against Negrín in February 1939

Companys, Lluis: leader of Catalan Esquerra and President of the *Generalitat*, executed by Francoists in 1940

Durruti, Buenaventura: anarchist militia leader, killed on Madrid front in November 1936

Franco Bahamonde, Francisco: youngest general in Europe, after early hesitation assumed leadership of Nationalist forces

Gil Robles, José María: leader of legalist right

Goicoechea, Antonio: leader of Renovación Española before return from exile of Calvo Sotelo

Largo Caballero, Francisco: Minister of Labour 1931–1933, became figurehead of Socialist left in 1930s, Prime Minister from 4 September 1936 to 17 May 1937

Lerroux, Alejandro: founder of Radical Party, became increasingly corrupt and conservative, Prime Minister from 1934 to 1935 in coalition with Gil Robles

Koltsov, Mikhail: Russian journalist close to Stalin

Martínez Barrio, Diego: centre Republican, left Radical Party in 1934, Prime Minister 18–19 July 1936, President of the Republic in 1939

Miaja, General José: general entrusted with organizing the Madrid Defence Junta in November 1936

Mola, General Emilio: director of the military conspiracy in 1936, commanded Nationalist northern armies until killed in a plane crash in 1937

Negrín, Dr Juan: moderate Socialist and Professor of Physiology, Finance Minister under Largo Caballero, Prime Minister from May 1937 to end of war

Nin, Andreu: one-time Trotskyist, leader of POUM, murdered by Communists in May 1937

Prieto, Indalecio: moderate Socialist rival of Largo Caballero, Minister of Finance in 1931, Minister of Defence from May 1937 to April 1938

Primo de Rivera, José: founder of the Falange, executed in Alicante in November 1936

Queipo de Llano, Gonzalo: eccentric general who seized Seville and set up a rule of terror in Andalusia

Rojo, General Vicente: Republican Chief of Staff, masterminded Teruel and Ebro offensives

Sanjurjo, General José: right-wing general, organized abortive coup in 1932, killed in air crash in Portugal *en route* to be the figurehead of 1936 rising

Serrano Suñer, Ramón: Falangist, Franco's brother-in-law, architect of the Nationalist political structure

Varela, General José Enrique: Carlist sympathizer, led attack on Madrid

Yagüe, Colonel Juan: Falangist sympathizer, field commander of the Army of Africa

Zugazagoitia, Julián: Socialist newspaper editor, executed by Franco in 1940

Glossary

accidentalist: a conservative prepared to work legally within the Republic on the grounds that forms of government are 'accidental' and not fundamental

Alfonsist: orthodox monarchist committed to the restoration of King Alfonso XIII who left Spain in 1931

alzamiento: military uprising

bracero: landless agricultural worker

bunker: the die-hard Franco supporters who went on fighting for years after his death to maintain Civil War divisions

cacique: political boss, usually rural

caciquismo: system of political corruption and electoral fraud

Carlist: extreme reactionary monarchist follower of the rival royal dynasty

catastrophist: rightist from the Carlist, Falangist or Alfonsist factions committed to the violent destruction of the Republic

Cortes: the Spanish parliament

Caudillo: military leader, became Franco's equivalent to *Führer*

faccioso: military rebel

Falange: Spanish fascist party

Esquerra: Catalan regionalist Republican party

Generalitat: autonomous Catalan government

Hermandad: State-run union or 'fraternity' encompassing both landlords and rural labourers after the Civil War

Jefe: Chief, the Spanish equivalent of *Duce*, rank held by provincial leaders of the Falange

jornalero: landless agricultural day-labourer

latifundista: landlord of a big estate

Movimiento: general term for the Nationalist war effort; more specifically Franco's single party which united all other rightist groups on 19 April 1937

pueblo: small town or village

pronunciamiento: military coup

Reconquista: the reconquest of Spain from the Moors in the Middle Ages, used by the right as an allegory for its struggle against the left

Regulares: brutal Moorish mercenaries who fought with the Army of Africa

Requeté: Carlist militia

retranca: taciturn peasant cunning, supposedly typical of Galicians

sacas: unofficial removals of prisoners from jail to be executed

Sanjurjada: abortive military coup of 10 August 1932

Sindicato: state-run vertical or corporate trade union after the Civil War

List of Abbreviations

ACNP: Asociación Católica Nacional de Propagandistas – the elite rightist group founded by Angel Herrera, later provided CEDA high command

CEDA: Confederación Española de Derechas Autónomas, the largest mass political organization of the legalist right in the Second Republic

CNT: Confederación Nacional del Trabajo, giant anarcho-syndicalist trade union

FAI: Federación Anarquista Ibérica, the insurrectionary vanguard of the Iberian anarchist movement

FJS: Federación de Juventudes Socialistas, the PSOE youth movement

FNTT: Federación Nacional de Trabajadores de la Tierra, the landworkers' section of the UGT

HISMA: Compañía Hispano-Marroquí de Transportes, the company set up in Morocco on 31 July 1936 to send Spanish goods to Germany in payment for aid received by the Nationalists from the Third Reich

JSU: Juventudes Socialistas Unificadas, Socialist youth movement created by the unification of the Socialist and Communist youth in 1936

PCE: Partido Comunista de España, the Moscow-orientated Spanish Communist Party

POUM: Partido Obrero de Unificación Marxista, a combination of anti-Stalinist Communist dissidents and Trotskyists who united in 1935 in an effort to create a bolshevist vanguard party

PSOE: Partido Socialista Obrero Español, the Spanish Socialist Workers' Party

ROWAK: Rohstoffe- und Waren-Einkaufsgesellschaft, the export agency set up in Germany in October 1936 to channel supplies to Nationalist Spain

UGT: Unión General de Trabajadores, the trade union federation linked to the Spanish Socialist Party

SIM: Servicio de Investigación Militar, secret police in Republican zone

Bibliographical Essay

The Spanish Civil War has given rise to an astonishing wealth of polemical, scholarly and memoir material. Among the 15,000 books and pamphlets on the war there are works of political, historical and literary importance. There is also an immense amount of rubbish. Some of the best writing has been in English and many important works have been translated, although there remain crucial works available only in Spanish. The following remarks are not intended to be comprehensive, but merely to serve as a guide to the literature in English for the reader who would like to know more about the Spanish conflict. Titles available in paperback are marked with an asterisk. Unless otherwise stated, all were published in London.

There are many general works on Spain which place the Civil War in its long-term historical context, but those by two English authors are outstanding. Gerald Brenan's *The Spanish Labyrinth* (*Cambridge UP, 1943) is unsurpassed for its sympathetic 'feel' and authenticity. Written in the most delightfully limpid prose, it reflects the long years that Brenan, a Bloomsbury exile, spent in southern Spain between the wars. Raymond Carr's monumental *Spain 1808–1975* (*Oxford UP, 1982) is a beautifully written account of the long-term origins of the Civil War based on a lifetime's reading and travel. Equally perceptive and teeming with insights is Carr's interpretative account, *The Spanish Tragedy* (Weidenfeld & Nicolson, 1977: new edition *The Civil War in Spain*, 1986). Other accounts of the breakdown of the Second Republic and the immediate social origins of the war are Edward Malefakis, *Agrarian Reform and Peasant Revolution in Spain* (Yale, New Haven, 1970) and Paul Preston, *The Coming of the Spanish Civil War* (*Methuen, 1983). An interesting general interpretation from a Socialist point of view is Antonio Ramos Oliveira, *Politics, Economics and Men of Modern Spain: 1808–1946* (Gollancz, 1946).

General surveys of the war itself also abound. Hugh Thomas's *The Spanish Civil War* (*Hamish Hamilton, 1977) is a long (1,115 pages), encyclopaedic and highly readable narrative account. It is especially good on the military and diplomatic aspects of the war. Its most obvious rival is by Gabriel Jackson, *The Spanish Republic and the Civil War* (*Princeton UP, 1965), an elegantly written and humane account from a liberal standpoint. It is summarized in his *A Concise History of the Spanish Civil War* (*Thames & Hudson, 1974). More recently, Ronald Fraser has given us *Blood of Spain* (*Allen Lane, 1979), a work of oral history which weaves together a mass of eye-witness accounts into something like a great novel. An unusual anecdotal re-creation of the war is provided by Peter Wyden's *The Passionate War* (Simon & Schuster, New York, 1983) which is at its best on the personal involvement of the Americans who went to Spain. Two eye-witness recollections of Spain in the 1930s which are well worth searching for are those by the American

Ambassador Claude Bowers, *My Mission to Spain* (Gollancz, 1954) and by the British journalist Henry Buckley, *Life and Death of the Spanish Republic* (Hamish Hamilton, 1940). The latest international scholarship is reflected in the collective volume edited by Paul Preston, *Revolution and War in Spain 1931-1939* (*Methuen, 1984).

Inevitably the Spanish war aroused political passion, and many books reflect a preference for a particular faction. There is a broadly Trotskyist account by two French historians, Pierre Broué and Emile Témime, *The Revolution and the Civil War in Spain* (Faber, 1972). Antony Beevor's *The Spanish Civil War* is very well written, especially good on the military side and politically sympathetic to the anarchists. Neither of the above is narrowly partisan, something which cannot be said for Arthur H. Landis, *Spain! The Unfinished Revolution* (Camelot, Baldwin Park, 1972) which is an unashamedly and narrowly Communist interpretation. The outstanding pro-Communist and pro-Socialist accounts of the war, the vivid diaries of Mikhail Koltsov and the important memoir of Julián Zugazagoitia, have unfortunately not been translated into English. However, there are vivid, if somewhat blinkered, works by the Republican Foreign Minister, Julio Alvarez del Vayo, *Freedom's Battle* (Heinemann, 1940) and by a remarkable woman, an aristocrat turned Communist, the early Spanish feminist Constancia de la Mora, *In Place of Splendour* (Michael Joseph, 1940). The memoirs of the Socialist Arturo Barea, *The Forging of a Rebel* (*Fontana, 1984) take the form of a slightly fictionalized, colourful and deeply moving trilogy. There exists no good right-wing overview of the war in English, although readers wishing to consult one might seek out Luis Bolín's hybrid memoir-cum-survey, *Spain: The Vital Years* (Lippincott, Philadelphia, 1967).

Of the many unsatisfactory biographies of Franco, the best is the short but sensible synthesis by J.W.D. Trythall, *Franco* (Hart Davis, 1970). The *Caudillo*'s admirers will enjoy George Hills, *Franco: The Man and his Nation* (Robert Hale, 1967) which is sympathetic without equalling the unqualified enthusiasm of Brian Crozier, *Franco: A Biographical History* (Eyre & Spottiswoode, 1967). There are two excellent studies of Nationalist politics. Stanley G. Payne's *Falange: A History of Spanish Fascism* (*Stanford UP, 1961) gives a clear and balanced picture of one of the central components of the Movimiento. Martin Blinkhorn's *Carlism and Crisis in Spain 1931-1939* (Cambridge UP, 1975) is a lucid and stimulating study of the other, and indeed of the right in general. Two accounts of life in Burgos and Seville during the war are Antonio Bahamonde, *Memoirs of a Spanish Nationalist* (United Editorial, 1939) and Antonio Ruiz Vilaplana, *Burgos Justice* (Constable, 1938). Arthur Koestler recounts his experience in a Nationalist jail in *Spanish Testament* (Gollancz, 1937). All three may be balanced by the rightist visions of Peter Kemp, *Mine Were of Trouble* (Cassell, 1957) and H. Edward Knoblaugh, *Correspondent in Spain* (Sheed & Ward, 1937). An enormous amount may be learnt about the Nationalist zone from Herbert R. Southworth's *Guernica! Guernica! A Study of Journalism, Diplomacy, Propaganda and History* (California UP, 1977), an astonishing reconstruction of the propaganda effort to wipe out the atrocity at Guernica. Extremely partisan accounts of Nationalist military campaigns may be found in Harold Cardozo, *The March of a Nation* (Right Book Club, 1937), Cecil Gerahty, *The Road to Madrid* (Hutchinson, 1937) and William Foss & Cecil Gerahty, *The Spanish Arena* (Right Book Club, 1937).

The Republican zone and the debate over the primacy of war or revolution have provoked a rich literature. The siege of Madrid is best described by Robert G. Colodny, *The Struggle For Madrid* (Paine-Whitman, New York, 1958). Dan Kurzman, *Miracle of November* (Putnam's, New York, 1980) is colourful but inaccurate; George Hills, *The Battle For Madrid* (Vantage, 1976) is good on the military side. On the demolition of the revolution, the indispensable work is Burnett Bolloten's monumental and devastating assault on the Communists, *The Grand Camouflage* (Praeger, New York, 1968) revised as *The Spanish Revolution* (*University of North Carolina Press, 1979). It should be read in conjunction with Noam Chomsky's polemical article in his *American Power and the New Mandarins* (*Chatto & Windus, 1969). George Orwell, *Homage to Catalonia* (*Gollancz, 1938) is a sane and moving vision of the May 1937 events in Barcelona written with a pro-POUM stance. Other Trotskyist perspectives may be found in Felix Morrow, *Revolution and Counter-Revolution in Spain* (*New Park, 1963) and Leon Trotsky, *The Spanish Revolution (1931-1939)* (Pathfinder, New York, 1973). The most compelling anarchist account is by Vernon Richards, *Lessons of the Spanish Revolution* (*Freedom Press, 1972). Other important anarchist versions are to be found in Gaston Leval, *Collectives in the Spanish Revolution* (*Freedom Press, 1975), Agustín Souchy, *With the Peasants of Aragon* (*Cienfuegos/Refrac, 1982), José Peirats, *Anarchists in the Spanish Revolution* (*Solidarity, Toronto, 1979), Abel Paz, *Durruti: The People Armed* (*Black Rose, Montreal, 1976) and Emma Goldman, *Vision on Fire* (*Commonground, New Paltz, NY, 1983). Defence of Communist policies is undertaken crudely by Dolores Ibárruri, *They Shall Not Pass* (*Lawrence & Wishart, 1967) and by José Sandoval and Manuel Azcárate, *Spain 1936-1939* (*Lawrence & Wishart, 1963), and with great intelligence and sophistication by Fernando Claudín, *The Communist Movement* (*Peregrine, 1970).

The International Brigades have an enormous literature of their own. The fullest general history, by Andreu Castells, has not been translated into English. A useful Soviet-produced volume is *International Solidarity with the Spanish Republic* (*Progress Publishers, Moscow, 1975) which may be contrasted with the hostile account by R. Dan Richardson, *Comintern Army: The International Brigades and the Spanish Civil War* (University Press of Kentucky, 1982). Vincent Brome, *The International Brigades* (Heinemann, 1965) is fanciful and inaccurate. The standard accounts of the British contingent are the splendid one by Bill Alexander, *British Volunteers for Liberty* (Lawrence & Wishart, 1982) and the earlier one by William Rust, *Britons in Spain* (Lawrence & Wishart, 1939). Vivid interviews with British volunteers are collected in David Corkhill and Stuart Rawnsley (editors), *The Road to Spain* (*Borderline, Dunfermline, 1981). Tom Wintringham, *English Captain* (*Penguin, 1941); Esmond Romilly, *Boadilla* (Hamish Hamilton, 1937) and Jason Gurney, *Crusade in Spain* (Faber, 1974) are important British accounts of the fighting on the Madrid front. The American volunteers are well served by Arthur H. Landis, *The Abraham Lincoln Brigade* (Citadel, New York, 1967), Alvah Bessie, *Men in Battle* (Scribner, New York, 1939), Steve Nelson, *The Volunteers* (Masses & Mainstream, New York, 1953) and Cecil Eby, *Between the Bullet and the Lie* (Holt, Rinehart, Winston, New York, 1969); the Irish by Michael O'Riordan, *Connolly Column* (New Books, Dublin, 1979) and Sean Cronin, *Frank Ryan* (*Repsol, Dublin, 1979); the Welsh by Hywel Francis, *Miners Against Fascism: Wales and the Spanish Civil War* (*Lawrence & Wishart, 1982). The memoirs of the German Communist dissident Gustav Regler, *The Owl of Minerva* (Rupert Hart-Davis, 1959) are informative and, at times, moving.

The diplomatic background to the war is covered in a number of important studies. The two general surveys, Dante A. Puzzo, *Spain and the Great Powers* (Columbia University Press, 1962) and Patricia van der Esch, *Prelude to War* (Martinus Nijhoff, The Hague, 1951) are now out of date. The scathing account of the Non-Intervention Committee by Ivan Maisky, *Spanish Notebooks* (Hutchinson, 1966) remains indispensable. British attitudes are covered in K.W. Watkins, *Britain Divided* (Nelson, 1963) and Jill Edwards, *Britain and the Spanish Civil War* (Macmillan, 1979). David Wingeate Pike's study of French policy has not been published in English but his earlier work has, *Conjecture, Propaganda and Deceit and the Spanish Civil War* (California Institute of International Studies, Stanford, 1968). The most substantial books on Germany remain untranslated. *Documents on German Foreign Policy* Series D, Volume III, (HMSO, 1951) are a treasure store of information. Denis Smyth's chapter on German policy in Preston, *Revolution and War* (see above) is essential. John F. Coverdale, *Italian Intervention in the Spanish Civil War* (Princeton UP, 1977) is unlikely to be surpassed. Russian policy is covered in Claudín (see above), E.H. Carr's sadly unfinished *The Comintern & the Spanish Civil War* (*Macmillan, 1984), David T. Cattell, *Soviet Diplomacy and the Spanish Civil War* (California UP, 1957) and, most recently Denis Smyth, '"We Are With You": Solidarity and Self-interest in Soviet Policy Towards Republican Spain, 1936-1939' in Patrick J. Corish (editor), *Radicals, Rebels & Establishments* (Appletree Press, Belfast, 1983).

Index

INDEX